Virginia Woolf and
the Power of Story

Virginia Woolf and the Power of Story
A Literary Darwinist Reading of Six Novels

Linda Nicole Blair

McFarland & Company, Inc., Publishers
Jefferson, North Carolina

LIBRARY OF CONGRESS CATALOGUING-IN-PUBLICATION DATA

Names: Blair, Linda Nicole, author.
Title: Virginia Woolf and the power of story : a literary Darwinist reading of six novels / Linda Nicole Blair.
Description: Jefferson, North Carolina : McFarland & Company, Inc., Publishers, 2017. | Includes bibliographical references and index.
Identifiers: LCCN 2017003976 | ISBN 9781476664392 (softcover : acid free paper) ∞
Subjects: LCSH: Woolf, Virginia, 1882–1941—Criticism and interpretation. | Storytelling in literature. | Human behavior in literature.
Classification: LCC PR6045.O72 Z56133 2017 | DDC 823/.912—dc23
LC record available at https://lccn.loc.gov/2017003976

BRITISH LIBRARY CATALOGUING DATA ARE AVAILABLE

ISBN (print) 978-1-4766-6439-2
ISBN (ebook) 978-1-4766-2721-2

© 2017 Linda Nicole Blair. All rights reserved

No part of this book may be reproduced or transmitted in any form or by any means, electronic or mechanical, including photocopying or recording, or by any information storage and retrieval system, without permission in writing from the publisher.

Front cover art: Kathryn L. Dreier, *Virginia*, screen print, 10" × 13", 2008

Printed in the United States of America

McFarland & Company, Inc., Publishers
 Box 611, Jefferson, North Carolina 28640
  www.mcfarlandpub.com

To my parents, who taught me to never give up,
To follow my dreams,
And to shoot for the brightest star in the sky.

Acknowledgments

This book has been a labor of love, sometimes more labor than love, but nonetheless, mostly a joy! Without the assistance of several wonderful people, it would not have happened at all. First of all, I must thank my good friend and amazing reader, Margaret Lundberg. Words cannot possibly express my gratitude to you—thank you, thank you, thank you.

I am also grateful to my teaching partner from a few years back, Sam Parker: it was in his course that my interest in the nature-nurture debate began. As we taught that class, I began to see connections between the sciences and the humanities that I had not seen before. Thank you, Sam.

I must go back further in time to thank Allen Dunn, who directed my dissertation, my first lengthy piece on Woolf. I learned more about writing from him than I had ever learned in the years previous: thank you for leading me through that process and for your guidance along the way.

I would like to thank the writing groups at the University of Washington, Tacoma. Without your support, I would not have even started this project, let alone finished it. My friends, you know who you are!

I also thank the Helen Whiteley Center in Friday Harbor for two beautiful weeks of writing, and re-writing, and re-writing. That time, that space—absolutely essential to the completion of this book.

To all of my friends and family who have encouraged me along the way to tell this story about Story: Thank you. Last, but certainly never least, I thank my husband, Michael. You are the most patient, understanding, and supportive human on earth. And I am one lucky woman.

Table of Contents

Acknowledgments   vi
Prologue   1

Part One: Theory of Story

INTRODUCTION: Virginia Woolf and the Evolutionary Power of Story   3

CHAPTER ONE: The Evolutionary Power of Story   29

Part Two: Practice of Story

CHAPTER TWO: The Power of Story to Comfort: *Jacob's Room* and *To the Lighthouse*   55

CHAPTER THREE: The Power of Story to Connect: *Mrs. Dalloway* and *Between the Acts*   90

CHAPTER FOUR: The Power of Story to Create: *Orlando* and *The Waves*   134

Part Three: The Past, Present and Future of Story

CHAPTER FIVE: The Power of Story in Human Survival   171

Epilogue: The Story of Our Future   191
Chapter Notes   197
Bibliography   205
Index   215

Prologue

What does it mean to be human? It means to love and lose, to laugh and mourn, to wake up every day into a different world, one that demands so much of us and sometimes gives back so little. It means to share our lives with each other so that we can keep waking up into this crazy world. It means that to explain our experiences, we turn to the oldest form of communication we have: Story. This book is about the evolutionary power of stories in human survival. It is also the story of Virginia Woolf, the power of story in her life, and in the lives of those who came after. In the end, the stories we tell are the stories we have lived to tell.

PART ONE: THEORY OF STORY

Introduction

Virginia Woolf and the Evolutionary Power of Story

> The story, from "Rumplestiltskin" to *War and Peace*, is one of the basic tools invented by the human mind for the purpose of understanding. There have been great societies that did not use the wheel, but there have been no societies that did not tell stories.—Ursula Le Guin
>
> Fiction is like a spider's web, attached ever so lightly perhaps, but still attached to life at all four corners.—Virginia Woolf, *A Room of One's Own*
>
> The Imagination is one of the highest prerogatives of man. By this faculty, he unites former images and ideas, independently of the will, and this creates brilliant and novel results.—Charles Darwin, *The Descent of Man*

What is the power of a story? Can a story cure a broken heart, or bring together people who misunderstand each other? Is it possible for stories to help us create a new world and a better life for ourselves and our offspring? In short, can stories, that most ancient of forms, help us survive in a modern world? From a literary Darwinist perspective, it is possible to see stories not just as cultural artifacts, but as deeply integral to creating and shaping human experience. From this perspective, it is impossible to dismiss stories as dessert for the brain, as Steven Pinker has insisted.[1] While much of what he says about why humans are drawn to the arts seems reasonable enough, I simply do not believe that the arts can be brushed aside as mere entertainments, or, in more scientific terms, *spandrels*, as Stephen Jay Gould may have argued.[2] On the contrary, Story is a deeply engrained behavior without which we not would be Human, or to put it more strongly, without which could not survive. To borrow a phrase from a popular toy store, "Stories R Us!" The notion that story is not only adaptive for human survival but that it has the potential to change our world has gained considerable popularity, especially over the past ten years. Many would agree with Brené Brown, author of *Rising Strong*, who has asserted, "Story is literally in our DNA."[3] The word *Story* as I use it here does not refer to the literary genre known as fiction. Rather, Story as I define it includes literary fiction, incidental stories, fairytales—in other words, Story consists of a broad category that includes all forms of narrative. Story is the tool we use to cope with problems, relate to others, and create a brand new world each day of our lives.

Virginia Woolf, whose novels provide the focus of my analysis, would have agreed that inventing stories fed her heart, soul, and mind. She lived during one of the most interesting and, some would say, chaotic times in modern history. As she said, the very nature of "human relations" and "human character" in fiction changed in 1910. It seemed to her that modern life had brought with it momentous changes to society and, thus, to fiction. In "Mr. Bennett and Mrs. Brown," she exhorts her contemporaries to not lose sight of the subject of their fiction: the human being.[4] In the midst of the clutter of daily life, she argues, the reality of the human being waits to be revealed. As her fictions cut through that clutter, the characters she created have left an indelible mark on her readers. To read a Woolf novel is to have a deeply personal, and for some, a transformative experience.

In an innovative marriage of literature and science, this book brings together Virginia Woolf, one of the foremost writers of the 20th century, and Literary Darwinism, an interdisciplinary theory of the origin and adaptive role of fiction, in order to illustrate the way stories can help us survive in increasingly turbulent times.

But before I go any further, I will stop a moment and explain exactly how this book about the evolutionary power of stories came to be.

My Story: Virginia Woolf and Me

Like most children, I lived on fairytales and dreamed of becoming the heroine of my own life: I slayed my dragons, poisoned my wicked queens, and won the heart of the handsome prince every time. Fairytales taught me that nothing was impossible, and that magic lived in the most unlikely places: in the heart of an ugly frog or in the tiny face of an unsuspecting mouse. These were my first stories, and I never forgot them. The patterns of thinking that those stories engendered in my mind left an indelible impression. My love of stories eventually led me to pursue a career teaching literature at a university. Stories affect all of us in myriad ways. You may not make your living telling stories, reading them, or explaining them to students, but that doesn't mean that you, too, don't play an integral role in this world of Story.

In the past when I've thought of powerful and transformative stories, I must admit that Virginia Woolf was not the author that immediately popped into my mind. In fact, I had not read much of her fiction until I went in pursuit of my Master's Degree in English. It was on a study abroad trip to London in 1981 that I *met* her for the first time. Standing outside of an enormous white dwelling at Hyde Park Gate, I began to picture her as a child surrounded by siblings and loving parents, not just as the author of novels like *To the Lighthouse*. She slowly began to come to life as I learned more about her childhood, and about the subsequent triumphs and tragedies of her family. I discovered that the Stephen family, although in some ways an island unto themselves, were very much like other families I knew: a father, mother, sisters, and brothers who loved each other despite differences in their ages and temperaments. When I finally read *Mrs. Dalloway*, I followed in the footsteps of hundreds of others who had encountered Woolf for the first time. As I soon found out, this novel, along with *A Room of One's Own*, is required reading for all blossoming Woolf scholars. When I visited Gordon Square, I envisioned Virginia, Vanessa, their brothers and friends, known as the Bloomsbury Group, deep in conversation about the latest literary trends. As I wandered around London that summer, taking it all in, I fell more in love with this group of writers and artists whose stories had captured my heart and my imagination.

On a tour of Knole at Seven Oaks, Nigel Nicolson piqued my curiosity further with his tales about this woman who was married, but deeply in love with his mother, Vita Sackville-West. I remember resisting the truth about that relationship. As a young woman of twenty-two from the conservative South, I didn't want to acknowledge Woolf's bisexuality. It was just too scandalous—I could not seem to justify it with my Southern Baptist upbringing. And yet deep inside I realized that I, too, had at times been half-in-love with many women in my life, women whom I had considered to be role models and heroines. My attractions had only differed in degree, not kind. At this point, my mind began to open up to the idea that there were different kinds of love. As I began to further investigate Woolf's essays, letters, and diary entries, I started to hear and respond to a voice that was at once insatiably curious and yet confidently knowledgeable. Here was a voice of one who was sometimes judgmental of herself and other people, a voice that exuded criticism and love in equal measure. I heard fear in her voice, as well as bravery; I heard hints of loneliness as well as the insistent tones of someone who craved her own space: in short, I heard a very human voice. And what I heard surprised me.

Based on my initial impression, I had imagined her to be a haughty woman of privilege, which she certainly may have been, but what I learned would determine my future as a literary scholar. When it came time for me to choose my dissertation topic many years later, I decided to write about *The Waves*, arguably one of her more challenging novels. I wanted to put into words the effect that novel had on my young mind, a story so unlike anything I had ever read: its meditative style mesmerized me. In preparation for that project, I read all of her novels, short stories, essays: in short, everything she had ever written. I was rewarded with a richer understanding of her imaginative life, and of the reasons behind her lifelong commitment to simply connect with readers by telling a good story.

The more I learned, the more I wanted to know, even though she and I couldn't have been more different from each other if we had tried. I was born in Mississippi in 1957—my father had been a sharecropper, while my mother had been raised from the age of about nine in a Baptist orphanage. Woolf's life, unlike my own rather ordinary existence, seemed to me tinged with intrigue and romance. She had known rich and infamous people; she had traveled widely in her young adulthood. No stranger to grief, having lost her mother, father, brother and half-sister all before her 25th birthday, she had also experienced her share of joy and laughter. My favorite story from her young adulthood concerned the infamous Dreadnought Hoax: it sounded like something my friends and I would have dreamed up. The account of this escapade became even more infamous after Woolf's brother, Adrian, published the account in 1936.[5] I couldn't believe that she, her siblings and their friends had fooled the entire British Navy! She seemed to be, like me, somewhat of a rebel, a troublemaker and a practical joker.

I had long been in love with all things British, from Shakespeare to the Beatles, but here was something new. Woolf and her contemporaries had lived during a period of history that seemed more daring and remote from my own. Even so, I felt I could relate; after all, my father had answered the call with the rest of his generation to join the fight in World War II, and was stationed for a time in both England and France, his first trip abroad. He had landed in Normandy only a few short years after Woolf had taken her life. Somehow, his stories of England, France and Germany became intertwined with my burgeoning awareness of Woolf and her life during that period of British history. She had become, for me, a gateway to the past. I became intrigued, and after thirty-four years, I still am. Her stories have somehow become my stories.

A few years ago, when my husband and I visited Rodmell, Virginia's last home near the ocean, I walked down to the River Ouse where she ended her life. As I sat on the shore of that river, I cried for a woman who had been dead for fifty years. What was it about her story that would not let me go? I had to know if other readers had been affected by her stories in the same way. What power did her story hold for me and for so many others? Reading more about her life and work over the years, I began to wonder what her novels could teach us about the value and potential power of Story for human survival.

The Critical Reception

During her lifetime Woolf's stories were carefully analyzed, praised, puzzled over and even condemned; in the months immediately following her suicide, and for years since, this scrutiny has grown more intense. Much time and attention has been devoted to excavating her every thought regarding subjects from A to Z. Of particular interest to most readers are her ideas about fiction, of course, but also intriguing are her opinions on issues such as the position of women in society, shifting power relationships between women and men, and the debilitating effects of mental illness. Judging from her rather large body of work, Woolf had rather a lot to say on a great many subjects. Yet we still don't fully understand her, perhaps in part because of the sheer volume of her work. Hermione Lee, in her masterful 1999 biography entitled *Virginia Woolf*, perhaps best expresses the way many people feel when they encounter Woolf: they feel somewhat anxious.

Unfortunately, as Lee rightly points out, Edward Albee's 1962 play *Who's Afraid of Virginia Woolf?* sums up the perception of Woolf's work as unapproachable and even a bit scary, even though the play has nothing to do with Woolf. Like Lee, and many others who have undertaken to write about her life and works, I do not want to be presumptuous. I recognize, as Lee does, that Woolf can be a polarizing literary figure for many people—from the scholarly experts to those Woolf might have called "common" readers, those who read for sheer pleasure. At whatever point in their lives readers find Woolf, they either seem to love her or hate her. Seldom have I encountered anyone who has read her work and feels only ambiguity over it. One reason for this extreme reaction may stem from the fact that because her diaries and letters have given us almost unprecedented access to her unguarded thoughts, we feel as if she is talking to us, baring her soul. While she certainly could be an egotist, as evidenced by her diary, she also had the ability to enter into the minds of her characters to an astonishing degree: she closely observed the world and the people around her and then used those observations to create unforgettable characters who moved through stories of extraordinary transformative power. It is this power that draws many readers to her work year after year. It is this power that motivated me to make her stories the centerpiece of my book about the continuing evolutionary role of stories in human life.

The Evolutionary Power of Story

Since *meeting* Woolf and getting to know her, I have found myself reading her stories not only for their intellectual and artistic beauty, but for their accounts of unique characters dealing with very real problems. Thus, when I began to search for a writer to help me explain the evolutionary power of stories, I realized that her body of work would provide me with a case study of unparalleled depth. Not only would I have access to her fiction, but also to her diary and letters. These texts have proven to be especially valuable to my research. Together with her fiction, the diary instructs us in the myriad ways stories give us comfort in times of grief, enabling us to get on with life. We learn how stories can connect us one to the other, bringing us strength in numbers for the tough days ahead. Lastly, we begin to more clearly understand how stories create new worlds, thereby giving us permission to play and to dream of the possible, not to just settle for the predictable.

Of all of the fiction writers in the 20th century, Woolf may be one of the most *human*—meaning both authentic and flawed—as well as one of the most misunderstood. One of the reasons we perceive her this way is because of how she died. Her suicide and the note she left behind created around her a mystery that has begged to be solved. Even though the circumstances surrounding her death have been explained and analyzed from various angles, we still want to understand why she walked into that river. For years, her readers have wondered why a woman who seemingly had so much to live for would just walk away from her life. Of course, we know from her note to Leonard that she was impossibly ill, and believed she had no choice. There was no Prozac for her, no easy fix. And yet, you might ask why she made that choice. After all, she had been ill many times before and had managed to recover. Why not stay and fight the demon one more time? I would argue that it is a testament to the strength of her will that she lived to be fifty-nine. And it is testament to the strength of her intellect and imagination that she left such innovative and engaging stories as her legacy.

One of the more popular critiques of her fiction is that it presents readers with maddening obstacles, such as the poetic style of her language and her use of non-traditional narrative structures, to name just two examples. Other writers from this period in history, although also experimental, have been deemed more accessible and readable. Her novels have been critiqued by those outside of a small circle in academia as being difficult to understand at best and elitist at worst. She has been accused of being out of touch with her own time, out of reach of the very *common reader* of whom she wrote. By making her work the centerpiece of a book that argues for the adaptive power of stories in our lives, I obviously disagree. When Woolf died, she left behind a reliquary of work—short stories, essays, diaries, letters, and novels—that provide a unique insight into why humans NEED stories to survive. Her stories have taken many forms, and like all others, they are unique to their author, yet somehow representative of how we all feel at different points in our lives. It is likely that we will experience the death of a loved one during our life time; we will experience love of various kinds and to different degrees; we will feel fear, joy, heartache and triumph, confusion and clarity, disappointment and determination. Woolf's fiction, which takes readers into a variety of familiar situations and feelings, gives us a unique opportunity to study the way Story can comfort us, connect us, and enable us to create ourselves and our world anew.

My theoretical approach is unapologetically interdisciplinary—I do not claim to be a cognitive or natural scientist. I have studied texts across several disciplines, borrowing terms from evolutionary science, evolutionary psychology and cognitive science such as *survival of the fittest*, *mirroring, mutuality, kinship, cognitive mapping*, and *cognitive play*. In light of these new interdisciplinary explorations and arguments, however, Ellen Spolsky has made it clear that we should take great care in how we apply terminology and knowledge from one field to another.[6] Interdisciplinary research can be a tricky enterprise if not done properly. Therefore, as I acknowledge my debt to a variety of sciences, I wish my readers to recognize that the terms and concepts as I use them are intended as broad meanings and applications. The argument I make about Virginia Woolf concerns ways in which her fiction reveals something more about who we are in this human-making enterprise. In short, I bring together the disciplines of science and literature in an attempt to get at something basic to all humans—Story.

One last caveat: in writing this book, I do not wish to prove beyond the shadow of a doubt the notion that fiction is adaptive to human survival. I am simply exploring the practical implications of such a theory through Woolf's fiction. The work of scholars from various fields—literary theory, Woolf studies, narratology, neuroscience, evolutionary psychology, cognitive science, cognitive aesthetics, Literary Darwinism, and Darwin himself—provide the overarching framework which has elicited the many questions I will address: Does storytelling have an adaptive function for our species? Do stories have a role to play in our continued survival? Why is narrative so central to who we are as humans? How did stories originate? Why did they persist and proliferate? Why did Virginia Woolf want to write stories? How was fiction a vital component to her own sense of mental, emotional and intellectual balance? How did her stories help her to survive for so many years with an often debilitating mental illness? Is it possible that stories help us to create structure, purpose, and meaning for our lives? Why is that when she felt she had lost her audience and had nothing else to say, she took her own life?

Chapter Preview

Six of Virginia Woolf's novels—*Jacob's Room*, *To the Lighthouse*, *Mrs. Dalloway*, *Between the Acts*, *Orlando*, and *The Waves*—form the nexus of my investigation. To aid in my analysis, I have consulted a number of her essays, letters, and diary entries in order to deepen and clarify my overall argument. I did not choose to include her first two novels, *The Voyage Out* and *Night and Day*, nor *The Years*, only partially due to issues of length. I maintain that these novels contain themes she developed with greater skill in the six novels I have chosen. Further, I chose to write about six of Woolf's most artfully written stories in order to call attention to their power as *artifacts*.

Chapter One, *The Evolutionary Power of Story* puts forward Literary Darwinism as the critical framework, a theory which sets out to explain the phenomenon of stories through the work of Charles Darwin, taking as its starting point especially *The Origin of the Species* and *The Descent of Man*, but I would add his other major work, *The Expression of the Emotions in Man and Animals* as being equally important to this discussion.

Not only is it useful to establish the primary tenets of this critical approach, represented by Joseph Carroll, Brian Boyd and others, but also to delineate the way in which these ideas differ from cognitive literary criticism, a position chiefly represented in my book by Ellen Spolsky and Lisa Zunshine. I also briefly address arguments against Literary Darwinism in an effort to situate this theoretical perspective within the larger literary critical framework. These various theories, which sometimes overlap even as they disagree, have helped me to understand the ways in which we can think about how Story is basic to the experience of being human.

Chapters Two through Four comprise *Part Two: Practice of Story*, in which I closely analyze the six novels in order to explore the roles Story plays in human life. Therefore, in *Chapter Two, The Power of Story to Comfort*, I argue that *Jacob's Room* and *To the Lighthouse* exemplify the power of stories to engender healing in the mind of the writer/storyteller, as well as in the mind of the reader. In *Jacob's Room* she remembers and mourns her brother, Thoby, while in *To the Lighthouse*, she memorializes her parents, finding in the telling of these stories a measure of comfort. *Chapter Three, The Power of Story to Connect*, in which I focus on *Mrs. Dalloway* and *Between the Acts*, further develops the idea that stories do more than entertain us: without the basic connective tissue of stories, which sometimes appears to be in danger of eroding in our society, we have little hope for survival. Specifically, these two novels create an interconnecting circle of relationships among the characters, what Darwin may have called the "inextricable web of affinities."[7] *Mrs. Dalloway* serves as a fitting companion to *Between the Acts* in that both novels focus on connections between characters as well as connections between the past and the present. My analysis of the novels comes to a close in *Chapter Four, The Power of Story to Create* with a discussion of *Orlando* and *The Waves*. In this chapter, I explain how stories can help us create a new vision of the kind of world we want to inhabit. These novels show us the power of stories to kindle the imagination, as well as to create the strong and resilient brain so critical to human survival. With these six novels, Woolf is at her most creative as she freely plays with the genre of the novel. Her imagination and intellect are in full gear, and she takes her readers along for the ride of their lives. Although some may believe that Darwin was concerned only with the biological origins of life, he wrote extensively of the presence of imagination in the lives of all animals. As the highest functioning animal on the planet, our imaginations are more highly developed, with stories playing a crucial role in this development. To put it simply, when we tell stories, but also when we truly listen, the possibility opens up for a better life.

Part Three: The Past, Present and Future of Story completes the book with *Chapter Five, The Power of Story in Human Survival* and a brief *Epilogue*. In concluding, I explain that these six novels, when read in chronological order, form the arc of a meta-story—briefly described below—of which Woolf herself may not have been aware, but that, from a literary Darwinist perspective, gives greater weight and meaning to her work as a whole. This meta-story corresponds to a kind of evolutionary "life story" structure, the themes of which are intertwined throughout Woolf's career as she considered how to navigate the ups and downs of life and survive, and how to understand her own mind. An evolutionary perspective not only sheds light on the central concerns of human life evident in these novels, but also indicates the way that these works launch a meta-narrative of Woolf's development as a writer. For instance, Jacob may be seen as a kind of forerunner to Clarissa Dalloway, Lily Briscoe, Bernard, Orlando, and Isa Oliver. As I have suggested, however, instead of looking at each of these characters as separate entities, or as the *heroes* of separate stories, it proves more useful to see each character as stepping out of the previous one as evolving iterations of the search for identity and meaning. In light of my original hypothesis, in the *Epilogue* I propose a new, literary Darwinist reading of *The Hours*, Michael Cunningham's novel based on *Mrs. Dalloway*. I find it particularly interesting that in his retelling of this story, he unearthed new implications and themes which had been latent in Woolf's stories. His novel introduces new themes that now move readers (and movie goers) of an entirely new generation. Cunningham has helped to give Woolf new life in a new century, and so, like Orlando in the novel of the same name, she lives on, her stories becoming an important link in a chain of stories that help us understand what it means to be human.

Virginia Woolf: Background, History and Context

Virginia Woolf's novels convey the power of stories to comfort us in grief, to connect us one to another, and to create a world full of possibilities for an as-of-yet undreamt future. Her literary masterpieces not only appeal to us through their artistic ingenuity and careful attention to style, but they bring to life the most basic of human emotions. Fortunately, a story doesn't have to be a literary masterpiece to achieve this feat: it just has to be concerned with the things humans care about: loss, love, and hope for a better future. Woolf is a writer's writer, long considered the academic's prime example of literary writing in the first half of the 20th century: artistic and infamously difficult. You might ask that if I am trying to argue that stories—regardless of what some may deem their *literary merit*—are powerful tools of human survival, why wouldn't I want to choose a novelist whose work may not be so *academic*? My answer is that if I am to argue that stories have an adaptive function for humans, I needed to choose a writer who not only wrote captivating stories with memorable characters, but also a writer who challenges her readers to think. I wanted to focus on the work of a writer whose work has outlasted the test of time. Woolf is one of the most widely read and controversial authors of the last century. She was not just a writer of fiction, but a master craftsman of the art of storytelling.

The daughter of a prominent philosopher and historian, she had been steeped in history and engrossed in fictional worlds from a very early age. She, her sister, Vanessa, and her brother, Thoby, produced a family newspaper called *Hyde Park Gate News*, published the first time in 2005 for public consumption. Within the pages of this little newspaper, they reported on the happenings in the family, and included some of their favorite poems and stories. In "A Sketch of the Past," Woolf recalls that she had loved nothing better than to place the newest edition of this newspaper on her mother's plate in the morning and wait with anticipation for her reaction.[8] Pleasing their parents with their growing knowledge of society and their developing wit, was undoubtedly one of the reasons the siblings conspired to create this newspaper. These early experiments in writing and art gave rise to habits in the sisters that continued for their entire lives. In particular, Woolf's willingness to experiment with style early on, delving into what we could term "cognitive play," proved crucial to her later development as a novelist. These early forays into writing seem to have given her the ability to explore many avenues of expression, as well as the courage to try on different voices in both her fiction and nonfiction.

Writing became a deeply ingrained habit, her primary way of discovering and then expressing her thoughts, pinning down the fleeting moments of life. The crucial piece of evidence is the fact that she kept a diary almost continuously from approximately 1918–1941. Woolf scholars have long considered the diary to be a goldmine of information that reveals the inner workings of her writing process, her love and practice of literary criticism, and her developing aesthetic philosophy. Not only did she faithfully keep a diary, but she also wrote copious letters, a literal treasure trove that yields almost unprecedented access to her opinions of society and her interactions with friends and family, not to mention her reactions to her own writing. Her ability to focus on the details of life and then to express those details in an unfolding narrative marked her nascent development as a storyteller.

As the years went by, the diaries and letters show the level to which she developed her skills as a keen observer of human nature and behavior, as well as a philosopher who thought deeply about why we were put on this earth. Despite the fact that she committed suicide, we see Virginia Woolf as a strong woman, outspoken in her belief that every woman needed not only a room of her own, but also a voice of her own in order to weather the storms that would surely come. From these documents, we know that the year leading up to her death was a time of great creativity for her, but also a time of increasing stress on her mental health, mainly due to the upsurge in World War II. Unfortunately, at the time of her suicide, some people reacted in a judgmental way, accusing her of selfishness and weakness. As we have learned more about mental illness in the past several decades, we have discovered that it is a disease that takes no prisoners, one often accompanied by a debilitating and deadly prognosis.

Celebrity suicides have brought attention to those who suffer to the point of death from mental illness, as well as to the fact that such individuals are judged harshly for this act, just as Woolf was all those years ago. The sheer number of artists who have experienced mental illness—a list which includes writers, painters, and actors—provides us with overwhelming evidence of its nature, particularly concerning the relationship between bipolar disorder and the creative mind, as we learn from experts like Kay Redfield Jamison.[9] As she and others have explained, Woolf's illness fueled the fire of her creativity and, in a way, drove her need to explain to herself her own mind. These "wounded storytellers" as Arthur Frank calls them, may not be able to achieve total healing, yet these brave souls carry the potential to heal others with their stories, a benefit of storytelling that I argue is necessary to our survival.[10]

When she started writing at a very young age, Woolf unknowingly discovered a tool that would help her cope with the many traumas she would face later in her life. She found writing to be the most important thing she could do with her time. She had a particular way of seeing life which she used as a lens for writing fiction; one of her most well-known is "that there is a pattern hid behind the cotton wool."[11] This singular point of view influenced her perception of reality and, at the same time, shaped it in her stories. For Woolf, writing was not a luxury, but an absolute necessity. In this passage from "Sketch of the Past," a memoir she began to write in 1939, she lists a number of ordinary things she could be doing, but instead chose to fill her days with writing in an attempt to get a peek behind the curtain of surface reality. Although her illness finally overcame her, her habit of writing stories served her well throughout her life.

Among other things, stories helped her to see that despite the horrors of war, despite untimely and tragic deaths in her family, human beings could be connected in a meaningful way. She was to struggle all of her life with the question of ultimate meaning, but in fiction she could, through a multitude of ideas, themes, and characters, explore this question, helping to lay bare for herself and her readers some of the mysteries of the human mind. Woolf's stories take as their subject varied experiences of human life and explain these experiences in new ways, bravely letting us in on what it must have felt like to inhabit her kind of mind. Her life story, which fuels her fiction, creates a doubled mirror for her readers—we see her and ourselves, as it were, twice. In reading Woolf's fiction, we become increasingly interested in unearthing what she called *real life* and in essence, join her on this quest in novel after novel.

Each of the six novels in this book provides an appealing subject for the analysis of Story from the Darwinian point of view for other reasons as well. Her stories, coupled with her focus on the craft of writing—testing theories, writing stories, struggling with her own inner critic—provide us a fully-equipped laboratory in which to work out this theory. Further, because the scientific method depends on the repeatability of an experiment, we can say with confidence that storytelling qualifies as such an experiment. In fact, the particular experiment we know as storytelling has been repeated millions upon millions of times throughout history, with as many variations. We have evidence that Virginia Woolf's work has merit, as proven by the fact that her works have been analyzed from almost every critical view imaginable: plot, theme, studies of imagery, connections to history and current politics and concerns with social issues. Unfortunately, in several scholarly studies of literature, the focus often falls away from the story itself and its connection to real people. Many critics have centered their comments on current political and social issues rather than on the connections between the stories, the practice of storytelling, or on why the origins and the practice of storytelling matter. Some of these critical practices, while they have proven both insightful and extremely useful in some respects, seem to have lost sight of something simpler: the basic evolutionary origin of Story and its usefulness in everyday life.

Woolf wondered about the conundrums of life, writing about all manner of issues in her diary, from questions about personal relationships to rumors of war. But it was not just a space for her to ruminate: she used it strategically, as a space for experimenting with new ideas and new structures. She did not take for granted her own practice of writing, but often acknowledged that writing fiction was an expensive occupation—in terms of time and energy—especially for her, given that she struggled with mental illness. She recognized that if she wanted to write good fiction that she had to take the time to hone her craft. In "Sketch," she writes of her own devotion to writing and wonders why a novelist like Dickens would have spent his entire life creating stories.[12] Her answer, at least in this instance, is that he wanted to create characters who were "immensely alive," his concept being to emulate the life he saw around him through characters who could be created with only "three strokes of the pen."[13] Significantly, the time and energy it takes to create a story is noted by evolutionary scientists, many of them using this example of the extensive time taken up by storytelling as a way to argue that stories could not possibly have been adaptive for survival: who has time to create a story when there may be a saber-toothed tiger to avoid while hunting for dinner? It seems to me that telling other hunters exactly where that tiger was located would be quite beneficial in the quest for survival! But I will return to this objection in more detail in Chapter One.

One of the more intriguing and important motives she could have had for writing novels could very well have been to keep loved ones *alive* through characters like Clarissa Dalloway and Helen Ramsay. Thus, her stories represent a kind of life writing in that as she wrote, she somehow preserved the lives of those she had known. *To the Lighthouse* resurrects both her mother and father in an attempt to, at the very least, begin to understand her childhood; after writing this novel, Woolf admits being no longer obsessed by her parents, that now she could move on. Writing *To the Lighthouse*, she says "laid them in my mind ... writing of them was a necessary act."[14] Although Mitchell Leaska, among others, has questioned whether or not this was entirely the case (i.e., her parents continue to show up in later novels), the fact that she kept writing about them only provides more evidence that stories played a significant part in helping her to grieve. There is also ample evidence to suggest that *Jacob's Room* was written, at least in part as a tribute to her brother, Thoby, who in 1906 suddenly died from typhoid after a family trip to Greece.

Her fiction certainly seems to have served a therapeutic role in her life, a way to work out her thinking about loss, as well as about her place within her own family, community, and society. Woolf comments in "Sketch" that writing was her own version of psychotherapy, and that in fiction she was able to express the "deeply felt emotions" that she had held onto for a very long time.[15] As she explains in "Sketch" creating scenes was her "natural way of marking the past," and so it is for the relationship between memory and being human.[16] In "Phases of Fiction," she declares that one of the delights of good fiction is that we can see "the mind at work," revealing the "relations in things" that are obscured by habit.[17] I would argue, however, that as a writer of fiction, she was neither unique in her impulse to tell stories, nor particularly in what that impulse consisted of: to preserve and explain her past to herself. Unique to Woolf is that heightened attention to language (perhaps brought on by her particular mental illness) applied to the craft of fiction. Writing stories helped her to know herself and test the limits of her creativity, as well as giving her a reason to live. Like other writers, she used and reused the same materials many times throughout her work. In fact, I would argue that she was basically telling and retelling one story in an attempt to answer, or to propose a series of answers, to some very basic questions: What does it mean to be human? What is the meaning of life? What can life mean in the face of certain death? Her growth in understanding herself, as well as a broader human nature, can be seen in the six novels that I will analyze. When read in chronological order, these novels reveal at least one aspect of how Woolf might have understood why we tell stories. As I will argue, she told stories not only to put into words her own theories about life and writing, but also to know her own mind.

The ways in which life had been presented in 19th century fiction, while in many ways admirable for its attention to detail, did not satisfy Woolf. She constantly sought new and better ways to express what she would have called *reality*. These six novels reveal what she was thinking at pivotal moments in her life regarding her own growth as a writer. Thus they serve as a perfect model for this kind of literary analysis. These particular novels, more than the others, provide a rich landscape for an exploration of why we tell stories in general. Each of the stories she tells poses a particular answer to the initial literary Darwinist question: "Why do humans tell stories?" In addition, the meta-story these works tell, a reflection or commentary on the process of telling stories, is also the story of her development as a writer and as a human. Woolf was uniquely positioned to ask these questions in her work given the early traumas that she experienced, as well as the kind of family she was born to—somewhat wealthy, educated parents who could afford to give her access to a wide range of life-changing experiences at a pivotal time in history. Her sexual orientation and her bipolar disorder also gave her a unique view of life. Of course, one could argue the implications of the word "access"—even she keenly felt the lack of access she had to university libraries and the university education that her brothers could pursue; on the other hand, in comparison to other young women her age, more doors were to open to her because of her class. Through her novels and the diaries that seem to act as their companion pieces, we are given an in-depth look at a woman who relentlessly seeks answers that would give her life meaning.

In addition to the power and potential of stories to enhance brain function, connect us to other people, and provide an avenue of healing from grief, stories help us survive, both as individuals and as a species. Woolf's own quest certainly enabled her to live through many a bout with suicidal thoughts in the midst of her deepest depressions. As Boyd has pointed out, storytelling possibly fulfilled one of its adaptive functions in her life by recalibrating Woolf's mind.[18] As we have seen, although she battled mental illness most of her life (most experts say it was most likely bipolar disorder and schizophrenia), she continued to write stories, essays, biographies, and literary criticism; in addition, she wrote and delivered public lectures, wrote hundreds of letters and faithfully kept a diary until days before her death. Writing was her life, her way into her Self and into a society comprised of her family and friends; as such, it was not an activity that she took lightly. Sometimes, she writes in her diary, she dreaded and even hated writing; at times it was even exhausting. She not only used her diaries as a way to vent her feelings, but she also used her non-fiction prose, such as "Modern Fiction," "Phases of Fiction," and "Mr. Bennett and Mrs. Brown," as a space in which to toy with innovative ideas, discovering techniques she would later put to use in her fiction.

Throughout the ups and downs in her life, she formulated narrative theories and later implemented those theories, providing us with further evidence of the power and functionality of the cognitive play of storytelling. As she was writing *Jacob's Room*, she speculated about her changes in style from novel to novel, concluding that in the final analysis, none of her readers seemed to notice, nor could she really say herself what those changes in style were or what they meant.[19] She acknowledged that after she finished that novel, she declared that it helped her to work "free" into a new and more experimental way of expression.[20] In 1926, she began thinking of *The Waves*, which began as a sort of mystical rumination about life and loneliness. She says of this novel that she wanted to "make note" of a state of mind.[21] And in 1937, the glimmerings of *Between the Acts* began as a note in her diary about a new novel that would be unlike any other story she had ever written.[22] A few days later, she formulated a theory about this same novel which would contain a center from which everything else in the novel would emanate.[23] To the end, Woolf valued experimentation and innovation as she searched for answers to her questions.

In fact, she seems to have written stories partly as an exercise in what we could explain as *cognitive play*,[24] not only to put into practice her concepts about narrative, but also as a way to explain life to herself. In *Jacob's Room, Mrs. Dalloway, To the Lighthouse, Orlando, The Waves*, and *Between the Acts*, we read six stories written at different phases of Woolf's life, all six of which reflect her evolving interest in "life itself going on."[25] In order to understand the entire arc of my argument, it is important to see each novel as emerging out of the last, progressing and changing as her vision shifted, and as she added to her reliquary of life knowledge. With *Jacob's Room*, she would try her hand at departing from the traditional style of narrative. This story tells of one young man's journey through life, but in a larger sense, it operates as a story of human consciousness, providing an intriguing example to analyze from the evolutionary point of view. As I will explain in detail in the next chapter, a literary Darwinist searches for the larger meaning that literary works provide in the relationship between author, characters and reader, but that relationship in *Jacob's Room* is difficult to discover. If the main character is more of a felt presence than an actual presence, then we are confronted not only with questions of the evolutionary adaptability of this story, but also of where and how meaning is derived. The role of memory, so indispensable to the quality of human life, is also vital to this story in that Jacob primarily lives in the minds and memories of the other characters. Not only does he occupy their thoughts, but they try to imagine where he is and what he is thinking at any given point, especially his mother and the other women in his life. Speculation becomes a primary activity in the story, thus emerging as an early formulation of Woolf's understanding of how her mind worked. As Carroll reminds us, meaning itself "is always located in some specific mind," defining the correlation between the individual mind and the idea of "point of view." This is, he says, how Story works: it comprises an "interactive" relationship between the reader, the author and the characters.[26] I would agree, adding only that in *Jacob's Room* the challenge becomes, for the characters and for the reader, how to construct a meaningful story from an assortment of fragments and what some have likened to a series of discrete snapshots. In this sense, Woolf's portrayal of Jacob is particularly interactive because it engages the reader in an exercise if not of futility, of great effort to glean the meaning Woolf intended.

Each of the novels begins with a problem or question, most often focused on style, form, or theme. In *Jacob's Room*, for instance, Woolf begins to expand her prose style, as well as to introduce a continuing theme which focuses on an over-arching question: what is this thing we call life? *Mrs. Dalloway*, Woolf's fourth novel, pushes the boundaries of fiction even further, putting into practice a method she referred to as "tunneling" behind her characters in order to more fully disclose the inner workings of their minds, thus revealing the realities of being human. *To the Lighthouse* calls to mind a eulogy, in essence, a farewell to Julia and Leslie Stephen. In addition to her mother and father, she was undoubtedly thinking of her siblings—Lily Briscoe is a reflection of her sister, Vanessa, while James is another re-embodiment of Thoby, or perhaps a composite of Thoby and Adrian. *Orlando*, her sixth novel, takes us on a playful romp through history. In this story, she writes her own creation myth of the perfect world. This novel has also been seen primarily as a love letter to Vita Sackville-West, but I would argue that, from the literary Darwinist standpoint, it accomplishes much more in terms of the benefits of cognitive play.

In *The Waves*, she returns to a more serious narrative style, showing her further progression from *Jacob's Room* in its style and conception. This is particularly evident as she develops a new rhythmic style which allows her to delve even further into the minds of her characters, adjusting the microscopic view of human life into sharper focus. Finally, in *Between the Acts*, her ninth and last novel, and most opposite in style from *The Waves*, she creates a style similar to *Jacob's Room*, but even more fragmented. Some have speculated that it seems unfinished, that perhaps she had planned to edit and revise one last time, but walked away from it all before she could finish. Whatever the case, the form of the novel reinforces what we surmise about her state of mind at the time. In *Between the Acts*, she returns to the basic questions with which she began her writing career regarding both individual identity and identity within a community. She raises once more questions regarding the relationships between men and women, as well as between women themselves, but more importantly, that one, crucial question: "what does it mean to be a human being?" It is this higher level inquiry that Woolf comes back to again and again, using the varied lenses of her fictional microscope to shed a bit of a different light in each story: putting first one puzzle then another then under her finely calibrated glass.

The Novels: A Brief Introduction

From beginning to end, *Jacob's Room* asks the reader to consider the idea that although we may think we know someone, we only know them through a limited view, which, I would argue, is one form of the kinship theme. How do we come to terms with the death of one we had hardly known, especially if that one is a sibling? The overall structure leaves us with a series of impressions of Jacob rather than a continuous, traditional plot in which the action rises, climaxes and finds a resolution. World War I provides the historical backdrop, giving to the novel a richly suggestive context. In this respect, she writes the story as a way of coming to terms with her brother's sudden death, the telling of it a means of both surviving and understanding loss. As the story of human consciousness in general, *Jacob's Room* narrates the growing awareness of a young man's emerging understanding of the shape of life, and is also, therefore, a variation of the traditional *bildungsroman*. This novel initiates Woolf's second "voyage out," as *Jacob's Room* is her first experimental narrative, a marked departure from both *The Voyage Out* and *Night and Day* which predate it.

To the Lighthouse tackles one of the hardest questions of all—how to make sense of life in the face of great personal loss. Stylistically, *To the Lighthouse* continues her mastery of free indirect discourse. To this narrative style she adds the *ekphrasia* of painting. Woolf famously said that words were not sufficient to express her ideas, that she needed a more malleable medium, like her sister's language of paint. As an artist, Lily Briscoe brings a lyrical perspective to the description of events and people, framing things more impressionistically than a writer could, tied down by necessity to language. Woolf tests one of her favorite ideas, that writers need both painting and writing to create what is really there—that not just one perspective or method will do to discover the reality behind the veil of that murky "cotton wool." As a central image, the lighthouse is burdened by, but also gifted with, the preponderance of symbolic meaning. The title, *To the Lighthouse*, gives the reader an address: a letter written "to the lighthouse," or perhaps an invitation to go to a specific destination, or as an answer to a question, "Where shall we go now?"

The symbolic significance of the lighthouse feeds into the basic human drive to find patterns in the world to which we can attach meaning. The titles of her other novels are also replete with these organizing tropes: *The Voyage Out* implies a journey, but doesn't say where we are going; *Night and Day* is, by its title alone, a study in contrasts. Jacob's bedroom, left empty after his death, becomes a symbol of that emptiness and the end of a promising life. In comparison to symbols found in the other novels, however, the symbol of the lighthouse is the richest and most suggestive of all. Connected deeply to mythologies of womanhood, motherhood, art, and beauty, the story Woolf tells in *To the Lighthouse* embodies her deepest feelings about her mother and about the power of creativity on a mythic level, creating a connection to more ancient stories.

The primary storyline in *Mrs. Dalloway*—her journey through London, her encounter with Peter, her reunion with Sally, and her confrontation with her own mortality at the party—is intersected several times over by other stories told by other characters, thereby destabilizing the primary narrative center. The reader, in fact, may wonder by the end who this story concerns, an effect similar to what we experience in reading *Jacob's Room*. The title leads us to believe that it is largely about Mrs. Dalloway, and in truth, it is, but it is not entirely about her or her own concerns. Peter Walsh, Miss Kilman, Sally Seton, William Bradshaw, and most importantly, Septimus Smith, enter her life, mixing their tales with her own, which complicates their search for meaning. *Mrs. Dalloway* becomes another vehicle by which Woolf again asks "what is life all about?" adding yet another layer to her knowledge. While the entirety of *Jacob's Room* revolves around the tragedies of life, perhaps the story of *Mrs. Dalloway* questions why life is not more tragic than it is, given the vagaries of living and the perils that we face from day to day. "Why Septimus and not me?" is a question Clarissa might have asked upon learning of his suicide at the end of the evening, immediately before she rejoins the party. The war is over, and yet casualties of that war remain, embodied in Septimus and other veterans, as well as in Rezia, his puzzled and frightened wife. Clarissa and her friends have grown older, and yet the uncertainties do not go away—if anything, more problems have emerged; for Clarissa, life had become more, not less, complex. The story of Clarissa Dalloway, like the story of Jacob, further explores the extent to which we do not, or ever can, fully know another human being. This impulse, the drive to connect, is basic to how we have evolved as social creatures.

The narrative style of her last novel, *Between the Acts* provides an interesting denouement to Woolf's life of writing because while it echoes the style we find in *Jacob's Room*, it is more fragmented—instead of one central presence, in *Between the Acts*, we find a story predicated on the concept of dispersal and disunity: thus, the novel feels more scattered, less unified than her previous stories. Its theme is the re-making of the world, a sort of re-envisioning through a critique of history. The historical backdrop of the novel is World War II, the threat of which grew closer to England as Woolf was writing. It is more than a little interesting that *Three Guineas* was written proximate to this last work of fiction, as this book-length essay takes up as one of its subjects the puzzle of human nature and the vagaries of war. Surely, she wonders in the opening chapter, human beings who are thinking clearly and rationally do not need to go to war. In classic Woolf style, she assigns blame for the war to men, which recalls her theory of the androgynous mind from *A Room of One's Own*, to which *Three Guineas* is the bookend. Likewise, because *Between the Acts* is set with World War II in the background, it represents a bookend to *Jacob's Room*, a story framed by World War I.

The main plot concerns the gathering of the villagers for a history pageant which was held on the lawn of the Oliver estate. Miss LaTrobe, the pageant's creator, takes on the role of director, while the citizens of the village, including the "village idiot," perform as actors and singers. Romantic intrigue, village business, gossip, and politics underlie the action, which revolves chiefly around the production of this pageant. Interspersed between the scenes of the pageant, we *hear* snippets of conversations in the audience which consists of gossip, commentary about the show, and local lore. None of the characters seem sure of their roles in life; each one ponders the meaning of it all, especially Isa, whose husband, Giles, is being pursued by a woman named Mrs. Manresa, a character Woolf had meant to represent her lover and friend, Vita.[27] Because this was her last novel, we see it differently than the others—she could not have known for certain when she began writing that it would be her last, and yet there are hints to that effect in her diary in the last months before she her final walk to the river. It is, as we say, the end which gives shape and meaning to the beginning and middle.

Above all of the others, *Orlando* achieves a kind of evolved thinking with regard to the role of gender in life. Its link to mythology can be traced through both Dionysius and Hermaphrodite, the ultimate heroic figure who dies and returns to life, as well as taking on the opposite gender, giving her a power to see life literally from both sides. A book that she intended as a fantasy has become one of the Ebenezer stones of the feminist movement, a marker to which we consistently refer when we encounter issues of gender and identity.

As in her previous novels, the context of her life reveals much that is essential in understanding the role of Story. In the period of time during which she wrote *Orlando*, Woolf had met and begun to fall in love with Vita Sackville-West, the wife of Harold Nicolson. The two women began a love affair that lasted several years. With this novel, Woolf pens an inventive biography and history of England, as seen through the adventures of Orlando, a character who lived as a man up until he turned 30; after a long and strange period of sleep, he awakens to find that he has been transformed into a woman. In this gender-bending tale, which Woolf wrote quickly in comparison with her other novels, she asks yet another version of her investigation into meaning in life, this time in the form of two related questions: what does it mean to live as a man, and conversely, what does it mean to live as a woman?

Classical mythology forms part of the cultural context for this novel: this was the question posed to Tiresias in ancient myth. One of the stories associated with Tiresias tells that Hera changed him into a woman after he saw her bathing. In another version, he was transformed because, after watching two snakes mating, they attacked him—when he struck and killed the female snake, he was in that moment transformed into a woman. Seven years later, after he witnessed these same snakes engaged in mating, he again struck them and was returned to his male form. Unfortunately, Hera later struck him blind because he sided with Zeus in an argument regarding which gender enjoyed the act of sex more: Hera claimed it was men, while Zeus argued that it was women. Having been both a man and woman, Tiresias had experienced both, and yet Hera obviously disagreed with his opinion. Although Woolf doesn't make the mistake of providing a definitive answer to this unanswerable proposition, if we are to take Orlando's words as truth, it would seem that to live as a woman, as Tiresias would have argued, is preferable, as Orlando exclaims: "Praise God that I'm a woman."[28]

Whether one sex is preferable over the other, however, was not Woolf's ultimate point. Rather, she wanted to play further with the idea of the androgynous mind, a concept she discusses at length in *A Room of One's Own*. In this text, she argued that the writer who has an androgynous mind is more likely to be expansive in her views and able to see life without the lens of anger, or any other impediments. The ability to unite the two parts of the mind in this way was a quality for which she admired both Shakespeare and Jane Austen, one quality she saw lacking in many women writers of her day. In *Orlando*, we see the androgynous mind fully fleshed out. The interesting thing about Orlando as a character is that although he becomes a she, the character's personality, philosophy of life, ability to think, etc., had remained much the same—gender does not appear to have changed the essential self of the character.

Finally, *The Waves* stands as a departure from traditional narrative structure in almost every respect. In some ways it takes up where *To the Lighthouse* leaves off as the story of human consciousness and the way in which we perceive, and are perceived by, others. In addition, this notion of "selves" and the effect of time and change on identity which she had considered in *Orlando*, is once more taken up in *The Waves*. As in her previous novels, however, Woolf's central inquiry in *The Waves* concerns whether meaning can be gleaned from life when all is said and done. We encounter six characters who speak in a series of monologues, separated by eight interludes. The characters do not speak to each other as much as they speak of themselves and about each other, situating themselves within a context or a scene or an event and then expressing their reactions and feelings about the events.

Narrated from an omniscient perspective, the interludes provide a generalized point of view: the novel opens with an interlude which describes the sun rising over the horizon of the ocean, its beams resting on a house; birds are singing, and waves are hitting the shore. Heavily symbolic, but resting squarely on realism for scenic details, the style is not exactly stream of consciousness, but it is also not a traditional narrative. As I will argue, *The Waves* is also the story of human consciousness, but the light of consciousness diffused through a prism made up of six characters. The inspiration for this group of characters was certainly, in some respects, members of the Bloomsbury Group, but the likenesses between the real people and characters is very slight, so slight that the characters can be understood and appreciated by someone with no knowledge of Woolf's life.

By the time she composed *The Waves*, Woolf had experienced the deaths of her mother, father, half-sister and brother, marriage to Leonard Woolf, an affair with Vita Sackville West, and the success of three novels and a book of essays based on a series of lectures, *A Room of One's Own*. She seemed at the height of her creative powers and of her experimental ideas. In 1931, she was writing with more confidence, yet continued to wrestle with her demons even as she created yet another method by which to represent the ways in which we experience life. For the structural framework, she returned to a sound from her childhood at St. Ives: the sound of waves hitting the shore, the elemental heartbeat of the beginnings of life itself. The meta-layer of this novel concerns the mythological connection to the hero's journey. Bernard is the ultimate hero, the Odysseus of her story—facing the struggles of life to close out his narrative, a collection of all of the voices within his own—with a challenge to Death itself to continue his journey to the bitter end.

The Meta-Story

As you read through chapters three through five, in which I provide an in-depth analysis of each novel from the literary Darwinist perspective, keep the following discussion at the back of your mind. I will return to it in more detail in the conclusion, at which time the theory will come full circle and my point will be made clear. Throughout her life, Woolf told stories of how to make sense of human experience, stories that could be said to form the arc of one, larger story. *Jacob's Room*, the exposition of this meta-story, introduces the basic conflicts of the plot, a young character coming of age, falling in love, going to war, meeting his death; in *Mrs. Dalloway*, the action of the plot begins to rise in a story that introduces competing and overlapping plot lines—the stories of Clarissa and Septimus, as well as a more complex contemplation on time and space. *To the Lighthouse*, part of the further rising action, returns to the more traditional view of a novel that addresses the lifetimes of its characters, but its structure as a triptych enables the reader to view Mrs. Ramsay, in particular, from three positions in time and space—the final frame holding just her image and not her physical presence. The two questions, "what does it mean to be human?" and "what is the meaning of life?" are further complicated by Lily's desire to hold on to the past and her inability to let go and move forward, though she is forced to do so. *Orlando* takes up the last piece of rising action with the story of a 16-year-old boy in the age of Elizabeth I and ends in 1928 with the 36-year-old woman, Orlando, a writer and wife of a sea captain. In this section of the meta-story, Orlando is both a man and a woman, the perfection of androgyny about which Woolf had written. In addition, the lifespan of this human has been extended into its own story of the evolution and development of the human species. *The Waves*, which works as the climax of the meta-story, shifts the focus from one character to six, although keeping the ghostlike figure of Jacob in the characterization of the absent Percival (absent except in the minds and words of the six characters). In this way, the issue regarding the "meaning of human life" has now been extended into the minds of six characters instead of just one or two. All of the issues from previous novels are at play—death, loss, the search for love, the fear of being alone—just multiplied six-fold. At the end of this novel, Bernard, the receptacle and voice for the other five characters, defies the finality of Death and vows to push on. *Between the Acts* provides the sudden and open-ended denouement of the meta-story, with the interrupted narratives of seven characters, accompanied by a chorus. But instead of Bernard's death-defying cry, we are left with questions and fragments, and a voice that is no longer as certain. This voice knows only that the curtain will rise again, and that, like Orlando, the world will go on without her.

This meta-story thus combines the elements of all six novels, such as archetypes of the Hero and Heroine, the Journey and the Quest, into an overarching theme: what does life mean, when considered from the point of view of its ending? What does it mean to live day after day and live to tell the tale? What difference will it make to future generations, these stories of survival? Woolf left a legacy of stories when she decided to leave the earth, stories that told us not of defeat, but of triumph and a stubborn will.

Conclusion

In the following pages, I pose the question: "Why stories?" to every writer and reader in my audience. Of Virginia Woolf, I would like to one day ask: why did you persist, in the face of great obstacles, in writing these curious but fascinating stories? As we close this chapter and enter into Chapter One which explains the literary Darwinist framework, I would ask you to keep in mind three basic questions: Why did Woolf write stories? In what way is her storytelling adaptive, for both herself and her audience? What is the larger, human purpose for her stories? Her stories reveal her to have studied human nature quite closely. She consistently sought explanations for why life was the way it was and theorized, in her stories, diaries, and essays, about the function of narrative in showing what she called *real life*. Her fiction evolves, even as she asks over and over again: "what does it mean to be human?"

I also ask that you consider, in light of several Darwinian themes, how Woolf's stories provide a space for cognitive play, in which she posed and answered questions for herself and her readers about the nature of life: "what does it all mean?" She wrote partly out of a deep need to understand her own life, but also the times in which she lived and the people of those times—each of the novels are firmly situated within the social and political issues of her day, particularly the two wars. I would argue further that her stories served as a kind of self-therapy—she worked over her childhood again and again, for example, acknowledging that in writing *To the Lighthouse*, she finally came to terms with the memories of her parents. In addition, she wrote as an artist, trying out various methods of writing fiction, another form of cognitive play. Finally, her stories are rooted in kinship and relationship, echoing what Darwin saw as the true nature of the world, one which is built on the principal of affinity rather than on a system of hierarchies.

At the end of her life, Woolf began to see death at her own hand as more and more of a possibility. After writing about it and talking about it for years, testing it out as a way to escape her continuing mental battles, she finally decided to spare Leonard more pain. Her decision to take that final walk, instead of an act of cowardice, should be seen as the choice of a strong individual, taking her fate into her own hands. In recent years, we have seen a few states grant their citizens the right to die. Woolf granted herself this right as a human being. Perhaps one thing her stories and her life can teach us about being human is that issue of choice, of human will and the human imagination. Woolf longed for a deep connection with life—she had lived a happy life with her husband, had enjoyed success as a writer, and so could be said to have lived a very successful and productive life in spite of her mental illness, perhaps in defiance of it. Her time of death was of her own choosing. As Hamlet wisely tells Horatio in Act Five as he prepared to face the poisoned sword of Laertes, "There is special providence in the fall of a sparrow. If it be now, 'tis not to come; if it be not to come, it will be now; if it be not now, yet it will come—the readiness is all. Since no man, of aught he leaves, knows what is't to leave betimes, let be."[29] At the very least she lived out her Story on her own terms, and by so doing added much to our understanding of what it means to be a flawed, and therefore perfect, human being.

Chapter One

The Evolutionary Power of Story

We—I mean all human beings—are connected...; the whole world is a work of art; ... we are parts of the work of art; ... we are the words; we are the music; we are the thing itself.—Woolf, *Moments of Being*

[The moment] is transitory, flying, diaphanous. I shall pass like a cloud on the waves. Perhaps it may be that though we change, one flying after another, so quick, so quick, yet we are somehow successive and continuous we human beings, and show the light through. But what is the light?—*Diary* III, January 4, 1929

There is grandeur in this view of life ... whilst this planet has gone cycling on according to the fixed law of gravity, from so simple a beginning endless forms most beautiful and most wonderful have been, and are being evolved.—Darwin, *Origin of Species*

The Human Story

Close your eyes and imagine what your world would be like if there were no stories: no novels, short stories, films, histories, biographies, autobiographies, or even video games. What would it be like if you did not possess the ability to tell a story that now seems to come so naturally? If it is difficult to imagine such a world it is because human beings seem to be natural born storytellers. We transform everything we experience into a story, from the iconic "first date," to the everyday trip to the grocery store down the street: all is fodder for the story machine.

The narrative formula we call Story is known to the very youngest child without ever having to learn it in school. On the first day of first grade, our teacher asked all of us to stand in the front of the class and tell our favorite fairytale. Although I can't recall which one I told, I know that

I began it "Once uponce [sic] a time" because this was how my mother began every bedtime story she ever told me. Although they weren't familiar with the exact story, the other children in the room immediately knew that I was telling a fairytale. The formula for Story has been ingrained in the minds of children before the first time they hear a tale. Such simple stories apparently have an important function: among other things, they carve a path in our brains that makes it possible to establish vital connections between our own minds and the world outside, a process that begins earlier than we had ever imagined. Alison Gopnik has explained at length the function of causal maps, the construction of which begins in early childhood—without them, it would be impossible to imagine the world as other than it is: it would not be possible to dream: "knowledge is what gives imagination its power, and what makes creativity possible."[1] Moreover, because Story is a tool for explaining the Self and for learning to comprehend and navigate the world, it is not a mere by-product of language as some have argued, but stands at the forefront of important developments in human cognition from the very beginning. Had I dropped the standard fairytale introductory language and simply launched into the story, not a child in the room would have been misled into thinking that I was doing anything other than telling a tale. And so it seems to have been for thousands of years.

Much of our knowledge of the prehistoric era is shrouded in darkness, especially when it comes to complex issues such as language and culture; however, based on the knowledge that we do have, we can intelligently speculate about why it is we have evolved to tell stories. Further, we might ask just why narrative developed as central not only to how we think, but also to whom we imagine ourselves to be. These questions might then lead us to analyze the conditions under which storytelling became such a central part of our identity and how we operate in the world. Do the functions of narrative, which began to evolve many thousands of years ago, still operate today? In what way does the phenomenon of Story as a part of our brain's structural design serve an essential or adaptive function? Every culture around the world enjoys a good story, right? What role might stories have played in the survival of our species, and what might that role look like going forward?

Given the time and the resources to analyze every story that has ever been told, we would likely recognize that stories serve many purposes in human life. We tell stories for all kinds of reasons: to entertain each other, to receive praise or attention, to explain a situation, to understand a problem, to make a connection with a new friend, to manage grief, to regain control, to celebrate, or to find a mate—reasons as endless and varied as we are. Over the years my students have told me how literature, and in particular, fiction, has meant to them. Just recently, I have been asking them to write down their responses to one question: Why are stories powerful in your own life? Here are a few of their responses:

"Fiction is a new way to try and untie the knots in our emotions" (Rocky).

"[Stories] have something in them that we as readers can connect to" (Amy).

"Fiction allows us to capture [the] pure essence of our being" (Hyung).

"Hope is what we seek to gain while we continuously run away into these stories, these places that are aside from our own reality" (Trey).

"Every time I read a new story, I learn something new ... about myself, or a new way of thinking completely" (Pam).

These comments, while anecdotal and incidental, indicate that stories communicate a Truth about human life that we are drawn to, time and time again. We might even venture to say that the history of humanity is itself one long unfinished Story overflowing with millions of smaller stories. As a central human activity, one that occupies much of our time, storytelling organizes our experiences and, thus, our lives.

So why do humans tell stories?

What compels us to create fictions to such a great extent that practically everything we know about the world comes to us through some form of narrative, whether scientific, philosophical, or literary?

How can we take our knowledge about fiction and gain understanding of not only the broad human story, but also the ways in which individual writers such as Virginia Woolf have contributed to that knowledge about who we are as human beings?

Finally, how can we use this knowledge to better understand each other, thereby creating strong and lasting bonds across diverse cultures? Despite the fact that, as Judith Rich Harris and others have observed, it is *human nature* to establish communities based on similar tastes in fashion, forms of behavior, beliefs, and language, stories have the power and potential to intervene in the sharpest of divisions.[2] That is certainly one way to define human nature—however, that picture only tells one side of a truth. Throughout history, in the most unlikely unions of diverse groups, stories serve to strengthen social bonds, increasing the likelihood of long term survival.

As I will explain throughout this book, stories entertain us in limitless ways, but they do more than entertain: they are the life blood of individuals and their societies. As Jonathan Gottschall has said, even when we sleep, we are telling stories to ourselves, stories that can't help but manufacture.[3] From the stories in our dreams to novels by writers like Virginia Woolf, stories shape who we are and give us the tools we need to fashion our world. Darwinian theory provides a way to explain the role of Story in human survival not only as individuals but on a grander scale, as a species. Literary Darwinism gives us new ways of understanding the role of fiction in everyday life. From this vantage point, we can see that an ability to create stories, like the acquisition of fire, would have given us an enormous evolutionary advantage: bringing a group of people together creates safety, security, and bonds of loyalty. Stories teach pattern recognition which aids in our ability to predict outcomes in unknown situations. Further, stories engage both hemispheres of our brains and involves several complex structures simultaneously, similar to why the brain responds to music. Contrary to the way many of us might think, while an interest in Story begins in childhood, storytelling is not just for children at bedtime: it is our "default mode" as human beings.

Darwin, Cognitive Science and Literary Darwinism

Since the day the first story was told, there have been listeners and readers of stories. Some of these readers are in the business of interpreting stories for others, based on various theoretical frameworks, known by such names as Formalism, Structuralism, Marxism, and Feminism and a host of others. Literary Darwinism, a relatively new theory, takes a view based in Darwinian science in order to address the questions concerning Story that continue to puzzle us: namely, how did the arts, and fiction in particular, originate and to what purpose? Why has this mode of communication (for that is it what a story is at its heart) continued to grow and develop through thousands of years? In short, just why is that we paint, make music, and tell stories? According to Carroll, the recognized leader of this new way of thinking, this theory may be best defined as "a modern evolutionary understanding of the evolved and adapted characteristics of human nature ... [Literary Darwinists] think that all knowledge about human behavior, including the products of the human imagination, can and should be subsumed within the evolutionary perspective."[4] This topic should not be a purely academic one, although it will continue to give academics a great deal to debate. My purpose in writing this book is to bring the discussion out of the Ivory Tower and into the living room in order to engage your imagination about the power of Story in everyday life. Specifically, in analyzing Virginia Woolf's fiction from an evolutionary point of view I hope to elucidate how stories help us to think more creatively, connect with our fellow humans, and overcome grief and trauma. The stories we tell about ourselves and each other *can* change us and, therefore, also change the world in which we struggle to survive.

Story as a phenomenon has pervaded modern culture in an unprecedented manner, through new platforms made possible by technology, such as computers, iPads, and cellphones; whether we write our stories out by hand, or whether we text, we can't seem to stop telling stories. According to a *New York Times* report in 2008, "a 21-year-old woman named Rin, wrote 'If You' over a six-month stretch during her senior year in high school. While commuting to her part-time job or whenever she found a free moment, she tapped out passages on her cellphone and uploaded them on a popular website for would-be authors."[5] We spin yarns every day to anyone and everyone who will listen. Stories bring the world to us in a way that has never before been possible—we can mourn with people thousands of miles away; our stories can create virtual friendships. Moreover, every story—those we tell and those to which we listen—constantly compete for our attention. We play endless games of "my story versus your story." Oftentimes, stories contradict each other, sometimes even contradicting our own intentions: it is typical that the storyline of one political party may seem stronger to one person than another; or the story that one child tells about her Superman dad might be more believable than that of her friend; or even one person's story in a court of law may override the story of an opposing witness, allowing one person to escape punishment while another is left to pay the penalty.

Stories serve various functions, even as they strive for our attention, in part because they represent individual versions of reality and truth. It seems that whoever wins this contest wins the right to make the rules and write *The Story*, commonly known as "The Grand Narrative." Some theorists believe that this Grand Narrative of humanity is detrimental, or that it does not exist at all: instead, they argue, there are only small stories that reflect individual experience. While I agree that there are individual stories, I would argue that Story, woven deep into human nature, not only exists, but that we contribute to it *every day of our lives*. If it is true that the winners write the story of human history, perhaps we should take more seriously the power we wield in the stories we tell. Through Story, I have the hope of understanding my next-door neighbor, as well as the person who lives halfway around the world.

One of the purposes of Story, and perhaps its origin in the first place, is to teach us the pitfalls of viewing the world from a limited vantage point. We see the world only through our own eyes, but what if I could see it through *your* eyes? What would change? Might I understand you more fully? Might I gain not only sympathy for you, but even better, empathy? Story affords us the opportunity to build connections with the Other, but only if we are *paying attention.* Some of the most innovative stories ever told have been those which place us in the position of a first person narrator. We have become so accustomed to this type of narrative that we don't notice it any longer, but even classic films have attempted this technique. In 1947, *Lady in the Lake* was shot entirely from the detective's point of view, letting us see everything through his eyes—the film's way of telling a first-person narrative. This little-known film provides a captivating example of the power of seeing from inside someone else's mind, as well as the frightening implications of being limited to only one point of view. *Being John Malkovich* and *American Psycho* stand out as two well-known modern examples of this narrative perspective. Tragic events of both domestic and civic violence in our communities and around the world underscore the crucial way in which our very lives depend on clear communication and on our capacity to listen to and empathize with someone else's story. If we do not listen, we do not learn. If we do not learn, we are bound to repeat our mistakes. Stories give us the opportunity to hear and to learn from someone else's experience, thereby creating connections that help us survive.

Our relationship to history and time is intimately and irrevocably linked to this storytelling function. As a matter of fact, our inclination—or maybe it is a compulsion—to tell stories may be said to be uniquely tied to the birth of modern man. Hundreds of thousands of years ago, stories taught us to predict the future, as it turns out, to the benefit of civilization. This development is important to who we are: you could argue that if not for the ability to predict future events with relative success, civilization may not have happened. Stories have helped us to map our own minds as well as to map the landscape around us. Without this ability, we could not function, either in the "real" world or, as it turns out, in the fictional world, as Zunshine has observed.[6] Using the data regarding autistic individuals, she determined particular connections between reading fiction and creating a workable Theory of Mind (Tom). Simon Baron-Cohen, drawing on similar evidence, concludes that "the capacity to imagine owes more to biology than to culture."[7] Thus, stories and the overall shape of narrative are embedded in our thinking, indeed in our very bodies. Through stories, we have learned to recognize a correlation between events, as well as to understand cause and effect. But there are no easy answers to the puzzle of Story's purpose in our lives. Critics of Literary Darwinism may well ask why, if stories are adaptive for survival, shouldn't they communicate something essential to that survival, some kind of factual information we could take stock in? Those who think the arts play a less important role in human life might ask "But aren't stories just child's play?" These same individuals may wonder what serious role Truth can play in stories, or, as cognitive scientists refer to them *counterfactuals*. Or they may question what Truth, or *whose* Truth, can be represented in stories, and whether this Truth is revealed or obfuscated? Perhaps, they might say, a story is the same as a lie; if this is so, how might a lie (a fabrication) be considered adaptive? Before we can think about the adaptive role of stories, or even begin to consider Woolf's works from an evolutionary point of view, we need to return to more basic questions: "Why do we tell stories, and how do they make us human?"

Spolsky, Tooby, Cosmides, Zunshine, and many others have explained the role and function of stories and other arts in cognitive development, breaking new ground in helping us understand how the brain operates, but more specifically, how it works to invent and understand fiction. Although these scholars may not agree on every detail of the evidence, I would venture to say that, at the very least, each of them have pushed scientific, literary, and cognitive research into new and promising directions. As we've seen, Literary Darwinism, which developed out of and alongside the integration of literary studies with evolutionary science, cognitive science, cognitive aesthetics, and evolutionary psychology (known as "ep"), has begun to offer some interesting answers, as well as even more illuminating questions by situating this *problem* of stories within an evolutionary framework. Taking a somewhat different view than other theorists, literary Darwinists claim that fiction is not only powerful in terms of explaining human minds and experience, but that it could be adaptive for the survival of our species.

We know that storytelling dates back thousands of years, and that while these ancient men and women certainly had more on their minds than sitting around the proverbial campfire telling stories to each other and to their children, we know that sometimes they did. Not only did their stories survive, but our species did as well. I do not mean to suggest that the survival of our species indicates that storytelling is *responsible*; only that it must have played a crucial role in both our evolutionary development as a species and in our everyday lives as individuals. The bold claim made by literary Darwinists about the role of Story urges us to consider various viewpoints from related fields, such as cognitive science and evolutionary psychology, as well as some of the earlier arguments by those who hold a different view. Key to the application of the literary Darwinist framework is a basic knowledge of Darwinian evolution, as well as an understanding of how and why the arts originated and how they later evolved. A literary Darwinist approaches the phenomenon of Story through questions such as: Why do we tell stories in the first place? What might have been the evolutionary advantage to the skill of storytelling in everyday life, or to the art of crafting popular or literary fiction for wider audiences? Why did a form that may seem like a rather useless entertainment emerge all of those thousands of years ago? Further, why did stories, once "invented," proliferate? And still more puzzling, why has Story as a structure perpetuated across vastly diverse cultures?

Because Literary Darwinism is rooted in an understanding of Darwin's writings, I will briefly highlight some of his ideas to which I will be referring throughout the book. The publication of Darwin's work—beginning with *On the Origin of Species* (1859), followed by *The Descent of Man* (1871) and *The Expression of the Emotions in Man and Animals* (1872)—marked a change in the grand quest to understand human nature and our purpose on the earth.[8] Janet Browne reminds us that with the publication of *Origin* came a mixed reaction: some praised it, while others were afraid of what seemed to be an attack on religion. Once *Origin* was published, Darwin waited for many years before including humans in his theory of evolution.[9] It has been speculated that he knew it would stir great controversy to even suggest that man had descended from apes, even without directly asserting that claim. This controversy swirled around Darwin's work for years (and for many, it still does). However, we may forget that even before *Origin* was published, people had begun to doubt the authority of religion on such matters. Instead of turning to religion for a story of human origins, many people began to turn to nature itself as a way of explaining our presence and place in the universe. A new story of our origins began to emerge with Darwin's theory.

One of the more significant breakthroughs in this area was his study of emotional expressions across various cultures, as described in *Expression*. In this illustrated book, he demonstrated that we can recognize emotional expression regardless of the cultural stimuli that may have caused them. Darwin showed that we expect similar emotions across diverse cultures to be evoked by similar stimuli, but even when the stimuli were vastly different, similar emotional expressions would arise. For instance, if I ingest something that "disagrees with me" in New York, like a Brussel sprout, my face may register disgust. In China, this same face of disgust may arise from eating a specific rice dish or shark tail soup: different stimuli, same emotional expression. This example is, of course, somewhat of an oversimplification, but my point is that in doing this research, Darwin helped to undergird a biological basis for an essential human nature, which did not result in a diminished view of life, but in one bursting with meaning and purpose.[10]

As I have suggested, the Enlightenment had already started to open up a space for a scientific storyline long before Darwin was born. Building on the work of a vast number of scientists and philosophers, Darwin and others provided more on-the-ground evidence for the story of evolution, essentially a new way to understand and explain ourselves to one another. Regardless of whether we were conceived by a divine being or whether we evolved from the microbes in the earth we walk on, this need to know and understand remains basic to our *humanness*. Science pulled back the curtain from the wizard's workshop, letting us see the inner workings of this mechanism we call LIFE, proposing new answers to puzzles like "How did we evolve into these communities of creatures who are dependent and interdependent?" What role did stories play in building community, and why? Have we always lived in community? What did the first human communities look like? It seems most likely that they were formed out of a need for safety and for purposes of sharing resources. As travel became more common, we started making connections outside of these small communities. Stories played a crucial role in breaking down cultural and communication barriers. Humans, regardless of variations in cultural habits, can relate to one another if given the opportunity. That ability to share who we are and to make connections with each other based on mutual understanding is vital to our social lives, but I would also add, to our very survival.

In order to understand the impact that Darwinian science has had on our understanding of human life, I offer this brief, and hopefully not overly simplistic, review of some basic ideas about human nature that had been taken as gospel until modern science and philosophy began to call them into question. The traditional view of human nature is that we all share the capability to reason, that we have a soul, and a self, or psyche. Although Western religious tradition claims that humans are made in the image of God, as evolutionary science emerged and developed, that understanding shifted from its central position to being one of many theories. In other words, the Biblical view of humankind was no longer the only game in town. Evolutionary science holds that humans are not a special creation of a higher power, but have developed along with the other plants and animals as part of Nature as a whole. From this point of view, humans are not specially designed apart from other creatures, but are deeply connected with all other living things. In addition, evolutionary science proposed that we are all—every living thing—in a constant struggle to survive.[11] Thus, the religious argument regarding human purpose was undermined by Darwin's theory.

This is not in any way meant to suggest that religion ceased to play a part in human life—to the contrary. The human story is intimately tied into religion and myth. As Gottschall points out, "humans conjure gods, spirits, and sprites to fill explanatory voids,"[12] similar to the reason we invent stories. It does mean, however, that human history took a different direction—we began to see ourselves differently, as part OF the natural world as opposed to being ABOVE it or apart from it. The growing angst in the late 19th century, continuing into the present day, has its roots in this revolutionary paradigm shift that began with the Enlightenment. Once humans were toppled from their special pedestal atop the hierarchical heap of creation, our place in the grand scheme of life was no longer one of undisputed authority. In some ways, the stories we told became richer and more complex as we began to search for and re-establish our identities along different lines.

What might Darwinian theory mean in terms of the function of Story in human culture? Literary Darwinism proposes that stories grow out of our need to understand our lives and our experiences, and ultimately to make meaningful connections with other humans. Stories enable us to see beyond our own limited perspectives and therefore to dream of what is possible. In creating and sharing stories, we are using an important tool in our species' survival. If we are all in a struggle to survive, this theory maintains that it may certainly have been adaptive to bond with other humans to increase the odds for survival. This potential for creating bonds and stronger social ties in and among communities may be just one function of stories.

Diverging from the work of Tooby and Cosmides, Spolsky and others, scholars such as Carroll, Boyd, Austin, and Gottschall have focused instead on the origin and function of stories for humans from an evolutionary perspective. Their investigations have yielded an ever-growing body of intriguing work as well as indicated fruitful pathways for further research. Situating story-making and storytelling within an evolutionary framework, as opposed to cognitive science in general, proves useful in not only tracing the origins of Story, but also in explaining why stories have been and continue to be central to human life. Returning to Carroll, in his early defense and explanation of literary Darwinism as a critical approach, he points out that although some may not acknowledge definitively whether fiction is adaptive—and this sentiment is not even shared by *all* Literary Darwinists—his evidence suggests that stories are certainly more than mere by-products of our evolved language abilities. Literary Darwinism, he insists, works in partnership with literary studies and the evolutionary understanding of human nature and human behavior, which includes our proclivity for telling stories.[13] Carroll laid the original groundwork in 1995 with his book *Evolution and Literary Theory*. This study marked a breakthrough in a field of study that has begun, especially in recent years, to gain more of a foothold in literary studies and in English departments throughout the academy. Although many scholars have contributed to this growing body of knowledge over a number of years, in synthesizing the tenets of this new approach, Carroll has provided a workable model for a new kind of literary analysis and interpretation. This basic critical framework is based solidly on both evolutionary science and literary studies.

Carroll has not been alone in this new way of thinking about literature. Prior to the work of Carroll and others, as early as 1940, Leo Henken, in his book *Darwinism in the English Novel*, describes the influence of evolutionary theory on such writers as Charles Kingsley in *Water Babies* and in *Transmigration* by Mortimer Collins. A sometimes overlooked analysis in this field is Randall Hood's text *The Genetic Function and Nature of Literature*, published in 1979, in which he presents an earlier version of the more recent studies such as Carroll's, linking the ways that literature helps specific "gene pools" to survive.[14] In such books as *Reading Human Nature: Literary Darwinism and Practice* (2011) and *Literary Darwinism: Evolution, Human Nature and Literature* (2012), Carroll has expanded and further developed his original thesis to describe in more detail the practice of this theory. Boyd's book *On the Origins of Stories* (2009), to which I have already referred, and Gottschall's recent work, *The Storytelling Animal: How Stories Make Us Human* (2012), bring to this discussion fresh insights regarding why we tell stories. Gottschall's book sets his account of Story within the history of human evolution, explaining that we are not only drawn to expressing ourselves in this form, but that it is fundamental to our identities.

Two works of literary criticism that have proven crucial in the formation of Literary Darwinism have been Gillian Beer's *Darwin's Plots*,

(1983) and *Darwin and the Novelists* by George Levine (1988). These two studies focus on Darwin's influence—either directly or indirectly—within 19th century fiction. Beer focuses on Darwinian influences in the Victorian novel, specifically in the works of Kingsley, Eliot, and Hardy. Her main point is to explore the ways in which Darwin's theory was assimilated by novelists who were experimenting with evolution as a "determining fiction by which to read the world," regardless of whether or not they were consciously doing so.[15] In her analysis, Beer identifies a few key evolutionary themes, gleaned from Darwin's writings, such as the "inextricable web of affinities"[16] and his concepts of time and history, fitness, descent, and sexual selection, using these as starting points to delve into particular novels. Beer develops a richly textured argument regarding the ways in which Darwin's theory illuminates the study of fiction and its evolutionary trajectory. Like Beer, Levine analyzes the work of Victorian novelists, Austen, Dickins and Trollope, as his primary targets of inquiry. He maintains that although Darwin's theories may have caught his own, and our, culture unprepared, his work has "transformed the way we can think about reality, about the way we exist in time, about what, after all, is possible."[17] Although Carroll has noted that Levine may have, in some ways, misread and/or misapplied evolutionary theory to fiction, I find in Levine's argument a meaningful foundation on which to build my own emerging ideas regarding this view of fiction, and a fruitful context in which to develop Darwinian arguments about Virginia Woolf's fiction.

In *On the Origins of Stories* (2009), Boyd, who designates himself as an *evo-critic* and not strictly as a *literary Darwinist*, offers significant insights regarding why we choose narrative as our go-to explanatory tool, or, why are there millions of books of fiction and non-fiction narrative in the world today? He argues that the presence of storytelling in human cultures helps us to be less restricted by the here and now, by only what is given and in front of us, unlike the other animals with whom we share a similar evolutionary history.[18] In *The Descent of Man*, Darwin was careful to build his argument from the premise that humans ARE animals that share many traits, even sympathy. Only in the areas of imagination and the higher intellect do we differ, he claims.[19] Our ability to tell stories arises from our imaginations. This ability, says Boyd, helps humans to cope with life more flexibly, as well as to imagine and then design possible solutions to problems of ever-increasing complexity.

Furthermore, Boyd contends, although narrative implies the use of language, a story need not even use words—it is a practice deeply embedded in our minds and bodies.[20] Our gestures and body language often tell a story we can't verbally express. This idea in particular opens up the possibilities for the adaptive function of Story in a way that rings true with what we can observe about stories in our everyday lives. We tell stories, Boyd further explains, because we are social creatures, and sharing stories has social benefits. We tell stories because we like to pretend and imitate the behavior of others. Storytelling, he theorizes, can help us make better decisions: as we look into the past, we seek patterns to help with a problem in the present, and then we look into the future to project the consequences or outcomes of our actions. Stories, in short, provide a testing ground for all sorts of ideas.[21] Boyd argues that because we are wired for what he calls "emotional contagion," we engage in three primary behaviors: we "imitate," we "empathize," and we seek patterns that look human, a face we can recognize and relate to within stories. Finally, I would emphasize two more functions of story that Boyd highlights: storytelling as a form of "reciprocal altruism," and as a way to garner "social status."[22] All of these roles and functions can be identified in Woolf's stories.

Adding to this growing body of knowledge, Michael Austin, in *Useful Fictions*, focuses on how stories help us cope with anxiety. More striking is his argument that storytelling itself is born of anxiety, reaching back thousands of years into our evolutionary history. What is evident is that deep-seated patterns of thought, which we organize into narrative form, have emerged through our continuing fascination with and dependence on stories. Although, as Austin points out, such narratives are "contingent, relative, fragmented and incomplete," they reflect the experience we have of the world. Stories engage both intellect and imagination in the search for meaning. Our *petits récits*, as Lyotard called them, may be "messy, gappy, biased, and highly subjective," but they serve an important function, says Austin, in that they help us to ease our anxieties.[23] I would maintain that even though we may view the Grand Narrative with suspicion, this does not mean that we won't continue to seek a kind of transcendent meaning in our lives through stories.

Despite the fact that they have distanced themselves from literary Darwinists, cognitive scientists and cognitive aestheticists have provided compelling evidence that reveals not only why we tell stories, but explains the functions of stories for human beings which includes pure entertainment value alongside complex brain processes. Zunshine, Ellen Dissanayake, and Denis Dutton, three such experts, have put forth related arguments regarding the way in which Story could possibly play an adaptive role. Zunshine argues that in *Mrs. Dalloway*, Woolf expresses a particular Theory of Mind, which is an "ability to explain people's behavior in terms of their thoughts, feelings, beliefs and desires."[24] This ability, in addition to helping us form close relationships, also helps us extract from fiction the patterns of prediction we need to survive in the real world. She uses as her primary example those who are autistic, arguing that their inability to formulate a cogent ToM severely inhibits them as they try to travel through a deeply social world. The development of ToM dates back to the prehistoric era when any misinterpretation of signals could end in death at the hands of a hungry predator. Even today, misunderstandings lie at the basis of most of our problems as we navigate our day-to-day interactions in the world. Modern humans need to hone the skills inherent in a strong Theory of Mind, perhaps now more than ever. Story plays a significant role in our ability to achieve this goal to our greatest advantage. When humans invented the arts, including fiction, we unknowingly invented a powerful method for creating this useful tool for navigating through the world.

Above and beyond the positive effects on our minds, in *Arts and Intimacy*, Dissanayake tackles the evolutionary concept of mutuality and affinity, identifying these as possible underlying motives for the creation of the arts. Perhaps she is picking up on Darwin's concept, as stated in *On the Origin of Species*, "Let it also be borne in mind how infinitely complex and close fitting are the mutual relations of all organic beings to each other and to their physical conditions of life."[25] Steven Pinker and many others, including Jared Diamond, have claimed that the arts were formulated as part of the bid for a sexual partner, which may be true, but Dissanayake takes issue with this notion, arguing instead that the arts stemmed from the mother-child relationship—specifically the mirroring of emotions and expressions between them. She argues, at least in part, that we need the arts to build a sense of interdependence within our communities. Expanding this argument concerning the functions of art, Dutton claims that because our imaginative life is fundamental to humanity, the creation of fiction is an evolved adaption that sets us apart from all other animals.[26] The imagination plays a crucial role in our day to day lives, he argues, helping us strategize tasks from the most mundane to the most complex. He further reasons that strategic planning (imagining a beginning, middle and end) is an adaptive function with crucial advantages to the modern human. Citing Tooby and Cosmides, Dutton argues that the prime case study for this is in children's play, in which they invent and inhabit imaginary worlds. A child's ability to "de-couple" fiction from reality goes a long way towards explaining how storytelling plays an adaptive role in human life. Without this ability to play out situations and scenarios, we would face nearly insurmountable difficulties in navigating in the world. This kind of *brain-play* makes it more feasible that fiction may be adaptive for survival. Humans have evolved as social creatures, and anything that facilitates this social function might be considered adaptive. Stories certainly fit the bill.

Although these cognitive scientists, cognitive aestheticists, evolutionary psychologists and literary Darwinists disagree on many points, they may concede that because stories are basic to the way humans think, we should, at the very least, continue our research into this phenomenon, especially since stories are ubiquitous in cultures around the world. Theories regarding the origins and uses of stories have proliferated into popular culture, becoming part of the way we have all begun to think about the arts and the evolution of human life. Jared Diamond and Leonard Schlain, two of the more well-known writers in the popular science genre, have explained the emergence of language and the arts in terms of human evolution. Diamond reminds us that it took millions of years before the Great Leap Forward propelled humans into the creation of art on a broad scale.[27] In other words, many upheavals in human development had to happen before art even appeared on the human stage. Diamond includes tool-making in his analysis, while Schlain argues that our leap forward was tied more directly to sex and childbirth.[28] He further explains that art, literature, rituals, and all forms of linguistic and musical innovations began out of the simple biological need for sex on the part of men and the need for iron on the part of women, asserting that "language evolved primarily because men and women had to negotiate sex."[29] The men who were the "most convincing talkers" would be most successful in gaining mates and having the most offspring, thus ultimately securing the survival of the species, one set of family genes at a time.

As similar arguments go, once our brains had developed to a point at which we could begin thinking in more complex ways, we began to tell stories. Ancient mythology illustrates this point particularly well—the earliest written records of storytelling include the epic poetry of Homer and the story of Gilgamesh, not to mention ancient religious texts, stories of creation that are surprisingly similar. Why might this be so? How is it that people from various cultures developed seemingly one story of creation and origin? If all language and all stories are situated in a cultural, historical context, how did these ancient myths, so similar in ideas and images, emerge to become universal in meaning? Furthermore, these myths contain the seeds of stories that have become new again, their deeper meanings instantly recognizable by people from diverse cultures. One need not look too far to find a plethora of examples in film and literature of the hero-cycle, for instance: *Star Wars*, *Harry Potter*, and *The Lord of the Rings* trilogy are among the most well-known, but the list is endless—the familiar structure of the hero's journey informs virtually every story.

Foundational to the heart of the literary Darwinist approach is an understanding of the familiar nature/nurture debate which underlies most of the recent political uproars concerning issues such as abortion, arts in the schools and affordable health care. We know, of course, that biology can only take us so far in life, and that culture's role is to shape and enhance our basic biological functions. Still at issue, however, is the degree to which biology and culture work together to shape human experience. Everyone has a vested interest in understanding human nature, an understanding which constantly guides our political, social, environmental, and other policies: how we raise our families, how we educate ourselves, how we view the role and function of entertainment in our culture, as well as our practice of the various arts in our daily lives. Since storytelling is basic to what it means to be human, we can then say that the very human ability to think narratively has implications that are far-reaching. Narrative thinking is based on pattern, speculation and planning, but also in *mind-reading*. If we were to lose even part of that ability, as some theorists have implied that we might with the explosion of a new visually based culture, the brain may experience changes to the way it processes information.

Could we lose the ability to build and/or extrapolate meaning if we no longer think through a situation with this narrative function guiding us? Are we at risk to lose the ability to make connection with others? With the unveiling of the genetic code, recent strides in cognitive science, and discoveries in neuroscience with regard to the way in which human beings act on a daily barrage of information, we should be closer to understanding some of the ways in which human nature both shapes and is shaped by cultural forces. Any assertion about storytelling and its motives assumes a basic human nature that we can all relate to. Of course culture does its part to shape us, but humans seem to have come into the world hardwired with certain proclivities which emerge from deep-seated structures within our brains. We are understandable to each other across cultures because we share basic human traits and behaviors, art being one of the more significant.

Arguments Against Literary Darwinism

Although the evolutionary view of stories may be compelling for some of the reasons I have reviewed, many literary scholars, evolutionary scientists and cognitive scientists remain unconvinced. One enduring argument against Literary Darwinism has been that stories are not adaptive because they serve no significant purpose—that they are entertainments at best and mysteries at worst. We don't really know, the argument goes, why stories matter. In particular, critics might ask whether stories teach us anything about how to live? Exactly how are they adaptive for survival? The whimsical nature of stories would seem to work against my hypothesis, especially a text like a fairytale. According to those who oppose this position, a thing can either be adaptive for a particular purpose, or it can be a side effect or "spandrel," to borrow a phrase from Steven Jay Gould. The purpose of language is to communicate information, others would argue, and so is relatively easy to explain as being an adaptive trait in human beings. But the language of storytelling is different. Not only is the language often of an elevated quality, the difference between a work of literature and a work of "ordinary" impact, such as a brochure or a magazine article, often runs from structure to content.

In addition, a work of fiction refers to situations that are not "real" or what we might consider factual. Certainly situations that COULD happen make for the intriguing stories, yet they have NOT in fact happened. Stories, while speculative in nature, take us into, as Gottschall says, Neverland, a place we do not want to leave behind.[30] While we are there, this "Neverland" becomes real to us, so much so that some would say we never really leave it—it remains in our minds long after we close the book. Neverland is, of course, populated with adults as well as children, both of whom enjoy reading the exploits of Harry Potter. Where else would we find such a hero except in a kind of Neverland? Adults also need to *make believe*, although they usually prefer more mature subject matter than we find within the *Harry Potter* series, adults also use stories as a way to escape. Regardless of whether there is a happy ending, the simple fact is that, as many people have observed, fiction helps humans to know themselves. Stories afford us ways to ameliorate confusion, grief, and stress, and to establish imaginative connections with other minds. The power of Story lies in its compelling ability to explain life's entanglements on both a more basic level and a more mysterious one.

One of the strongest arguments against Literary Darwinism comes from those known as post-structuralists. In the latter part of the twentieth century, this school of criticism emerged through the work of Jacques Derrida and later, Michel Foucault, the result of which has been a cultural and philosophical shift concerning, among other things, the important question of human nature and identity. This shift takes us far from a world we can know into one which we construct and still cannot know. Derrida argued that meaning in a text is continually deferred, and that there is only difference (or *differánce*). Difference, of course, is most certainly basic to being human and to the way we experience life. But difference is not all. In order for there to be difference, there must first be similarity. In order to recognize the dark, we must first see the light. The more difficult concept to grasp is the word's meaning "to defer," in that meaning is constantly *deferred* in a play of signifiers.[31] The binary formulations which Derrida and others demonized comprise a pattern that our brains create in an attempt to understand our surroundings. We have been hardwired to find similarities and patterns in the world around us, as well as to stay alert to crucial differences in the landscape. Our primitive ancestors used this ability to help them to survive. As a default mode of thinking, it is not perfect, but it served a specific set of purposes and continues to do so. Apparently, the way we make sense of these patterns, on many levels, is through narrative, which operates on tension and the resolution of tension.

While post-structuralism does not account for why there are stories in the first place, literary Darwinism attempts to unearth answers to these first kinds of questions. Spolsky, in her most recent book, takes issue with Carroll's critique of Derrida and post-structuralism. I mention it here to point out the fine points of difference between a cognitive literary theorist and a literary Darwinist. She argues that "Darwin's notion of fit is in fact a biological description of the central deconstructionist claim—namely that there is no stabilizing center but that iterable meaning, including its inevitable swerve, is, like adaptation, dependent on its function within a context."[32] The only stability that counts, from the Darwinian standpoint, is the one that is "good enough." While I agree that we cannot fully know *Truth*, we can know some *truth* which is grounded in real, lived experience. In addition, while I do not wish to align myself with social constructivists, I would agree that meaning is, by necessity, contingent. Nothing exists in a vacuum—contexts constantly shift. Life would be impossible if we had no markers, no path to follow in order to navigate. I would maintain that stories help to enact those markers, and in some cases even generate them.

Who among us can't recall where we were at a tragic or momentous occasion in the past? We have no doubt told story after story about such experiences which have sometimes become part of the *official* history reflecting the experience of people long dead, as well as those still living. Stories say to us *pay attention—this is important!* Mark Turner calls the ability and tendency to tell stories "parable," a term that refers not only to the genre, but to its biological function in our brains—Turner argues that we "parable" our existence on the earth. As he points out, parables are one of the most basic kinds of story forms that demonstrate this very point. A parable says to its readers/listeners: "Listen to this tale of a widow and her lost coin so that you too may understand who God is." A fable says "Listen to this story about the dog who dropped his bone in the river because he saw something he wanted more." We project onto these stories the lessons we need to learn about life.[33] While the stories themselves may give rise to an imaginary world, they refer to real life, although a life that is often unstable and contingent upon context.

According to this view, human nature does not reflect an essence but is, in fact, a cultural construct. Not only is reality a social construction, this argument goes, but meaning itself is contingent and thus constructed. There is no *Truth*, they claim, only small *truths* which are always suspect because such truths are always mediated by language—another social construct. Furthermore, a text is the representation of a world *always already* mediated by language, itself a representation, and so the circle goes, round and round. The world that we once knew has become unknowable and none of us, apparently, occupy an objective reality. Not only is the world unknowable, but also, when we do construct meaning, it is immediately undone and undermined. This is a particular point which Carroll takes up in full force in his book entitled *Evolution and Literary Theory*.[34] When he refers to post-structuralism, he means "the whole array of schools and methodologies that have clustered around two central concepts: that words make the world, and that all meaning is self-contradictory."[35] In other words, "Language shapes reality"; "reality is a social construct": these are the tenets of a post-structuralist view of reality and human perception.

If, as some would argue, we take this assertion to its logical conclusion, we would become free of judgment and more tolerant: the virtue of having no singular *Truth* to agree on enables us all to construct our own *truths*. But if this singular *Truth* does not exist, it would also seem logical to conclude that we will eventually become further divided from each other. To put it another way, if there is no *central* human experience we can all share, diverse cultures will one day be unable to understand each other and thus to communicate with each other on any meaningful level. As their argument would apparently have it, there is no basic, knowable human nature outside of culture. In short, proponents of this theory argue that we are who we are only because of *created culture*. The boundaries of biology exist of course, but culture alone does not produce the human essence. Such theorists take the view for instance that at birth we may be male or female by virtue of our sexual organs, but *masculine* and *feminine* are cultural constructs, a point I am willing to concede: if you have female sexual organs, you may identify as a male, or vice versa. But has Biology/Nature, and thus evolution, been subsumed by Nurture/Culture: is everything contingent? I would argue that sexuality is only one dimension of what it means to be human: regardless of sexuality, human nature has an identifiable essence. Without that common ground, we would not be able to communicate or transfer meaningful ideas. Literary Darwinism is the interdisciplinary response to what Carroll and others deem the relative emptiness of post-structuralism.

The Argument for the Evolutionary Power of Stories

Post-structuralism cannot account for why there are stories in the first place, but literary Darwinism attempts to resolve these perplexing questions. Practitioners contend that the text is NOT all—that the world is a real place and that words have an impact in the real world. Specifically, in contrast to the idea that everything is representation, that a text, in particular a literary text, refers to nothing but itself and other texts, stories instead reveal a real world that humans inhabit and with which they interact, reminding us of their power to shape us AND our world.[36] Both Turner (*The Literary Mind*) and Austin (*Useful Fictions*) in their discussions of this phenomenon use the stories of Scheherazade to illustrate an important point about stories and human life. Austin points out that one of the lessons readers can learn from Scheherazade's *One Thousand and One Nights* is that stories are deeply embedded in who we are as humans, and as such are vital to our existence.[37]

The notion that language actually points to something other than itself, however, undermines the concept of a world that has been emptied of substantive meaning. Although the tenets of post-structuralism have been absorbed by culture at large, due in large part to the wide dissemination of Michel Foucault's work, this critical practice has begun a slow decline in popularity. I would argue that this philosophy has not delivered on many fronts, its primary short-coming being its inability to account for the basis of the truth of being human, what we share, what we all know as human beings to be the essence of our very natures. The literary Darwinist's argument, on the other hand, shows us how stories return us to who we are, how they connect us to each other in an almost primal way.

In her own way, Woolf plays the part of Scheherezade as she weaves story after story to challenge the way we think about the world and our place in it.

One of the reasons we tell stories, I would argue, is for their explanatory power. The sequence of cause and effect initiates a pattern through which the inexplicable becomes a bit clearer, bringing comfort to the reader. The simple pattern of tension followed by release forms the basis of plot, as well as melodic and rhythmic structure in music. In order to show how story works on this level, Gottschall, Robert Storey, and others take us into the childhood realm of make-believe in order to demonstrate the primacy of pattern and the power of Story to explain our lives. Far from taking us away from reality, fiction allows us to think about it more efficiently. Although children immerse themselves in imaginary worlds, they ultimately know the difference between fantasy and reality, but the interesting thing is, they learn from their fantasies lessons that they apply in real life. Children's stories are often full of "catastrophe—sometimes violent conflict" says Storey. These "narratives are, in effect, rehearsals of possibility" that are "stimulated by imaginative rewards."[38] The playground of the mind serves a more serious purpose as we mature into adults.

Important in this theory is that stories are about more than conveying information. A story is, instead, fertile ground for the replication, in miniature, of the very arc of a human life. A story dramatizes, from a safe distance, some of the dangers inherent in human life. Fairytales in particular help us see how stories work. These tales portray a fanciful yet dangerous world in which anything can happen: think of the stories of Little Red Riding Hood and Hansel and Gretel. While Red does encounter a talking wolf, which is pure fantasy, children understand that this wolf stands for danger. Seen from this perspective, stories ease the transition from a literal to a figurative understanding of the world as well as enriching our experiences of daily life. Further, the tale of Hansel and Gretel allows a child to face danger from a safe distance, enabling her to consider what one might do in an insecure situation. While mothers and fathers may not always be kind and nurturing, sometimes the guy who wears the black hat may be the good guy.

Moreover, a story calls attention to an instance of human life in which we can picture ourselves and judge the choices of a particular character. Even video games now come complete with stories through which the player can participate in solving a puzzle or living out a fantasy. What is the purpose of all of these stories? A Lacanian critic may concede that a fairytale could serve as a way for a child to enter into the symbolic realm, and thus into culture as a whole human self, but the tales themselves are not seen as having a more basic, human function, and no ultimate meaning for us. If there is no significant answer regarding what it means to be alive, then there would be no purpose for a story: at its most basic level, this is what a story asks. A purposeless life would have no need of fiction, the very foundation of which is the resolution of conflict. Surely one of the reasons we tell stories is to give ourselves direction and hope, a reason to believe for the future.

Mysteries such as "Why do we have art?" and "Why do humans tell stories?" have begun to emerge as central concerns in understanding the phenomenon of stories and their importance in our lives. Perhaps this new exploration into the origin and possible adaptive feature of stories is a backlash against the tenets of post-structuralism, but there are ways in which Literary Darwinism and some of the basic theories of post-structuralism intersect. As we saw, Spolsky recently discovered an interesting connection between Darwin's ideas and the theories of post-structuralists, particularly Derrida, with regard to the concepts of contingency and context. Contrary to what Carroll claimed in 1995, that these theorists make any claim to truth or meaning incoherent,[39] Spolsky points out that Derrida was, in fact, correct in postulating that all truth and all reality are context dependent.[40] We can't know anything outside of a context. Instead of undermining the idea of meaning, then, contingency and context are what GIVE meaning. I would agree—this insight may even help to explain why we conjure stories out of the most mundane of situations: we must make meaning out of the stimulus around us: the elderly man at the bus stop with a baby carriage, the woman crying in the grocery store, the child walking down the street alone, wearing only one shoe; or even an ant carrying a piece of grass—all of these become material for a potential story. It takes very little for humans to see a story in everything around us.

Conclusion: We Make Stories Out of Everything

As a way of illustrating this fact, I offer a well-known film with has been cited by many as an example of the way the human mind is a story-machine: In 1944, Franz Heider and Marianne Simmel made a short animated film that we now call the *Heider-Simmel illusion*. This film, which they made as a part of their research into a phenomenon called "attribution," illustrates the way humans invent stories out of very sparse information because of our deep need to understand the world. First, I will attempt to describe in objective terms the action in the film. As the film opens, we see a Large Triangle, what I will refer to as LT, in a rectangular enclosure. LT moves to close the open end of the rectangle. Out of the top left hand corner of the screen appear a Circle, what I will refer to as C, and a Small Triangle, which I will refer to as ST. These shapes move rapidly toward the rectangle. LT leaves the enclosure to move towards ST. These two shapes collide and bump each other: LT pushes ST, after which C enters the rectangle. ST stays outside of the enclosure as LT enters, following C. As C tries to leave the enclosure, LT blocks its path. ST opens the side of the enclosure, C dodges and then makes its way around LT, joining ST outside. LT then leaves the enclosure to follow ST and C; eventually these two shapes exit upper left. LT returns to the rectangle and breaks it apart.

It is difficult to describe the action in this film in a strictly objective manner. As I watched, I realized I was constructing a narrative in order to make sense of the shapes on the screen. I began ascribing emotions and intent to what I was seeing. I could not help myself. Heider's research further underscores the role of narrative in human life. What I wanted to say about the actions in this film was closer to the summary of a popular soap opera, which might go something like this: Stephanie, the daughter of Larry, and Charlie are young and in love. They come home late from a date. Larry scolds and chastises Stephanie severely, taking her aside and away from Charlie's hearing. Charlie goes inside the house to wait for her, but Larry shoves her aside, entering the house alone to confront Charlie, who is quaking in a corner. Stephanie lurks outside, as if looking for a way to enter the house and help Charlie. She finally opens the door to find Larry glowering, hovering over Charlie in a threatening manner, blocking his path to the door. Charlie is trapped at first, but then manages to dodge Larry. He makes it to the door, and runs outside to join Stephanie, where the two lovers rejoice at being reunited. Meanwhile, Larry, frustrated and angry, runs outside to confront them both, chasing them around the house, until the two escape from the house and leave the area. Larry turns back to the house in anger, breaking down his own front door and smashing all of the windows. This is where the "story" ends. Of course, another person seeing this film might craft a different scenario that would fit these actions. The point is, however, that we would both have told a story in order to bring meaning to what otherwise would be a few meaningless shapes moving around on a screen.

How does my ability to build a story from three shapes on a screen have anything to do with my survival? Is Story adaptive, as Carroll argues that it could be, or is it merely a by-product, as Steven Pinker has claimed? For his part, Carroll argues that all knowledge is, at the root, a "biological phenomenon," and that stories are a "form of that knowledge."[41] One of his most compelling arguments most relevant to my book is the concept of storytelling as "cognitive mapping," one of the primary functions of Woolf's writing. She was able to formulate a theory regarding the workings of her mind, and to use that knowledge to sketch out ideas for her fiction. As I will discuss later, when she was ill, she kept close track of the permutations of her own mind, as much as she was able, in order to better understand herself, and thus tap into her creative impulse. Carroll's point, that stories both mirror and express our basic human nature, is also a direct response to relative empty arguments made by poststructuralists.[42] Stories are not only adaptive, but also they make us human. I agree with Gottschall, who has argued that Story is the one element that separates us from other mammals as nothing else in human culture. For our species, he says, story is all-encompassing, like the air we breathe—we are fully immersed in the land of make-believe.[43]

Stories provide for humans a way to bring structure and understanding to our experience. With stories, we can explain the world to ourselves and others, and these tales range from the most mundane to the most grandiose. Boyd insists, as well, that we are just plain compelled to tell stories—we can't stop. Why, he wonders, since evolution is the "richest" story of all, hasn't it been used to help us understand the importance of narrative in our lives?[44] Why not, indeed? One of the evolutionary advantages of Story is that it operates on several levels simultaneously, transmitting a special category of information, creating bonds within a community and between communities that are seemingly different, training the brain through cognitive play to predict future situations and outcomes based on contextual information, to seek patterns of meaning in the "real world" and learn how to navigate moral and ethical dilemmas within a safe space: basically, stories teach us how to survive in the world. Kinship, mother-child mutuality, sexual attraction and fitness, as well as cognitive play and mapping all operate within stories to varying degrees as Darwinian themes.

Critics may argue that a novelist who is not consciously aware of using such themes cannot be pulled into this kind of perspective. I argue to the contrary, that because these themes reflect the foundations of human experience, they are ubiquitous, all-encompassing, and appear to varying degrees in all of fiction. Both writer and reader benefit from stories, but in different ways. When the writer sees her "mind thinking," as Woolf does, she discovers what this mind is made of and how it operates. Stories lift us above the mundane to expand not only our minds but our souls. That land of make-believe has a purpose: to expand our minds and lift the boundaries of our bodily experience. This last idea harks back to the theory and practice of such authors as Shakespeare, Wordsworth, Keats, and Emily Dickinson: literature and its appreciation are about more than just a love of language. As for this idea, what would be the evolutionary advantage? Does the fact that stories help us to become smarter, to build connections with each other, and comfort us in times of grief, also mean that stories are thus adaptive for survival? In the next three chapters, I will offer up some answers as to why stories matter in our everyday lives.

So why did we evolve in this way? Why are stories our default mode for understanding and explaining the world? Questions that spring from the literary Darwinist perspective situate my reasons for writing about Virginia Woolf from an evolutionary perspective. She most certainly experimented with language and structure, as have many other writers, but her goal as a writer was to get closer to representing a world as human beings experience it, not further away. As we've seen, the mediation of reality which language provides is unavoidable because writing is doubly mediated, a double bind of which Woolf was aware. But that is the human condition—the only way to express ourselves is through language so that what is inside can be represented and expressed to a larger audience. A deeply embedded set of connections, established through this medium we call storytelling, binds us together in the common Human Story. In the following section, *Practice of Story*, I will explain how six of Woolf's novels correspond to three primary powers of storytelling: to comfort, to connect, and to create new ways of thinking about ourselves and the world in which we live. Far from being mere entertainments, stories ground us in lived experience and have the potential to act in our lives as agents of change.

PART TWO: PRACTICE OF STORY

Chapter Two

The Power of Story to Comfort: *Jacob's Room* and *To the Lighthouse*

> Listless is the air in an empty room, just swelling the curtain; the flowers in the jar shift. One fibre in the wicker arm-chair creaks, though no one sits there.—WOOLF, *Jacob's Room*
>
> What is the meaning of life?—WOOLF, *To the Lighthouse*
>
> Sympathy with the distresses of others, even with the imaginary distresses of a heroine in a pathetic story, for whom we feel no affection, readily excites tears.—DARWIN, *The Expression of the Emotions in Man and Animals*

Because human beings experience a broad range of events during their lifetimes, stories necessarily come in all shapes and sizes and serve multiple functions. Speaking in evolutionary terms, stories have served the purpose of everything from entertainment to purposeful deception; some, but not all, of these functions, may be adaptive for human survival. Although we may hold the entertainment function in higher regard than other possible functions, stories are not all just for fun; sometimes the overarching entertainment value of stories includes their value as *catharsis*. It would be difficult to find a story that did not afford us the opportunity to express our emotions in a relatively safe manner and allow us to become, once again, the heroes of our own lives. Holding a box of Kleenex in my lap while reading a sad novel can be a most satisfying way to spend a Saturday night. Reading a story that makes me cry alleviates—even if just for a moment—my grief over a lost lover, the death of a loved one, the loss of my job, or even just a bad day. As I read, suddenly I'm not alone any longer because I have found *someone* within the pages of my novel to share my grief, *someone* who understands me. This recognition lets me know my pain will end, and I will triumph over my circumstances, if only temporarily. Moreover, from reading that novel, I have learned a new way to think about my loss because I've been given a way to reframe it. Instead of feeling defeated by loss, I can feel empowered by sharing my pain with someone else, even though this *someone* is in a story. I may even pick up the phone and call a friend who has had a similar grievous experience to tell her about a novel I just read that brought me great comfort.

We know this pattern of behavior so well that we have organized book clubs that categorize our favorite stories for easy access, according to the ones we need most at certain times. In fact, in 2014, Ella Berthoud and Susan Elderkin published a volume called *The Novel Cure: From Abandonment to Zestlessness, 751 Books to Cure What Ails You*. Apparently fiction is better than a psychologist at helping us deal with a broken heart. The writer of such a story benefits as well, finding relief from the heaviness of grief. Stories that have the power to evoke our tears thus serve a practical function: they aid in the grieving process, bringing comfort and thereby helping us to heal. We are *cured*, if only momentarily, from pain that is all too common to human experience. Most important to my point about the evolutionary power of this kind of story, stories born of grief are stories at their most human, vulnerable and intense. As soon as we read or hear such a story, we feel its impact down to our toes. I would add that grief over a loss and illness—whether loss of health, either physical or mental, or a general feeling of *dis-ease*—makes us hyper-aware of the freedoms and the limitations of our bodies. After the losses of her mother, step-sister, brother and father, Virginia Woolf experienced periods of intense physical and mental illness. She wrote stories throughout these periods of illness, however, finding a sense of release as she confronted the demons of loss, trying to lay her ghosts to rest.

When we suffer loss, life as we have known it comes to an end and the grieving process begins. Grief looks different for everyone, but generally, any kind of loss, be it death, divorce, illness, or just moving to a new home, causes a disruption in the routine of our daily lives, and in the *life story* we have *written* up to that point. In order to survive this kind of trauma, we must create a new storyline: one with a new plot, a new purpose, and new main characters. Sometimes, one of those new main characters is ourselves because we inevitably become new people as we grieve. Regardless of how long it takes, we are building a bridge, one shaky, wooden plank at a time, on our way back to a new reality. As a child, Woolf suffered what she called a "shock" upon hearing about the suicide of a man whom her parents knew. As she walked into her garden that night, she came upon an apple tree which she was unable to bypass: "It seemed to me that the apple tree was connected with the horror of Mr. Valpy's suicide.... I seemed to be dragged down, hopelessly, into some pit of absolute despair."[1] She wondered how she would get around that tree which had become, in her mind, symbolic of this suicide.[2] After this jolt to her system, she needed a path back into her everyday routine. Years later, after she had suffered the loss of many family members, she used stories as a bridge to cross over from grief to healing. The new story we write after a loss can bring back a sense of normalcy, relief and solace. This is storytelling as praxis; time after time, we can count on the grief story to bring comfort and a sense of order back into our lives.

One type of comforting story is the traditional fairytale. Children are generally drawn to these stories that inevitably end happily after a tragic event has ensued: the princess, once a prisoner of the wicked witch, is rescued from the tower; the wicked witch, who had thought to inherit the kingdom and enslave the people, is punished; Snow White, who appeared to be dead, is awakened, and what looked like death turns out to have only been sleep after all. Although the stories we encounter as adults do not always end happily, we are nevertheless drawn to them for their power to heal, to impose an order upon situations that can feel confusing. Narrative structure, especially when coupled with the journey archetype, connects us to the deep history of humanity. As Joseph Campbell and others have explained, this archetype has been used across time by every culture as a way to express the basic notions of what it means to be human: the overcoming of obstacles and the sharing of wisdom within the community at large. It is a literary motif with which we readily identify, and we see it everywhere in our culture, from children's cartoons to financial investment advertisements, such as Fidelity Investment's image of the green arrowed road, prompting the viewer to "turn here" for the good life. Coupled with journey, hero, and heroine archetypes, the grief story enables the sufferer to face their loss because it holds out the promise of a positive resolution. Just how does this account of the role of stories in the alleviation of grief fit into an evolutionary explanation of why we tell stories? How could stories about grief, used as a tool for healing, be considered part of an adaptive function for humans? Why does the imaginative act of going through the cycle of grief and healing within a story help us survive actual grief and enable us to heal? The ultimate question in this discussion becomes: how do grief stories comfort us and help us survive our own lives?

First, grief affects our physical as well as mental health, causing an interruption in our lives, from slight to life-threatening. Depending on the severity of the loss and the intensity of the grief, it can take years to regain our balance, but perhaps longer than that to completely recover. Psychologist and author Elizabeth Kübler-Ross is perhaps most famous for her explanation of the Five Stages of Grief.[3] While some may disagree with her formulaic approach, she does attempt to provide some kind of structure to what can seem chaotic to the person who is grieving. Jamison relates accounts of depressive illness in creative people, including herself, revealing important insights into the impact of depression on the human mind and body.[4] Arthur Frank, the author of *The Wounded Storyteller: Body, Illness, and Ethics*, has studied the stories of patients for many years in an effort to understand how such narratives enable the ill to cope with their *dis-ease*.[5] These experts are just three are among the many psychologists and medical doctors who have shown the ways that our bodies, minds, and hearts can be harmed when we do not process anxiety, stress, and grief in a healthy manner. Second, when we are in the midst of grieving, we need a way to regain agency and re-establish control in our lives.

Telling a story, and thus bearing witness to the grief one feels, is one of the more important ways in which this healing takes place. Though loss takes away our sense of control, itself only an illusion, creating a story about loss returns to us that necessary illusion, so that we can regain a sense of balance and go on living. In fact, expressions of grief in the form of stories have become part of the ritual of healing itself. We have made an art form of it: elegies are one of the most popular forms of poetry, and popular music has made an institution of losing one's lover. Third, a grief story serves an important social function as well, bringing people together who have suffered similar losses or who have suffered in similar ways so that together, they can find a way to recover. Writing *Jacob's Room* and *To the Lighthouse* enabled Woolf to confront her grief in a safe manner and indirectly pass along her knowledge about how to cope with the sadness we feel in the face of inevitable loss. Finding a way to grieve—in this case, telling a story—enables the sufferer to come to terms with the loss, regain an illusion of control, and discover a path to a more balanced outlook.

Having suffered the shock of suddenly losing a brother, I can attest that grief after a loss can feel like a chronic illness, to the point of manifesting as physical symptoms of pain. As I tossed and turned in bed the night before his funeral, my body sweated out a high fever, the cause of which was nothing but pure grief. My mother's death felt like more of a long goodbye: diagnosed with a malignant brain tumor in 2001, she finally succumbed in late 2002 after two surgeries and many rounds of chemo and radiation. Although I do not remember feeling physically sick during that time, I remember that I gained weight and lost hair by the handfuls due to stress. Having family to talk to about our mutual loss was crucial: sharing our grief lightened the burden, enabling us to heal together. The traditional Irish Wake is a good example of this function of stories: families of the deceased find comfort and strength in telling stories of their loved ones. Because grief can feel like a kind of illness, stories about illness are useful as a way of explaining the role that a "grief and healing" story plays in the adaptive function of fiction. In his book, Frank groups such stories into four categories: the "restitution" narrative, the "chaos" narrative, the "quest" narrative, and the "testimony."[6] Each narrative tells us something significant about the person who tells that kind of story, but also about the nature of illness, and for my purposes, the *grief* he or she is experiencing.

While I argue that *Jacob's Room* is a kind of chaos story—which I will explain in that section of this chapter—*To the Lighthouse* most closely resembles the quest mode. Each of these types of stories serve a slightly different purpose. In the restitution mode, for instance, the teller seeks healing and a return to health. She must believe that complete healing is possible, and so she lives as if she is healthy. For every kind of illness and suffering, according to the restitution plot, "there is a remedy."[7] The trick is to find the answer to the puzzle that death produces for us, a problem that can be solved through the *restitution narrative*. The correlation to death in a grief story would be the urge to simply give in and give up. If one is telling a restitution type of grief story, one is looking for a resolution so that the *cure* can take effect.

Boyd claims that one of the effects of art, and therefore fiction, is its ability to form bonds between people, a function he calls *attunement* which arises out of shared attention. He argues that this phenomenon is in direct relationship to the importance of social cohesion.[8] I think of attunement in terms of general social cohesion as well, but in the context of this discussion, I will place an emphasis on the kind of attention shared by those in grief. For reasons I have already described, people who grieve feel cut off from society—it has even been reported that after a loved one dies, the one left behind may feel shunned by his or her friends (this happens especially after a spouse dies).

For purposes of my argument, I wish to appropriate Frank's categories to explain the important role that stories play as they bring healing and comfort. I must also stipulate that the four kinds of illness/grief narratives he describes provide a general framework to talk about how grief stories like *Jacob's Room* and *To the Lighthouse* illustrate the evolutionary feature of attunement. *Jacob's Room* occupies one end of a spectrum as the chaos narrative that expresses the sufferer's struggles to understand her loss and assign it a meaning of some kind, while *To the Lighthouse*, more of a quest narrative, borders on testimony in that the teller understands that her journey through grief can end in a blessing. The loss is felt deeply, but the sufferer comes away having gained an insight into her grief; any kind of meaning, even if it is provisional, brings relief. Stopping short of the moral imperative of a testimony that Frank describes, *To the Lighthouse* ends with an affirmation. Attunement is achieved with both stories, however, in that the sharing of grief brings people together as they seek comfort. Just as the characters in both novels come to terms with their loss both individually and as a group—in this way they are both storytellers and audience—Woolf's family was the immediate audience that was brought together, even though Vanessa found the novel to be a particularly painful story to read because of the vivid memories it evoked. The larger audience is comprised of Woolf's numerous readers, both then and now.

Attunement is one of the highest forms of social cohesion because it engenders sympathy and empathy which makes all of society stronger. As Darwin says, humans are "impelled to relieve the sufferings of another, in order that our own painful feelings may be at the same time relieved," noting also that communities in which sympathy is practiced "would flourish best."[9] In *Jacob's Room* we read of a man who shuns the connections of his own community, leaving behind friends and family to grieve their loss together, seeking answers and hoping for comfort.

Jacob's Room (1922): Plot and Introduction

Woolf completed the first draft of *Jacob's Room* on November 14, 1921, embarking on her second "voyage out."[10] The novel that Kate Flint has described as "stylistically adventurous" marks the beginning of a series of experiments, each one progressively pushing the genre of narrative fiction a bit further.[11] As she wrote each of these stories, she discovered the content and structure that enabled her to express the nuanced feelings and thoughts of which she was capable. The innovative structure not only complements the subject, but also signals, in some ways, the stirrings of the Modernist experiment in literature, including such works as Pound's *Cantos* and Eliot's *Waste Land*. For this new world, signaled by World War I and other events, new kind of story was needed, a new way to describe a new reality. The reality of 1922 was one for which the old ways of explaining things, through religious belief in particular, no longer seemed tenable. Reality would not consist, for this new type of story, of something cut out of cardboard and arranged on toy stage, but something that would reveal itself as a process, the way life itself unfolds. Woolf had written in several essays and in her diaries over the years, of her frustration with realist fiction which had failed to capture reality; *Jacob's Room* is her answer. The plot is notoriously difficult to summarize because its structure challenges the traditional form of a novel.

The plot involves a young man named Jacob Flanders who *flounders* around in his life and *founders* early only to die in World War I. He wanders from childhood into young adulthood with about as much purpose as the butterflies he pursues. Jacob appears to have been born with a broken heart and a sense of loss. Like the crab that cannot crawl out of his childhood sand bucket, he cannot seem to crawl out of the trap of his life and find a clear path into the future. While in school, he floats from one party or one girl to another, never staying for too long in one place. After university, he gains a position at the Bar, but he makes little use of his opportunities. The high point of his brief life occurs when he takes a journey to Greece and falls in love with a married woman. Predictably, that relationship ends up a dead end. Eventually, he drifts into the war and disappears. In the closing chapter, the story comes full circle, with Jacob having died and answered the call to come home at last. The closing sentence reads: "She [Mrs. Flanders] held out a pair of Jacob's old shoes," Jacob having left his room with all of his belongings.[12] In a way, he never really left that room, just as the crab in the bucket never really succeeds in its attempt to escape.

The author and narrator of *Jacob's Room* tell this disjointed story out of the initial chaos of grief. From Frank, we learn that the ill person who is in the midst of the chaos narrative is lost and confused, not even able to put into words what they are experiencing. They may need restoration, a return to health, but this is not possible because in the moment, all is confusion—there is no past and no future—only the present of suffering. The one who tells the chaos story has no chance to reflect or think—they see no end to their suffering, let alone any chance for healing. This kind of narrative emerges not only from personal loss, but also from public trauma such as occurred on 9–11 when as a nation we were glued to the television, watching over and over as first one and then another airplane deliberately collided with the World Trade Center. During these moments and for months to come, it seemed that an entire nation was living in chaos. Persons in chaos feel that they have no agency and are therefore powerless to change their situation. On an individual level, we hear the chaos narrative as a narrative of grief being expressed after the sudden and/or violent death of a loved one, or even the loss of property after a natural disaster like a flood or a forest fire. If the trauma is severe enough, the person affected will continue to live in the throes of the chaos narrative. The plot of a chaos narrative expresses little to no hope of things ever getting better, and as such is vastly different from the restitution narrative which focuses on the fact that one day all will be as it was before.

After this description, it appears evident that *Jacob's Room* is a classic chaos story on two levels: narrative voice and plot. This is the story of a hero who seeks meaning in his life but is doomed to try without success to find it. He never makes a meaningful connection with anyone; instead, the narrator describes him as a wanderer, an identity symbolized from the outset by his obsession with chasing butterflies. Jacob wanders miles from home in search of various species to add to his collection, just as he collects experiences and an assortment of women throughout his journey. He resembles these butterflies more than he does a man with a specific goal, in that he floats from experience to experience, absorbing the sweetness of it before moving on to the next flower: he appears in the lives of friends and family just long enough to stir their curiosity, but not long enough to build relationships. From the first few pages, we are presented with a symbol of aimlessness that is identified directly with Jacob: an "opal-shelled crab" left inside Jacob's sand-bucket, "trying with its weakly legs to climb the steep side; trying again and falling back, and trying again and again."[13] Jacob is similarly described as having "weakly legs" as he plods uphill through a sand dune.

In this regard, Jacob is very much like his mother who seems to plod through her life, unable to find stability after her husband's death. She seeks love, but never finds fulfillment. Early in the novel, she considers her decision to fabricate her husband's occupation on his grave marker in an effort to make his life's work more meaningful; yet, she wonders if he had really amounted to nothing. Had their life together been a lie? These questions could also be asked of Jacob, as well as his mother. The end came quickly for his father, and it will for him as well. Throughout the story, images of death emerge from mundane conversations and actions, indicating that the fine line between life and death was not far from anyone's mind. Unlike Jacob, Mrs. Flanders does not wander far from home, but in her relationships with men she is like him (and his butterflies) in that she does not *light* on any one thing and appears to live, on the whole, without much meaning or purpose. Also, like the other characters, she tries without success to gain and hold Jacob's attention.

Within the plot, Jacob is in chaos, but the narrator of this story is also in chaos, unable to express her feelings in a straightforward manner. The structure is episodic and disconnected, as if the narrator has little control over the events.

Diary and Background

Early on in life, Woolf became well-inured to grief and illness. By the time she was 24, she had lost her mother, step-sister and father and brother. The early loss of her mother hit her the hardest, sending her into a dangerous depression. When Stella Duckworth, her beloved step-sister, died soon afterwards, Woolf was once more devastated. Her father, Leslie Stephen, whose health declined after the deaths of his wife and step-daughter, died in 1904, adding further to her grief and mental instability. In "Sketch," Woolf reveals her ambivalence about her father, saying of him that he was "a man in prison, isolated" because he had not acknowledged his own feelings, hiding behind "violent displays of rage."[14] She had to have felt both relief and grief at his passing, a normal reaction given the intensity of his personality, but he never fully left her. The death of her brother also hit her rather hard. In 1906, after a family trip to Greece, her siblings, Vanessa and Thoby, became ill with typhoid fever. Vanessa recovered, but Thoby died. Woolf grieved in the years that followed his death not only the loss of this brother, but also for the promise of a young life cut short.[15] After this series of losses, Woolf found it difficult to stave off bouts of depression and anxiety, and in February of 1915, Woolf was thrown into yet another period of mental illness.

She was to write often of her struggles with the illness which finally took her life. In the diary she wrote about what lay beneath the surface of everyday reality in order to discover and then make manifest what had been hidden, even to herself. The diary provided that necessary *room of one's own*, affording her the ample space in which to navigate and manage her thoughts. While the novels became works of art, the diary was her studio and workshop. Here she studied her craft, unimpeded by the voices of the inner and outer critics she eventually learned to live with and manage to some degree. She learned the content and structure of her own mind, using it as a repository out of which she unearthed idea after idea, which she then perfected in her published stories and novels. The diaries lay bare her process of writing over a number of years. In addition, the diary evolved to become a marriage of philosophy and fictional strategy, demonstrating Woolf's keen mind for observation and for language.

On September 28, 1926, she records that she was feeling intensely depressed, and had been for several days, a condition that seemed to cause her to feel a so-called "blankness" in her mind, robbing her of her ability to think and write. The reason for the depression eluded her. A few years later, she notes that she was in a "black despair" and felt that another wave of depression had her in thrall.[16] It wasn't until many years after Thoby's death, in mid–April of 1920, that she could began to tell the kind of story that would both pay indirect homage to him and help her to grieve this loss. She had looked up to Thoby and had just begun to have "grown-up" conversations with him when he died. Thus, it was natural for her to have built an almost mythological significance around her brother's short life, out of which Jacob's story was born. After she wrote *Jacob's Room*, Woolf remarked that readers may think the novel "Mad ... a disconnected rhapsody."[17] Nowhere in the diary, however, does she discuss the fact that this novel was in any way a remembrance of Thoby; it certainly is a work of fiction first and foremost, and in her mind, a space in which she could work out new ideas and methods for writing fiction. However, *Jacob's Room* is a work that was generated, at least in part, from her grief over the sudden loss of her oldest brother: it freed her, by her own account, to imagine new ways of telling a story. The power of *Jacob's Room* for Woolf was that she found her own voice, and a way to express the chaos she felt after losing Thoby.[18]

Unlike *The Voyage Out* and *Night and Day*, in *Jacob's Room*, she tunnels into her characters' minds but rapidly shifts perspectives, which can be rather unsettling for a reader. This style has been described as being like a portfolio or comparable to the freestyle of jazz.[19] Furthermore, this innovative style, while it opens up access to the characters' minds, also gives to the novel a sense of being a bit off balance because it is difficult for the reader to perceive a narrative center. Even though the plot line moves forward in time, unfolding in a sequence natural to narrative form, in the telling of the tale, Jacob's movements are not linear, but circular (at best), and fragmented to an extreme. Further, the characters with whom he interacts seem interchangeable, but the scenes' structure remain relatively the same, in that nothing much is ever said or accomplished. Jacob may appear in Greece, or on a boat with his school friend, Timmy Durrant, but it becomes difficult to make any connections between these events. As a way of reinforcing this aspect of the structure, Woolf shapes Jacob in such a way that he does not seem interested in, or capable of, making personal connections or sustaining any kind of lasting relationships, not even with his mother.

Theme and Structure

It is in the nature of chaos that it operates only as undirected energy. In order to be creative, energy must be harnessed and given a purpose. Because Woolf begins this novel with images and sounds of the ocean, it seems fitting to focus for a moment on this image as an example of the kind of energy that, although it can be destructive, is both directed and purposeful. When we first encounter Jacob, he is small boy playing on the beach at the Isle of Skye, the waves crashing to the shore in the background. Although waves illustrate the power of harnessed chaos as a creative force, this problem of how to control and direct his energy is one that Jacob never quite overcomes. His life-force never seems to achieve a purpose. Gillian Beer has noted that in writing *Origin*, his own "creation story," Darwin substituted the sea for an image of a garden (Woolf uses a similar move in *The Waves*), the ocean seen as elemental in the creation and sustenance of life.[20] In the beginning of her story, Woolf describes the sea as "something alive," like a wild horse "expecting the whip," establishing a sense of driving restlessness that pervades the rest of the novel.[21]

Like these ocean waves, Jacob seems driven towards some unknown goal, but as the story unfolds, this potential is never realized. In the opening chapters, she establishes Jacob's role as the hero who is not-a-hero, absent in mind and often in body. She introduces the recurring themes of death and emptiness, and focuses on many of the thematic images that will appear in varying forms as his story progresses, such as the sheep's skull, the futile journey of the crab, and his penchant for butterfly hunting. The fact that the seashore symbolizes Darwin's "sea of creation" will become ironic by the last chapter of the novel because the object with which the ocean, and thus with Jacob, is associated almost immediately is a skull that washes up onto the sand. What is being created is destruction, the beginning and the end, represented in this one image.

Jacob's role in this chaotic drama is the young explorer who never listens or responds to anyone who calls to him. His brother's voice calls out to him in "extraordinary sadness ... solitary, unanswered, breaking against the rocks," yet Jacob, wandering on the beach hunting for crabs, ignores his searching voice.[22] As he walks in a directionless manner, distracted by everything he sees, he is startled into tears at the sight of a couple sun-bathing, having come upon them suddenly. What calms him is not the sight of his mother or his brothers across the sand looking for him, but the skull of a sheep, whitewashed by the sand and the wind, which, oddly enough, he insists on taking to bed with him.[23] While Archer, his brother, cannot fall asleep because of the skull—he must have his mother's comfort and stories of fairies—Jacob grasps this very skull and sleeps soundly, "profoundly unconscious."[24] It is as if he is grasping his fate at this moment, determined to embrace it rather than hide from it. Instead of the skull giving him strength or confidence, however, he seems lost throughout the story. This sense of loss and impending death saturate the story from the first chapter.

The disjointed, unpredictable style of *Jacob's Room* reveals Woolf's pain in a way that a more traditionally structured novel never could. On a level involving both the structure and tone, this story grasps for a sense of purpose out of the chaos of loss. In fact, the structure produces a visual montage in which Jacob is seen only in brief glimpses. A fitting analogy for this phenomenon is one that I alluded to earlier in this chapter: Jacob likes to collect butterflies. The butterfly flitting from flower to flower aptly describes the episodic structure of the novel, as well as his behavior with women and his inability to find satisfaction in his employment as a lawyer at the Bar. This structure thus appeals to the spatial sense rather than to the temporal: Woolf strategically arranges the text, the gaps between paragraphs lending to the novel an added sense of discontinuity and chaos. Jacob moves around rather aimlessly, his lack of stability and sense of timing leaving readers somewhat confused. The story feels like the present, the sense of loss always at the forefront of the reader's mind. Just as the narrator of a chaos story seems to have no control or agency, the narrator of *Jacob's Room* is struggling to find the words to express her grief. The comfort in the act of telling, emerges.

The method Woolf uses to capture the muddled effects of grief presents difficulties for the reader, but also is in keeping with her subject and theme. Not only does the narrative thread become more demanding to follow as one reads, but as the purported hero of the novel, Jacob himself proves almost impossible to keep track of: the reader wonders where he will end up next. He may remind us somewhat of Waldo from the famous cartoon books—finding him in a crowd can be next to impossible—but when you do locate him, he quickly disappears. While Jacob doesn't disappear from the plot entirely until the end of the novel, he makes only brief and rare appearances. The story seems to be one long search, with everyone—brothers, mother, lovers, and friends—looking for him. In Chapter One, his brother, Archer complains that Jacob "doesn't want to play," or to even be found.[25] Mrs. Flanders, in frustration, wonders where that "tiresome boy" can be, a complaint that that prevails in the text.[26] He lives up to the expectation set from the first page of the novel when he goes off on his own beach-combing in search of treasure, the sheep's skull with which he falls asleep. From the beginning, this story concerns itself with a lack of closure or endings, as well as the futility of even living at all. The structure of *Jacob's Room* seems designed to confuse the reader. The maze-like structure turns in on itself, pushing readers along with Jacob to wonder that if life is one long goodbye, what is the point of all of the machinations we create in order to find a purpose?

The constant presence of loss is intensified by that fact that someone is always leaving, many times prematurely, or so it may appear to those left behind. The looming presence of Death, especially in the lives of the young, seems to empty out the meaning of life. Not only do stories provide catharsis for all manner of events and emotions, but they also provide a much-needed structure, useful in stories of course, but perhaps even more useful in life. If we can put boundaries around an experience—and plot is nothing but a form of boundary—then we can begin to understand it. While writing a story may provide some kind of therapy for the one who is grieving, putting into words the depth of their feelings, the act of writing also literally enacts the process of trying to find meaning again after a loss. With *Jacob's Room*, the journey motif is interrupted and then fragmented, so that our expectations for the connections between characters and events are frustrated. The hero is not a hero in the traditional sense; his quest never becomes clear because he lives only for the present moment. This new kind of pattern that is "not-a-pattern" helps Woolf to somehow reorganize her life story in order to ameliorate the pain of her brother's death. Further, Woolf's new iteration of the journey motif reveals her own struggles to understand the meaning and purpose of human life from her perspective of grief. As we will see in the second part of this chapter, *To the Lighthouse* serves a similar function, but by the time she composed this later novel, she had further developed her prose style and had its own distinct purpose, resulting in a story which is more tightly structured.

Chaos vs. Predictability

Although *Jacob's Room* projects chaos, it coheres through this same series of loosely connected thematic episodes. The meaning is literally in the medium. As a result of this effect, we see Jacob as if in a montage of film clips, the wandering hero who lacks purpose, and a man who has lost his agency, absent from the relationships in his life, haunted by disappointment and doomed to disillusionment. His own sense of disarray emerges through the fact that his power to act has been thwarted. The future seems hidden from him; he has been anchored to the present moment. He has little agency because he is never fully present in what is going on around him. In place of stability, he opts instead to wander, preferring to sample life in small bites instead of feasting on the whole. In fact, it is fitting that although the title of the novel bears his name, he is suspiciously absent from the action, appearing in a little over half of the novel—we hear *about* Jacob more than we hear *from* him. When he is not present, the characters are occupied in thinking of him, speaking of him, or looking for him. When he is fully present in a scene, he says so little that the other characters mark his uncanny silence. At a dinner party, Jacob speaks only twenty-three words in the midst of other chatter and nonsense. The impression is that he is being overly careful with his words, speaking only when he felt that there were important things to say, perhaps another oblique reference to Woolf's brother.

Predictability gives to life, and to stories, a sense of stability and confidence. Instead of seeking stability, Jacob fights it, refusing to be defined or to follow the rules that other people have laid out for him. His refusal to be predictable adds another layer to the sense of chaos. With respect to his love life, he chooses partners that are marginalized by society: in particular, Florinda, a young friend of his family, and Fanny, who is a prostitute. Jacob pretends not to need anyone, ignoring the idea of social cohesion, but is hurt when he sees Fanny on the arm of another man. He floats from woman to woman, looking for a relationship, and yet at the end of his journey, he has given his heart to a married woman, leaving behind Clara, the one young woman with whom he might have had a future. The result is that Jacob never finds a satisfying relationship in his short life—always searching but never finding what he seeks, an unsettled not-a-hero who plans a journey, but never arrives at a destination.

The futility and frustration of trying to make meaningful connections with other human beings is Woolf's central concern. At the end of his travels in Europe, Jacob finally reaches his pinnacle, symbolized by the Acropolis, which ironically—and true to the rest of the story—leads nowhere. In this part of the novel, Jacob is described as a young god who has been cut down in the prime of his youth.[27] Sandra Wentworth Williams, the woman with whom he falls in love, is only a dead-end for him, a fact which he sadly acknowledges once he returns to London. Sandra identifies him on sight as an "English boy on tour," someone with whom she could find a diversion, much to her husband's dismay.[28] Although she has more luck than the other women in Jacob's life, even she cannot hold onto him for long. As the two lovers go on a tour of the Greek ruins, she does most of the talking, while Jacob's responses are muted or completely missing from the conversation. Sandra makes him feel like a hero waiting to be called upon to save her.[29] When he sees the statue of a goddess, he thinks of her and is "extraordinarily moved" by the sight.[30] In the end, he remains as aloof as always, a ghostly figure which floats out of her life, just like he has in the lives of everyone he has ever known. Their entire affair is elided in the text: "They had vanished," never having reached the Acropolis.[31] After Jacob returns to London, he gradually fades away and becomes that shadow he has been all along, merely a thought left behind in the minds of his family and friends. When he attends Cambridge, which Woolf describes as the ideal place for the young hero to learn who he is and what will be his destiny, the narrator claims that he is a "man of substance," which he echoes by saying "I am what I am and intend to be it."[32] However, he never realizes his potential: his identity remains virtually unformed, the meaning of his life suspended by an early and unexpected death.

In seeking resolution to her pain in *Jacob's Room*, Woolf creates a philosophical puzzle as well, her grief taking a specific turn: would the world make more sense if one could simply absent oneself from the action of life—to be passive, not to act but be acted upon; to be seen and yet not really heard; to be called but not really ever found? If one could become a moving target and remain unattached, then perhaps one could survive the griefs of life. Jacob represents that moving target; as his story progresses, it becomes more difficult for the reader to pin him down. Moreover, as he makes his way through life, he becomes even more uncertain of his destiny, even though early in the novel, after he arrives at university, he declares a strong identity. The narrative thread, like Jacob himself, meanders from page to page. This is not the story of life lived with purpose. Instead, Jacob lives by chance: whoever or whatever happens to cross his path receives his attention, while the reader is left with the task of making sense of the fragments. Nothing is stable; everything is contingent.

Jacob's Room emulates the process by which the grief-stricken family member or friend remembers their loved one, only in bits and pieces that, to anyone else would seem unrelated. And yet, out of those bits and pieces, memory is created. It feels as if we are looking at a series of photographs within specific kinds of frames, as one critic has described it: "[Woolf] seemingly sets the scenery of a traditional hero's tale, but uses the snapshot form in order to mark the deviance of that life."[33] This description enables us to emphasize the lack of a framing voice—since Woolf gives us little to no context, we must piece together each scene, creating our own significance and contextual meaning. In reading this story, no authoritative voice guides us in our own grieving process. Just as we must "remember" Jacob in scattered memories, the memories of our loved ones come back to us in bits and pieces: a face, a gesture, caught forever as a split second in our minds. There are rarely words to express the way we feel as we grope to make sense of what has happened.

After we lose someone, some days are okay, while other days are not. Grief washes over us in waves; it does not hit us all at once. Because there is no moment when grief ends completely, there is always a tension between calm and chaos, times when we are present in the moment, able to experience joy and normalcy, and times when grief empties us out. Similarly, a tension between absence/presence drives the rhythm of *Jacob's Room*: Jacob is often pictured as emerging out of or receding into the shadows. This novel is about his empty room, a gaping space left after his death. L. Koulouris has noted, "Jacob is only present through his absence ... evidenced by the half-finished sentences, his eerie reservedness, [and] his aloofness."[34] Because the plot hinges on a tension between absence and presence (Jacob's absence recalling his presence) the story seems to resist closure: the characters—and the reader—engage in a frustrating search that leads nowhere. The less present he is in body, the more present he becomes in our minds, but he remains just out of reach. These vexing feelings are all too common after losing a loved one. You see them everywhere you look, but then, just as you walk towards them, you remember that they are no longer with you. In this manner, they achieve a kind of immortality. In *Jacob's Room*, this kind of immortality is embodied by his deserted room and his empty shoes. Jacob survives in the memories of those who continue to catch glimpses of him after he has died.

It seems as if the grief of the characters at not finding Jacob overshadows their grief at his death, evidenced by the fact that Woolf writes only one sentence to indicate that he is gone, and devotes only one page to the aftermath of his death.[35] Thus, *Jacob's Room*—the tale of a hero who goes missing from his own story—may seem an odd example of the kind of story that provides comfort: how does this happen? Seeing Jacob through sidelong glimpses, sideways angles, and shadows gives to the story an unfinished feeling that deflects the pain of a full-on portrait. The novel thus becomes the embodiment of the missing or absent brother, a symbolic reliquary of Woolf's memories and feelings. Like Thoby, Jacob can never now be fully grasped or fully known, a feeling I understand quite well. Having lost my brother to sudden death, I wonder every day how he might have turned out, what his life would have been like had he not died relatively young—only 47—just as he was finding a measure of success and happiness. *Jacob's Room* offers comfort through inciting mutual sympathy with the reader. This feeling of absence—like being gutted—must be common to those of us who have lost someone, in particular if the death was sudden, because we were denied the chance to say goodbye. Certainly this was how Mrs. Flanders must have felt when Jacob suddenly disappeared.

Jacob's Room as a chaos narrative provides us with a vivid example of the way in which Story is embedded/embodied in human beings, adding further evidence to the evolutionary, adaptive function of this story as a vehicle for coping with grief. Like Thoby, Jacob exists mostly in the minds and memories of other characters. In the scenes in which Jacob is at school, Woolf describes the kind of intellectual discussions Thoby might have had with his mates, the kinds of talk that she and Vanessa were privy to on their Bloomsbury evenings. His death left a hole in all of their lives, just as Jacob's death leaves an empty space. Thoby's shoes, like Jacob's, were left to be filled. Unlike Woolf's brother, however, all that Jacob leaves behind is a pair of shoes and a room full of books, clothes, and furniture. His life, unlike Thoby's, does not seem to have amounted to much. The question we are left with at the end of this novel may well be "why bother?" Why bother with love? Why, if all we have left are a pair of empty shoes in an empty room, did we go to all the trouble? Upon learning the news of Jacob's death, Mrs. Flanders and his friend, Bonamy, go to his room and find that it is just as he had left it—virtually empty. Neither Mrs. Flanders nor Bonamy can comprehend what to do next or how to move forward. When Jacob died, his room still looked as if he had expected to return. His death seems to leaves his friend bereft, but interestingly, his mother just seems lost.[36]

The story of Jacob's life can be summed up in the image of those shoes, held up, pitifully, in his mother's hands. Because it is elliptical and elusive, Jacob's story becomes embedded in the reader's mind, just as the memory of a loved one becomes embedded in our own minds and bodies. Based on my experience of reading *Jacob's Room*, I would argue that stories are deeply connected to the very nature of what it means to be human since the experience of being human is a Story that is literally embodied. Even though Jacob's *body* is missing—he is an ethereal character who refuses to become corporeal, fully embodied—he comes to life in our minds.

Conclusion

Cut short in his prime Jacob Flanders never had the chance to fully realize his potential as a human being. When he died, he left unfinished affairs behind him, his family and friends left to piece together what they could. But isn't this the way death affects us all, left as we are with empty shoes in an empty room? After my brother died, I walked into his lonely room, randomly picking up objects that had belonged to him, marveling at their ability to conjure him so clearly. I grabbed clothes he had worn, holding them to my nose to breathe in his scent one last time. Grief makes you do strange things. The sudden disappearance of a loved one is the worst kind of loss because there was never a chance to say goodbye. Jacob's sudden absence had a similar effect on his family and friends. He had only begun to discover his identity when he died, or as Woolf puts it near the end of the novel, he "walked away" from life—from Clara, Timmy, his mother.[37] He simply vanished. It is odd that there is no death scene for Jacob, just a sudden absence. When a loved one dies suddenly, that is the way it feels—there one minute, while the next, they are simply gone. As Woolf knew, all that is left after a death are the voices of those who knew the loved one, trying to make sense of what is left. The story of Jacob's life is one of unfulfilled potential. As his consciousness awakens, he drifts off to fight in the war and by then, it is too late. It is left to the living to embody the memories of their loved ones, through shared memories and stories.

Although the story of Jacob Flanders concerns a hero who is not-a-hero, a man with no calling, his wanderings tell a story of their own. Just as we all carry within us our own story, created as we go along, we see Jacob piecing together his life from one experience to the next. It is frustrating that we seldom hear his voice or see inside of his mind—we don't know what he thinks about the events in his life. He reflects little about what is happening to him or around him. This is another aspect of the chaos narrative—Jacob does not reflect on his own actions or ideas. We only gather, little by little how he feels or what he is thinking, from the things that he comments on to his friends and from the narrator who tells us what he is doing at any one point. It is unusual that his story is not told from his point of view, but from an omniscient one. We know what other characters think of Jacob, but the narrative style deflects us from Jacob's thoughts in any one situation. Since he is present, but silent, for much of the novel, his story becomes embedded and intertwined within the stories of his family and friends who cobble the story together for the reader. At the end, although it feels like all we have left is emptiness, the story of Jacob is one that had to be told, comfort emerging in the remembered moments.

Because *Jacob's Room* represents the first truly innovative novel in Woolf's career, it marks a more mature view of the world and of her ability to express herself in that world. At this point in her life, she is beginning to find a way to tell the story of what happens behind the "cotton wool" in both content and form: *Jacob's Room* is an Everyman's story as much a tale of one young man's journey through life as the Story of human consciousness. In the sequence in which he slowly awakens to his life, Jacob's experience parallels the way in which human beings become gradually aware and sentient. Woolf's main concern is to explore the meaning of one human life: how one person is viewed by others in his life and how his life impacts the lives of so many others. Jacob is more of a presence than a character, seen from various points of view as the story develops, his image constructed by the various characters.

From beginning to end, the novel asks us to consider that although we may think we know someone, perhaps we only know them through a limited and biased view. This view is echoed in the overall structure of the novel which leaves us with a series of rather unrelated impressions of Jacob. It thus seems to be a kind of anti-*bildungsroman* in which the motif of the hero's journey, one of the oldest story patterns in history, is turned inside out, as Jacob literally walks away from his own life, time after time, and finally, for good. His potential for greatness is never realized because he was never really there to begin with. While *Jacob's Room* reflects the nature of the chaos story in its structural design and narrative form, and while I would argue that *To the Lighthouse* is a quest narrative, in both stories the narrator and her characters yearn to discover the meaning behind the suffering and loss and rediscover purpose. *To the Lighthouse* takes the potential, undirected energy of the chaos of loss as experienced in *Jacob's Room* and channels it into a successful pursuit of comfort and closure.

To the Lighthouse (1927): Plot and Introduction

To the Lighthouse is the story of Mr. and Mrs. Ramsey, their eight children, and an assortment of their close friends: Paul Rayley and Minta Doyle, Charles Tansley, William Bankes, Mr. Carmichael, and Lily Briscoe.

The plot concerns their stay at the Isle of Skye over two summers, approximately 10 years apart. The novel is divided into three sections. In the first section, we find the Ramseys and their houseguests at the seaside. Much of the action in the first section has to do with a boat trip to the lighthouse to visit to the keeper and his family and whether it would be fine enough to go. When the trip has been cancelled because of bad weather, family and guests leave, and the house is closed for the summer. Little did they know it would be ten years before anyone would return. Section Two concerns those ten intervening years, during which Mrs. Ramsey, Prue, and Andrew have died and the youngest of the children, James and Cam, have grown into sullen teenagers who do not like their father. In the third section, Lily returns to the seaside with Mr. Ramsey, James and Cam, the three of whom finally undertake the boat trip to the lighthouse, partly as a tribute to Mrs. Ramsay and partly as a way to reconcile their relationship with each other. Lily, who had been deeply affected by Mrs. Ramsey and regarded her as a kind of mother figure, grows to understand more about her own life. At the end of the novel, Lily experiences a vision of the older woman, whom she memorializes in a painting.

To the Lighthouse, the very title of which indicates a destination, tells of a journey that takes characters and readers from one side of grief to the other, from loss to a returned sense of wholeness—all in search of healing. The quest narrative, which Frank describes as occupying the opposite end of the spectrum from the chaos narrative, expresses hope in the face of illness, and in our case, grief: "I am deathly ill," or "I have lost a great deal, but I will learn something from this and become a better person." In the quest, there is a lesson to be learned and a blessing to be gained from the suffering. While the restitution narrative expresses hope for a remedy, the quest narrative speaks from a position of power. Agency has been restored because the person has identified a purpose—to understand what is to be learned from the illness, or in this case, grief.[38] The quest story, which may begin in chaos and confusion, eventually returns to the sufferer a sense of agency and a renewed sense of purpose. While the quest involves a journey, in testimony mode, the individual goes beyond a mere quest, turning illness "into a moral responsibility," creating a narration of what happened, bringing to light the moral lessons for an audience outside of oneself.[39]

The quest narrative is ancient in its origins—Campbell explains that the hero's journey begins with a call, followed by other stages, such as "Crossing the Threshold" and a "Road of Trials." The hero is accompanied on the journey by helpers and aids, but the burden remains on the hero to overcome the obstacles in order to return home with a blessing and a renewed sense of life's purpose, not only for herself, but also for her community. The trials of the hero may have left an indelible mark on her, but she returns only after a transformative experience, bearing a gift of strength which she bestows on the needy community. In Frank's description, the hero uses illness, in our case grief, as a path to increased understanding—the journey itself, then, becomes the gift.[40] The story of the Ramseys and their friends, in which Woolf may be partly represented by Lily Briscoe, is a gift of healing not only to herself, but more importantly, to her readers.

As we discover from reading her diary and other writings, this novel is loosely based on Woolf's family holidays at St. Ives in Cornwall where she recalls that they spent many happy times together. Unfortunately, after the death of Julia Stephen, they never returned. The place lived on in her memories, however, and she returns to it to compose this story. The occasion for the fictional gathering of family and friends is a late September holiday. The culmination of Part I, entitled "The Window," concerns a dinner party at which Mrs. Ramsey wonders what she had done with her life. Part II, entitled "Time Passes," provides a bridge between the two sections, the ten-year period in which Mrs. Ramsey suddenly dies; in this short section, we also learn of the deaths of Prue and Andrew, two of the Ramsey children. Reading more like a prose poem than fiction, "Time Passes" is heavy with symbolism and a dense repetition of images such as lamps, darkness, wind, dust, and emptiness. The entire section feels dreamlike: it begins on the last night that everyone is in the house and ends with Lily waking up in the house on a morning ten years later. The closing section, entitled "The Lighthouse," brings Lily, Mr. Ramsey, Cam and James back to the seashore. At this gathering, Ramsey and the children complete their journey to the lighthouse which they started in Part I, finding closure at last. The opening sentence of section three, "What does it mean then?" sets the tone for the actions that follow, bringing up more uncertainties: "Where do we go from here? How do we go on with our lives after such a loss as this?" Rhetorical questions like these are typical immediately after the loss of a loved one. Ten years after the fact, Lily and the other characters seem to have found a way to reconcile their feelings of loss.

The quest narrative is all about the take-away: how can I find meaning in the face of loss, and how can I take my lesson to the world? *To the Lighthouse* is suffused with Woolf's own brand of mysticism, revealing her need, almost a compulsion, to revisit this past, lay her unsettled emotions and memories to rest, and achieve a measure of inner peace. Recovery from loss and the trauma which such loss engenders carries universal appeal, relatable to all people regardless of culture. This novel taps into powerful emotions in a manner unique to Woolf, but common to every person who has lost someone. *To the Lighthouse* reminds us of a simple fact about being human: sometimes it hurts. If you want to know what this kind of hurt is like, listen to a grieving person tell their story.

If *Jacob's Room* typifies the chaos story—the one that can make no sense of what has happened and offer no meaning, no vision, and little hope—*To the Lighthouse* represents the quest story, bordering on what Frank designates as testimony.[41] After suffering a loss, the debilitating effects can be felt for a long time, not only in the mind but also in the body. If that pain can be expressed in the form of a cohesive story, it is a sign that some healing has occurred. The sufferer has internalized her pain and has recovered agency. She can organize her loss and share it to the benefit of others. Long after their deaths, Woolf continued to miss her parents, but had accepted their absence by the time she wrote this novel. She wanted to honor their memories, and in so doing, find a way to lay them to rest, at least in her own mind.

As a quest story, *To the Lighthouse* expresses a creative vision of unity. As a tribute to her childhood memories, this story goes far beyond a personal tribute in becoming what we acknowledge as a great piece of literature that cuts across cultural, gender, ethnic and national boundaries. We could assign many evolutionary purposes to this novel, but one seems to exceed the others—the expression of a quest to achieve peace of mind (as Frank has defined it), and to find comfort by sharing her grief with others. While *To the Lighthouse*, like all of Woolf's novels, ultimately questions the meaning of life, it also suggests an answer: the meaning of life can be found in the living of it day by day in the presence of friends and family; while we may not have all of the answers, we keep walking, placing one foot in front of the other in a delicate balancing act.

As we will see, the structure of *To the Lighthouse* reinforces the importance of acquiring purpose and direction in the face of loss, and acknowledging the notion that life goes on, and we must go with it. In place of the chaos of the present which contains only an empty room and empty shoes, *To the Lighthouse* concludes with a sense of hope, as an aging father and two teenagers journey towards healing and reconciliation. More importantly, Woolf invites us to share Lily Briscoe's sense of hope through the completion of the painting of Helen and James. The positive note at the novel's end, reverberating well past its last page, not only brings into focus the role of the arts in our lives, but reminds us of the power of Story to return to us a sense of meaning in the midst of sorrow. Its message stands in stark contrast to the nullifying effect of Jacob's death, that loss of life's energy. I would maintain that this does not take away from its power to heal—*Jacob's Room* exemplifies a different response to grief, but one that feels more chaotic. Lily Briscoe, having put the finishing touches on Mrs. Ramsey's portrait, knows that her journey's purpose has been fulfilled.[42] Just as the "not-a-pattern" structure of *Jacob's Room* revealed the instability of Woolf's thinking at that time, the tightly focused structure of *To the Lighthouse* reveals a more settled mind and a more highly developed perspective on loss and grief. Having had the time to reflect gave to Woolf the tool she needed in order to fulfill her personal quest for peace. Within the space of her novel, she discovered strength and a space to complete her own vision.

Writing this novel no doubt took a toll on Woolf's psyche, as did all of her writing to varying degrees, but it is evident that the act of writing also helped her to heal from the loss her parents, particularly the loss of her mother. Although she claimed to have laid them to rest in writing this story, some years later she revisits this notion. She thinks that perhaps she had not put them to their final rest, admitting that the presence of her father continued to haunt her. She even says a few years later that he continued to hover over her the rest of her life.[43] She realized what most us know who have suffered personal loss: one of the most frustrating aspects of the grieving process is that it is *process*: grief never really completely subsides. We think that the grief has been handled, put in its box and placed on its shelf. But these feelings have a way of escaping, triggered by a sight, a sound, or a place. The feelings we once had for a loved one never entirely disappear, but continue to return to us in different forms—sometimes amusement, sometimes wistfulness, sometimes hurt and sadness. I would argue that like the story of Jacob, which commemorated her chaotic feelings after losing Thoby, this quest story commemorates her parents, reflecting her hard-won peace.

Diary and Background

Woolf was not simply memorializing her parents in *To the Lighthouse*; she was also trying to establish herself as a serious writer. She began writing the novel in 1924 with a scene concerning her father whom she dubbed "The Old Man."[44] Later in 1925, she writes that she would include her mother, father, her childhood at St. Ives as well as themes of life and death into this new story. It is interesting that she would remark that she saw her father as the central character when it feels to most of her readers that her mother occupies the center of the narrative.[45] She was, in essence, trying to exorcise her parents, and as many critics have noted, come to terms with her unhealthy obsession with her father, as well as her mother. Because a theme of death runs throughout her stories, Woolf quipped in June of that same year that her new books needed a new designation, to which she queries "Elegy?"[46] Woolf missed her mother; 24 years after her death, she writes that the scent of wreaths in her hallway often made her think of Julia. These flowers, she says, create "as good a memorial as one could wish."[47] She had suffered a great deal at the hands of their domineering father, a reflection of whom we see in Mr. Ramsey.[48] After *To the Lighthouse* was published, she remarked in her diary that if her father had lived, she would not have written novels, that his life "would have entirely ended mine."[49] She also records in her diary that her father returns to her but differently, as a peer and not as a father. Vanessa remarked to Virginia that bringing back the dead was almost too painful to bear.[50] Her out-of-balance feelings for her parents were somewhat righted by the composition of this novel. This was a story that Woolf had to tell in her pursuit of a way to understand her life.

By Monday, July 20th of that same year, she had chosen a structure for the new novel which would become *To the Lighthouse*, a story that would stretch her writing abilities in yet another new direction. She writes of being challenged by her friends to include a more impersonal section in the book concerning the "flight of time" which would result in a break with her original design structure.[51] This kind of problem, she says, stimulated her mind and kept her thinking fresh. Throughout the writing process, she was seeing Vita intermittently, their relationship forming a significant part of the writing situation for Woolf throughout 1925 and 1926. Early in January of 1926, she enjoyed a visit from Vita; mixed in with her elation of once again seeing Vita is her excitement about the new book. She feels invigorated and energized by the entire process. This energy may partly explain the relatively positive tone of *To the Lighthouse*. By February, she felt that the story was flowing freely and is happy that she has shown her theories of storytelling to have been successful, that she may now grasp the "fruit that hangs in [her] soul."[52] The diary once more provides evidence that Woolf theorized about her own fiction, cognizant that her own process reflects her particular turn of thought. Writing allowed her to grieve her losses, to unearth her innermost feelings and memories. While she often speaks of the pain of writing, she also writes of the relief that it brought to her when a book was finished. Like Lily Briscoe, she also faced criticism: J.M. Murray once told Woolf that her novels would not be read ten years after they were published, designating her work to be a failure. In spite of the threat of criticism, she risked introducing art as a vital part of the story. Like Lily, she persisted in the face of criticism in order to work towards her own vision.

In the summer of 1926, she explains that human life is "infinitely precious stuff" given to us to spend, but that she often feels that this precious gift is wasted on trivialities. Her philosophy drives her to try new "tricks" in her stories to keep herself engaged. She "survives" each iteration of her story by keeping it fresh and "making it new," to echo Ezra Pound's advice to the modern writer. She alternately enjoys and dreads the process, calling *To the Lighthouse* a "python" and wonders why she continues to write at all.[53] As she neared the conclusion she wonders how to bring all of the elements together, finally admitting to herself that in comparison to *Jacob's Room* and *Mrs. Dalloway*, *To the Lighthouse* was "more human," meaning deeper, more connected, and more fully fleshed out than her previous stories.[54] The "human feeling"—the centrality of the mother, the effect of her death on all of the characters—seems to make the story what she called *more human*. After its completion, Woolf judged her process and experiments, which she calls her "method," to have been successful.[55] She was learning to narrate human experience from her own perspective and to her own satisfaction.

Structure, Theme and Character

The themes of life, death, love, and loss which she feared would be seen as sentimental are the very things that make the story appealing to readers. This novel's embodiment of her grief brings comfort and helps our souls to heal. As Lily says, getting at Life—the "thing itself"—is the purpose of art, whether it be verbal or visual. Artistic expressions of all kinds provide a popular vehicle through which to reconcile a seeming contradiction between the real world and an individual's perception of that world, from the everyday to the extraordinary. Throughout her essays, diaries, and fiction, Woolf claimed that the ultimate work of an artist was to express moments that seemed inexpressible. Many of her stories, and *To the Lighthouse* in particular, expand the boundaries of the traditional novel to include not one such moment but many. Through the structural framework of the novel, Woolf offers us a window onto a timeless, yet time-bound, view of life in all of its permutations.

Woolf once more manipulates the basic elements of fiction to tell familiar story of loss and her own struggle to come to terms with that loss, using indirect discourse as a way to open up an intimate space between the reader and the characters. As in the other novels in which she utilizes this technique, the reader becomes part of the group of characters as they struggle to understand themselves and each other. Using the metaphor of painting, the physical layout of the novel resembles a triptych at the center of which is Mrs. Ramsey. On one of these virtual panels we might see Mr. Ramsey and the children, while on the opposite panel would appear the figures of Charles Tansley, Paul Rayley and Minta Doyle, William Bankes, Mr. Carmichael, and Lily Briscoe. We might envision that on this center panel, standing closest to Mrs. Ramsey is her husband, while all around her, the other characters gather, from Lily Briscoe to Minta Doyle, the youngest to the eldest child, the widowed Bankes to Charles Tansley. As I am describing it, this triptych may seem both familiar and iconic. Mrs. Ramsey has become a religious figure, a Madonna: all of the other characters surround her and take their energy from her. Throughout the first part, the characters draw life from her, but even after she is gone, Lily, Ramsey, Cam, and James gain their purpose from their memories of her. Although throughout her life she willingly gave away her energy to those who needed it most, once she is alone she nestles down into herself so that she can find that powerful psychic energy once again. Helen Ramsey's behavior at these times reflects how Woolf might have imagined her mother to have lived in her private moments.

In writing *To the Lighthouse*, Woolf embarks on a personal quest not just to remember her mother in a particular way—as an energetic, inspiring, self-sacrificing woman—but to locate the kind of mother she never had. Julia Stephen, about whom she wrote so eloquently in her memoirs and diaries, was the mother she lost at far too young an age, the mother who never seemed to be hers alone but belonged to everyone else. She recollected that she often found her mother alone only for brief moments at a time. Julia always seemed otherwise occupied with her community work, with her husband, or with her other children. In spite of her mother's sporadic attention, the two had formed a close bond in her childhood, as Woolf's memoirs testify. Her death left an unfillable hole, not just in the family, but in her mind and heart. Although she eulogizes at least four members of her family in this novel, it is primarily her mother for whom she grieves the most and to whom she devotes most of the novel's attention. When midway through the plot Mrs. Ramsey dies, it seems ironic that we learn of the momentous event in such a brief sentence.[56] The lack of detail may strike readers as hardly the reaction they would expect, but perhaps by the time Woolf wrote *To the Lighthouse*, and twenty-two years had passed, she had allowed her feelings and attitudes to coalesce and settle around that first shock of loss. This understated death of Mrs. Ramsey in many ways emphasizes the significance of such a loss more than an overt expression of grief. Woolf sees Helen Ramsey's death as a natural event, death being something that happens as time passes. Physical and psychological distance had allowed Woolf to gain a sense of perspective: the years that had passed gave her time to write a version of the story in her mind long before putting pen to paper.

To the Lighthouse hinges on a tension between absence and presence, somewhat like *Jacob's Room*. Although absent from the second half of the story, Mrs. Ramsey remains, nonetheless, present in the minds of the characters. In the last section of the story "The Lighthouse," Lily conjures Mrs. Ramsey's spirit as she calls out to her in grief, indicating that Woolf's mother, although long dead, stayed ever-present in her mind. The constant push and pull of this tension between absence and presence connects the quest story to the chaos of *Jacob's Room*, and suggests that *To the Lighthouse* is also a story in search of a hero. Even though Mrs. Ramsey dies midway through the story, she remains its heroine. She is the spiritual center of the novel, bringing everyone back to the island ten years after her death based on a promise she had made to James years before, to row him out to the lighthouse. This story of a journey towards healing includes Lily's awakening consciousness. Moreover, this quest takes Lily, Mr. Ramsey, James, and Cam from light to darkness and back into light, from the safety of knowing one's identity and place in the world to an unsettled unknowing, and then to a new kind of knowing, a new definition of what is means to be safe and a part of the human family. The reconciliation to grief that occurs for these remaining characters provides a *happy* ending in spite of the grief that death creates.

It is clear that Woolf's search for comfort was realized in writing *To the Lighthouse*. Mrs. Ramsey remains the story's heart and soul throughout, symbolized by a beam of light emanating from the lighthouse. In Part One, she watches the pulsing light out of her window and connects herself with its "long steady stroke."[57] When the beam finds her, she doesn't just see it. She inhabits it. Light and warmth thus seem to emanate from her. In this way, she represents the light around which the characters hover like so many moths, a light that provides reassurance and safety.

As the Goddess of Light, and as the Earth Mother, she wants her family to find love and fulfillment. She wishes her children to stay young always, because she fears that when they mature they may lose that state of innocence and sense of adventure about life.[58] On the other hand, she admires her children, Rose and Jasper, who remind her of the various jewels they choose for her to wear to dinner, each one glittering in a more vivid color than its neighbor.[59] Simultaneously, she worries that they are too critical, that they indulge in too much "strife" and division for as young as they are.[60]

As her "adult child," Mr. Ramsey occupies the center of her world. She must stop what she is doing to see to his inexhaustible need for attention and support. When he sees himself as a failure, he goes to her to be soothed and propped up once again. As he leaves her alone, her energy sinks a little, but instead of feeling ill-used, she admires and loves him deeply, and can't imagine life without him.[61] This aspect of the novel reflects the fact that Woolf knew her father to be a tyrant in many ways, but she also knew that Leslie Stephen loved his wife completely and utterly, as she recounts in "Reminiscences."[62] When Julia died, Leslie was devastated and the children were lost without her. In this story of healing, the father and two of the children pay final tribute to her by completing the journey to the lighthouse. Closing the novel with the completion of this journey refocuses our attention on hope: the symbol of the lighthouse appeals to the recognition of our basic need for light, warmth and comfort in that a lighthouse is a beacon of hope in the darkness, a universal sign to all sailors and travelers. In addition, that steady, pulsing light brings to our minds the deepest rhythm of all, the heartbeat. As long as it's there, as long as that light can find us, we are still here, still finding our way in the world. The light reassures us that we will land safely on shore. I would argue that it is a universal desire to feel safe and loved on the journey of life. From the evolutionary standpoint, the structure, theme and characters of *To the Lighthouse* communicate the power of Story to comfort, giving voice to this deep-seated human desire.

Lily's Painting: Grief Turned to Hope

As we've seen, stories of grief can cleanse our minds. Human beings use many forms of narrative as a method of explaining this grief to ourselves, our friends, and our families. In the case of *To the Lighthouse*, the grief story is disseminated to an even wider audience, one which would have exceeded Woolf's own expectations. My analysis would not be complete without acknowledging that something more is happening in this novel, however; as we've seen, *To the Lighthouse* operates on two levels: verbal and visual. The initial quest narrative is mirrored Lily's painting; it is a *mise en abyme* which establishes the process of narrative creation and the completion of the painting as nested together within the text and emblematic of the whole.[63] The story of Woolf's parents was difficult for her to write about, but it was a story that she felt she had to tell. Everyone who has lost someone can relate to this impulse. Even when the story is difficult—maybe especially then—the telling of it brings relief. Moreover, if telling the story comes at a high price and we struggle to find the words to express our deep emotions, we will look for anything to help us tell what must be told. It is often the case that people who have suffered great trauma have no words, but can draw pictures to illustrate their pain. As Lily's painting focuses on her view of Mrs. Ramsey and James, the focus of the story emerges out of Lily's perception of Mrs. Ramsey and on the relationship between the two of them, the iconic Mother and Child. Although Mrs. Ramsey plays the part of surrogate mother, to Lily she is much more than that—Lily loves her very soul. As she contemplates why this is so, she thinks of words like "willful" and "commanding" but also "wisdom," "knowledge," and "beauty"; the other characters seem to worship her as well. Bankes conjures images of the three Graces, while Charles Tansley sees "stars in her eyes and veils in her hair."[64]

Lily plays handmaiden to a goddess who may be likened to a number of mythological figures: Artemis, the goddess of children and families, Hestia, goddess of the hearth, and Aphrodite, goddess of love and marriage. Woolf reveals the mystical portion of this quest story when Lily meditates on Mrs. Ramsey, trying to capture her soul in paint. The strongest of such mystical passages occurs at the end of the novel when Lily calls out to her to come back. At that moment, she imagines Mrs. Ramsey sitting next to her as she paints. Lily then sees herself not only as a daughter to Mrs. Ramsey, but also as her spiritual student.[65] She sees within the older, married woman a power that connects people of all ages and backgrounds, bringing them together in one place around one table. Lily longs for this ability, but falls short, at least in her own mind. In spite of the fact that she feels inadequate, she musters the strength to complete her quest. Like Mrs. Ramsey, she brings together those whom she loves, not around a dinner table but into harmony on a canvas, a space she can control.[66]

Helen Ramsey, the fictionalized Julia Stephen, thus becomes an idealized version of Woolf's mother with whom she had longed to have a close relationship as an adult; thus the story becomes a bridge between her and her mother, just as Lily's painting provides a bridge between herself and others around her. Although Lily guards her canvas jealously and initially feels afraid to show it to anyone, her painting expresses her deepest feelings, just as storytelling does for Mrs. Ramsey who reads stories to James and Cam (notably the fable of the Fisherman's Wife). Recall that in the first section that in *Jacob's Room*, Woolf played with structure and characterization to achieve the effect of fragmentation; any sense of attunement in that novel is achieved only by her readers because the characters do not achieve it. On the other hand, comfort, attunement and reconciliation become the entire focus of *To the Lighthouse*. Woolf incorporates art into the novel in order to express the inexpressible desire for comfort. The final effect is *unity* as opposed to *chaos*. As LaCourarie has argued, Woolf "put [the tools of art] to use so as not only to give a new tint to her prose, but also to approach those meanings she sought more closely."[67] Lily's painting, although a tool that is extrinsically connected to the narrative, affords Woolf the language she needed to complete her own quest for peace of mind.

This tension between painting and writing plays out through Lily's struggle to realize her vision. Even though Lily often felt that her art was inadequate to the task of explaining her perspective of the world as she would like to see it expressed, she chose to paint rather than to write. Mrs. Ramsey, on the other hand, who reads stories to James and the other younger children and weaves tales of love for Lily, feels most comfortable within the linguistic mode of expression. Mrs. Ramsey crafts stories about herself, her husband, and all of the children, as if prophesying their futures or trying to hold back the effects of time. For example, when Prue finds it hard to sleep in the presence of the skull, Mrs. Ramsey weaves a tale of fairies and beauty in order to put her mind at ease. She comforts Prue with a story, just as Lily comforts and heals her spirit with art. Because painting and writing are integral to the telling of the story, *To the Lighthouse* uniquely reveals the inner Self, and illumines our understanding of the mind through artistic descriptions of moments that reveal our humanity. One of the hallmarks of the flexibility of human brain is its ability to make associations between ways of communicating, as well as concepts, ideas, and people. It is clear that Woolf was especially adept at this skill, although she quite often vented her frustration with the limits of language.

Because she felt that words were inadequate to the task of expressing the transcendent moment, she was attracted to the more flexible medium of painting. In an essay about Walter Sickert, Woolf suggests that words were somehow "impure" and that she wished to have been born into a "silent kingdom of paint." She rightly recognizes that the two modes of expression had much to teach each other about the common art of storytelling, and that perhaps, in the end, they actually share more in common than not: the ability to bring to life a lost memory or loved one, and in so doing helps us find a sense of peace.[68] Moreover, she had the perfect partner for this kind of experimentation, her sister. Virginia and Vanessa regularly discussed the merits of one form of expression over another, although both acknowledged the power each form had to express as different ways of understanding the human experience. From Vanessa, she drew both the inspiration and the energy, perhaps in part derived from envy, which propelled her forward in her experimentation with language. As Jane Dunn argues, although Virginia wrote to Vanessa, telling her that she would perhaps "laugh at the painting bits in the Lighthouse," she wanted Vanessa's opinion, which, as it turns out, was very high.[69] Woolf had finally found a way to communicate emotions which she perceived to be incommunicable through words. Similarly, Lily creates meaning through her painting. Indirect discourse perfectly represents Lily's attempts to express in the "right words" her experience, in this case, colors and brushstrokes. Adding the narrative art of painting into the novel gives Woolf another way to express her understanding of *real life* and human experience. Her potential problem—how to find the "right words"—is worked out through the relationship between Mrs. Ramsey and Lily Briscoe, framed within the narrative structure as well as within the painting. As LaCourarie further observes, the "picture is a specular doubling" of not only the relationship, in my estimation, but "of the novel under construction."[70]

Our most hidden feelings may remain inexpressible on some level, despite our best efforts. Woolf's narrative style lines up closely with what neurobiologists have discovered about the way our brains function, especially as regards using Story as an explanatory tool, a point made so clearly by Jonah Lehrer in *Proust was a Neuroscientist*. The quest to discover and then to reveal the inexpressible emerges as one of the goals of Story with which most readers can identify. In *To the Lighthouse*, we enter an interconnected subterranean realm that runs counter to the daylight world of factual knowledge. Although painting is silent, we perceive it in a parallel manner to the way we perceive fiction: like painting, within the silence of the written word is ample space for reflection and the creative imagination of the reader. The power of this novel transcends both time and individual ego and takes on a universal appeal: we recreate the plot within our own minds, marking it with a significance that is unique to our own experience.

Even with all of our modern knowledge about the brain and its innerworkings, we may not fully understand how the brain works, but we do know that Story provides it with a powerful tool with which to comfort ourselves and others.

Furthermore, stories help us express our innermost selves and a vision of the world in which we live. Lily uses paints to tell her story instead of words, and the story she tells is the completion of a quest. When she insists that on creating her own view of Mrs. Ramsey and James, holding onto that vision with both hands, she simultaneously acknowledges that not everyone will see it the way she does; in fact, they may try to take it away from her. Even in the face of Charles Tansley's criticism—"Women can't paint. Can't write"—she remains loyal to her own story.[71] Lily regards her story to be of importance, if to no one else, to herself. She has the ability to create out of meaningless clods of color a particular vibrancy, life, and meaning. She insisted that she would continue to work in that medium until she perfected it, much like Woolf continued to write stories, searching for the right way to express herself.[72] As she struggles to keep hold of her vision, she subdues "all her impressions as a woman to something more general; becoming once more under the power of that vision which she had seen clearly once and must now grope for among hedges and houses and mothers and children—her picture."[73]

This vision of Mrs. Ramsey remained uppermost in her mind; even while at dinner she is thinking of her picture: "that matters—nothing else."[74] Lily is completely absorbed in her work, just as her subject, Mrs. Ramsay, is absorbed with her son, James. Painting doubles as a metaphor for procreation, for continuance, for strength, and for the idea of vision itself (as the novel and the painting are representations of that vision). Furthermore, painting represents Woolf's idea of "the moment," a perfectly captured instance of *real life* which she developed over a number in years in various stories and novels, as illustrated in "Moment: The Summer's Night."[75] The question for Lily, and for Woolf, was "Where to begin?"[76]

For both painter and writer, knowing precisely where to place the line or the word is the first hurdle. After that come innumerable other decisions about the fleshing out of an idea, either in words, or in lines and colors. As a more mature storyteller in *To the Lighthouse*, Woolf speaks through Lily in her belief that regardless of the risk, she would continue to concoct stories and make her vision known to the world. Lily realized that although phrases and visions would always come to her, what she was really after was the "thing itself before it has been made anything."[77] Like Woolf, she was continually frustrated at the inadequacy of art to capture that thing itself. The "human apparatus" for painting a picture, Lily said, was inadequate and "inefficient," too rough for the purpose of capturing the ineffable spirit. She sees the activity of *making art* as a heroic effort to keep trying to communicate. In this way, I would argue, Lily further embodies a version of Woolf herself, heroically attempting to put into words to her own grief and bewilderment. Lily may be echoing Woolf herself when, at the beginning of "The Lighthouse," she wonders "What does it mean, then, what can it all mean?"[78]

Conclusion

This seemingly simple question becomes the most important question of all, one that most people don't think about until their time on earth begins to grow short. Instead of a "great revelation," Lily decides one gets small moments, built up over time, which may resolve into something meaningful. In her painting, she captures for all time such a moment between Helen Ramsay and her son. The most important point for Lily was not whether anyone would ever see the painting, but that she could tell the story of Mrs. Ramsay in her own way. "In the midst of chaos there was shape," she finally declares.[79] Out of that apparent chaos, she emerges with a gift of unity. She establishes a link between herself and her subjects that is both physical and metaphysical—the now dead Mrs. Ramsay completed her painting, just as her vision had completed Lily's life. While painting is the central creative activity in *To the Lighthouse*, nurturing is the central maternal act—the two coincide in Lily's completed quest to find comfort and unity.

In the novel, the experience of being human rises close to the surface—Bonnie Kime Scott has pointed out that Woolf's style is not concerned with a single "moment of Truth" but with moments of "confluence ... the moment of ... pure existence."[80] Just as Impressionist paintings seem "on the brink of a—rather than the—next moment,"[81] Woolf's story pulls readers into the story of a family on the brink of a long journey of familial love, mother-child mutuality, sexual attraction, marriage, a journey punctuated by loss, grief, anger and anxiety. But the journey does not stop there. The rifts opened up by death and loss resolve into a need to find a sense of attunement, even between a father and children who had ceased to communicate. Making a life out of what is there—that is the trick. What we see with our eyes is not always what is true. For that, we need a new kind of vision, one that sees to the inner truth. In *To the Lighthouse*,

Woolf's brand of *trompe l'oeil* emerges through subject, structure, and colorful language which together engender a culminating vision of *real life*. She recreates an impressionistic move in her use of reflection, refraction, and the play of light. Lily paints to capture what is beyond her reach—Mrs. Ramsey's soul—just as Woolf tries to grasp her mother's soul in words. In this "House of Light," Woolf transforms the inner world of her grief into a portrait, and by so doing, achieves a sense of peace. When Lily sees that Ramsey, James and Cam have reached the lighthouse at last, she simultaneously completes her painting and declares, "It was done; it was finished. ... I have had my vision."[82]

The painting, Lily's interpretation of a particular moment shared between mother and son, is larger than that; it contains her vision of love, unity, and completeness—in other words, Lily's painting is an instance of attunement.[83] Although she dabbles with the canvas in the opening section, she does not fully capture her vision until the end, at which point it is unveiled for the reader to see it within their mind's eye. While Lily's artistic vision brings to an end a private quest to mourn and then connect herself to Mrs. Ramsey, Woolf suggests that need to come to terms with grief is universal, going beyond a single person who has suffered a personal loss. By laying her vision on canvas Lily constructs a bridge between herself and an audience—this, she says, is what love looks like between a mother and child, and between friend and friend. Although she had felt, up to this point, that connections between people were doomed to be tenuous, her art allows her to build associations between herself, her world, and her audience. Ultimately, just as writing the story empowered Woolf, as well as her readers, to recognize and reconcile loss in order to rejoin the human race, completing the painting, in the face of harsh criticism and self-doubt, gave to Lily not only an inner peace, but also a sense of agency. Her last act—a portrayal of unity and love—coupled with her last words, "I have had my vision"—conveys that she is ready to move on with her life, to embrace what will come next. Moreover, I would argue that "It was finished" does not mean that her journey is over, only that she has completed the necessary first step towards healing and integration with community.

Jacob's Room and *To the Lighthouse* not only exemplify the power of chaos and quest stories to facilitate healing and comfort, but also to forge connections between us that strengthen society. Once we have shared our story with those who are willing to listen without judgment, it becomes possible to build meaningful, lasting relationships. As Frank argues, if we could get beyond *sympathy*, something one person "has for" another and move instead into *empathy*, what one person "is with" another, we could build true, caring affiliations, seeing each other as partners and co-creators of community.[84] *Mrs. Dalloway* and *Between the Acts,* the novels that I focus on in the next chapter, illustrate the power of Story to create and strengthen connections between humans that are so vital to our survival.

Chapter Three

The Power of Story to Connect: *Mrs. Dalloway* and *Between the Acts*

> Or did it not become consoling to believe that death ended absolutely? but that somehow in the streets of London, on the ebb and flow of things, here, there, she survived, Peter survived, lived in each other, she being part, she was positive, of the trees at home ... being laid out like a mist between the people she knew best ... but it spread ever so far, her life, herself.—WOOLF, *Mrs. Dalloway*

> "Pre-historic man," she read, "half-human, half-ape, roused himself from his semi-crouching position and raised great stones."—WOOLF, *Between the Acts*

> We can clearly see how it is that all living and extinct forms can be grouped together within a few great classes; and how the several members of each class are connected together by the most complex and radiating lines of affinities—DARWIN, *On the Origin of Species*

We've seen how stories like *Jacob's Room* and *To the Lighthouse* can comfort us and facilitate healing, but that is not all they can do. They also have the power to build connections between us, strong enough to promote survival among individuals and their communities. All we need do is to listen as survivors of the Holocaust tell of their trauma in order to recognize that stories not only forge bonds within like-minded communities, but also build bridges between diverse communities who may have little day-to-day contact, except perhaps through social media. The world listens in shock as immigrants and refugees tell stories of alienation, fear, and their desire to live in safe, permanent homes. The numerous accounts of pain, loss, and suffering that emerged following Hurricane Katrina made thousands of us across the country and world aware of the inequities of the 9th Ward in New Orleans: that awareness led to a path of change for that community and many others like it. These large scale examples can show us the power of stories to bring us together. But we really need not look any further than next door. When we listen to someone's story, we can't help but be drawn into a sense of communion with them. History continues to teach us that, unfortunately, a failure to listen often results in a breakdown in communication, as evidenced by the fear and misunderstanding of the Civil Rights era conflicts, as well as racial violence in more recent times. We have yet to take heed. Stories have the power to tear us apart or bind us together. We should never forget that all of us are in a lifelong struggle to survive. If we want the next generation to not only survive, but to thrive, we must teach them these principles. We must encourage them to listen to the stories that are told of people who are different from themselves. When survivors tell their stories as a way to find refuge and relief, in that telling they establish bonds with those who most need to hear them.

Stories connect us to each other in a variety of ways: imaginatively, cognitively, emotionally, psychologically, and socially. They tell us who we are at the present moment, but they also forge links to our individual and collective pasts. More to the point, stories communicate the very desire for affinity so vital to our survival, an underlying purpose that lies at the heart of every story. In telling the tales of Clarissa Dalloway (*Mrs. Dalloway*) and Isa Oliver (*Between the Acts*), women for whom the search for meaning is all-consuming, Woolf writes of the possibilities, as well as the missed opportunities, for connections between human beings. This chapter explores the evolutionary advantage of storytelling in creating powerful evolutionary affinities.

Myth as Foundation of Stories: Seeds of Human Connection

Myth is as old as the human imagination: virtually every story we know of has somehow evolved from this ancient form. The Hero's journey, one of the oldest story patterns of which we are aware, emerges again and again in cultures around the globe. In *The Hero Has a Thousand Faces*, Joseph Campbell explains in great detail the way myth spans every culture.[1] By harking back to the pattern of an ancient myth for her narrative framework, Woolf positions the stories of Clarissa Dalloway and Isa Oliver within a tradition that seeks to explain why we are here—what is the meaning of life in all of its variations when all is said and done? Woolf answers this question through the voices and stories of these characters and through the one thing they all desire: LOVE. As the highest form of human friendship, love occupies the narrative center. Both novels consider the various ways in which human beings create affinities: woman to man, woman to woman, mother to daughter, friend to friend. What kinds of love are okay? Why isn't everyone loved, or even capable of loving others? Can love save us?

Of all of the faculties humans possess, our imaginations—coupled with a facility for language and an ability to reason—have enabled us, for thousands of years, to find creative ways to communicate our thoughts, feelings, and experiences. Stories go beyond the mere transmission of factual information, crossing over into territories better defined as inspirational, aspirational, and artistic. Over thousands of years, we developed different kinds of stories to suit various audiences and purposes: fairytales, epics stories of battle, love stories, murder mysteries—the list could go on ad infinitum. Underlying all of these stories is Myth, a type of story which communicates most deeply who we are as human beings because it connects us at a primal level. What, then, is the link between Myth and the evolutionary theory of the survival of the fittest? What later becomes a myth, told and retold, generation after generation, began first as a lived experience. Likewise, at its most basic level, a story explains something—a phenomenon, a feeling, a need. Beneath the surface, Myth adds a deeper level of meaning to the basic explanatory role of stories. Because myths generalize they can be inclusive of an entire culture or a people. In pulling the focus away from realistic details, a myth shifts our attention to the larger significance of a specific situation. The result is that a higher truth emerges. As the basis of all stories, ancient archetypes of mythology emerge in characters like Clarissa Dalloway, making her accessible and always relevant to us. Regardless of the fact that she was invented in 1920s England, in some ways she represents all women of a certain age.

Myths—repeated and passed down from one generation to another—unify the members of a community. From one family unit to an entire nation, myths have the potential to form a tight social cohesion, giving us an identity and a place to belong. Furthermore, Myth and ritual are intimately connected: ritual involves actions—patterned behaviors associated with mythic beliefs. Myths are the result of shared values and concerns of people living in community in order to survive. Myth lies close to the surface in *Mrs. Dalloway*, a fact noted by many literary critics. Jean Wyatt argues that *Cymbeline* provides the primary literary reference in the novel, supplying "the novel's central structure," further arguing that "by pervading present events with echoes of the entire span of western culture, pre-literary as well as literary, allusion and mythopoeic image reinforce the novel's underlying theme: continuity between past and present."[2] I would agree that the link between past and present is one possible theme, but only one the ways *Mrs. Dalloway* illustrates the genre of Myth. As I will claim later on, the allusion to the myth of Persephone makes more sense. For now, it is important to understand how this mythic aspect of Story interacts with Darwin's assertions regarding human behavior.

The Darwin Connection

Engaging with other people is basic not only for day to day survival, but, to the survival of our species. If you can imagine a day in which you live completely independently of others, you either deserve a medal, or you need therapy! We need each other in ways that we don't always recognize. The ability to feel sympathy, of course, is key to human relationships. In *The Descent of Man*, Darwin asserts that if we cannot feel and communicate sympathy to each other, we will not survive: "...it should be borne in mind that however great weight we may attribute to public opinion, our regard for the approbation and disapprobation of our fellows depends on sympathy, which ... forms an essential part of the social instinct, and is indeed its foundation-stone."[3] Without sympathy, which builds a strong society, we simply cannot survive. Communities that practice sympathy are the communities that flourish. This capability for "fellow-feeling" is vital to strengthening bonds between individuals and communities within and among diverse communities. These bonds come in handy, especially in times of crisis: if we fail to communicate, if we can't share our stories, let alone tell a cohesive story of our own identities, what hope do we have?

Darwin speculated about "Man's place in nature" in series of ideas to which he gives full treatment in *The Descent of Man*. In particular, he speaks of the way the development of the imagination, in tandem with other intellectual capabilities, gave human beings the ability to not only come together for protection from other communities (Darwin's "savages" and "tribes"), but also to sympathize with each other. He also asserts that there is no fundamental difference in the mental capacities between Man and the Lower animals, that any differences are not in kind, but in degree.[4] He notes the similarity between the way humans feel happiness and pain and the way animals, and even insects, seem to exhibit such feelings. Animals, just like humans, feel curiosity, exhibit a tendency towards imitation, have the power to focus their attention, and possess a great capacity for memory. When you leave your home in the morning to go to work, and your dog stands with her nose at the window, don't doubt for a moment that she will remember you: the moment you open the front door, she is there to greet you with a slobbery kiss. You are firmly implanted in her memory.

Another humbling idea: according to Darwin, the capacity to reason, which stands at the top of human intellectual and mental capacities, is an ability also shown by some animals that seem to possess a sense of self-consciousness, such as elephants. Perhaps even more amazing is that he does not deny that animals have imaginations, only that they cannot utilize their imaginations in the way that humans can. However, as Darwin points out, the *creative power* of imagination belongs to humans alone: "By this faculty, he [Mankind] unites former images and ideas, independently of the will, and thus creates brilliant and novel results."[5] In the final analysis, a very fine line separates humans from the animals. If anything can be said to separate the two, it would be what Darwin calls the "moral sense." Darwin held a non-hierarchical view of Nature and humans' place in it. Humankind does not hold this high position because we are completely different from other animals. Rather, we are at "the top" because of the degree to which we can implement these faculties for our survival.

Mrs. Dalloway reveals the power of the imagination by exploring who we are and how we relate to each other in a shifting emotional, mental, and physical landscape within the negotiations of daily life. In *Between the Acts*, which I will discuss in the second half of this chapter, Woolf tells how stories about the past inform the present, as well as point the way to a future. These themes in Woolf's novels correspond to Darwin's argument that sympathy among humans promotes community, and ultimately, survival. Even earlier, in *On the Origin of Species*, when he referred to the *inextricable web of affinities* within nature, he was rejecting a strictly hierarchical view of humans and nature that had held sway for hundreds of years, opting instead for the image of an inclusive web: "We shall never, probably, disentangle the inextricable web of the affinities between the members of any one class; but when we have a distinct object in view, and do not look to some unknown plan of creation, we may hope to make sure but slow progress."[6] Years of observation and field research had led him to this revolutionary conclusion. As Gillian Beer points out: "These affinities he perceives sometimes as kinship networks, sometimes as tree, sometimes as coral, but never as a single ascent with man making his way upward."[7] The metaphor of a tree—its network of branches emerging from a single trunk—helps us to grasp the kind of affinities that are at work in *Mrs. Dalloway* and *Between the Acts* as well. The common "trunk" of Darwin's Tree of Life is Clarissa's family, and the intersecting branches are the characters with whom they come into contact and by whom they are influenced. What confuses some readers about this novel—the lack of a central consciousness and the shifts between perspectives—is the very element that encourages our sense of interconnected affinities within its content and structure.

Paired with Darwin's notion of the web is his observation regarding the struggle to the death for survival, the twin forces of nature at work in all of life. The extremes of affinity and competition surface in stories as two of the chief concerns of human life: everything we do is shaped by these forces which take different forms—love, warmth, food, shelter, money, or fame, just to name a few. Darwin in *Origin* concludes that "Nothing is easier than to admit in words the truth of the universal struggle for life, or more difficult—at least I have found it so—than constantly to bear this conclusion in mind."[8] Evolution teaches that struggle is an inevitable part of life. Many people find it depressing to see life as merely a battle for survival. What these individuals miss is that society, with all of its benefits, *emerged* as a result of this struggle. More importantly, despite the fact that we fight, we also need each other; there is substantial hope in that truth. In Woolf's stories, the struggle for survival often involves the inherent tension between sanity and insanity, the never-ending search for a balanced mental state. Not all of the struggles she portrays are so urgent: she also depicts day-to-day concerns, as reflected in her diary, such as choosing which books to read, which parties to attend, the ups and downs of the relationships with her family and friends, conflicts with her critics, and her varied social life. Regardless of the urgency of the struggle, the daily battle to overcome obstacles both large and small is part of human life. It never ends.

Many of Woolf's stories concern what happens when men and women fail to communicate, a struggle that has caused an almost unbridgeable rift in society. She was well aware of the boundaries a patriarchal society has fashioned both within the minds and around the bodies of women of every class. The power of patriarchy to either approve or censure women was, and still is to a great extent, undeniable and as such, constitutes not only a social, but also a physical struggle. Power structures in modern society, predominately male, weigh in on matters involving women's bodies, for instance, wanting to control their most intimate parts. In *A Room of One's Own*, Woolf exhorts young women to find their own voices, and of the benefits of doing so in the fight to be taken seriously. Woolf may have been especially sensitive to this issue, given her own social anxieties which were made even more intense by her bouts with mental illness. Although Darwin did not include humans in his description of the kind of affinity he found in Nature, I would argue that this organic web of relationships does indeed include humans. We are bound together by our common needs, as well as by a wide diversity across cultures, ethnicities, class, and gender, regardless of political rhetoric to the contrary. As we know all too well, it is sometimes in the best interest of those in political power to divide us in order to more easily pursue their own agendas. Our stories, told in our own voices, have the power to remind us of our very real connections, to renew those bonds, and in so doing, facilitate individual and community survival.

Mrs. Dalloway and *Between the Acts* illustrate the ways in which humans interact within various networks—mother-daughter, husband-wife, brother-sister, friends, and lovers. In these novels, Woolf reveals a common human desire to establish kinship and affinity in the midst of disconnection and disunity. To find that affinity is to survive: to miss it is to die. In the next section I will discuss how the network of mutual affinity between characters in *Mrs. Dalloway* enables Woolf to express her belief in the power of stories to bring us together, and simultaneously to expose the deadly results when we fail. The mythic significance of the novel and the connection to evolutionary theory will close out this first section. In section two I will turn to *Between the Acts* in order to further develop the idea that stories play an important role in human survival by binding us together in a common goal of survival.

Mrs. Dalloway (1925): Plot and Structure

Mrs. Dalloway provides readers with a story that emphasizes the absolute necessity of human sympathy in the struggle to survive. The following brief plot summary highlights the external "facts": when Clarissa Dalloway wakes on June 10, she decides to buy flowers for a party she will be hosting that same evening. Thus begins an adventurous morning in London, walking through the city that she loved. During this day of Clarissa's life, she will see old friends, fight for her daughter's love and loyalty, come to terms with her past and her marriage to Richard, and host a party in his honor. On this same day, Septimus Smith, a veteran of World War I, and his wife Rezia are in London looking for a psychiatrist because Septimus suffers from shell shock. Before he can get that help, however, he throws himself out of a window. Clarissa hears of this suicide at her party that same night, but the novel ends with an affirmation of life.

This apparently simple plot carries forward a complex theme of affinity through two main characters, Clarissa Dalloway and Septimus Smith, who in Woolf's mind, represent two sides of the human coin. On the one side is a woman who has been in delicate health, mentally and physically, and is trying to reclaim her life, while on the other is a young man whose delicate mental state sends him over the edge because he was unable to find a way to hang on. Although they are as different as night and day on the surface, the substance of their affinity lies underneath the surface of daily life and superficial human relationships. Even though they never meet face to face, they eventually inhabit a common space in Clarissa's mind, perhaps an early iteration of Woolf's theory of the androgynous mind as seen in *A Room of One's Own*. While Clarissa comes to terms with her demons and determines to live to fight another day, Septimus chooses another way to end his suffering. Although he ends his life after much agony, he lives through Clarissa by way of the psychic bond she shares with him on the day of his death.

With the opening statement "Mrs. Dalloway said she would buy the flowers herself,"[9] Clarissa begins a journey that profoundly changes her life. Her impulsive decision to do her own shopping marks a shift in the way things had always been for her, a middle-aged woman who had always enjoyed a life of privilege. Having been absent from her day-to-day life after a long illness, she wakes on this particular morning in June feeling strong and optimistic. Because Lucy, her housemaid, has her hands full of housework, Clarissa readies herself to shop for her party later that evening, an adventure she is excited to take, as evidenced by her thoughts: "What a lark! What a plunge!"[10] The *lark* is of course in reference to her pending journey into London, while the *plunge* she takes into the day will acquire a double meaning. The connection between Clarissa and Septimus echoes throughout the book: as she *plunges* back into her life after a long illness, Septimus will *plunge* to his death, unable to resist the voices any longer. What Clarissa encounters on her journey that day—the people she will meet, and the conversations she will have—opens up her life in ways she couldn't have imagined. She witnesses events and has conversations that evoke questions about the meaning of her life she had never thought to ask.

Mrs. Dalloway is narrated from several different points of view, although the primary perspective belongs to Clarissa. This unique method highlights the central importance of a story's power to connect us. Whether we designate the narrative style as stream of consciousness or indirect discourse, the structure creates a virtual labyrinth: as the story unfolds, her thoughts are intersected by those of other characters, connecting their individual stories into one.[11] The heroine has lived through a long history of unfulfilling relationships, all of which she reviews on her walk through London. She feels that the one shining moment in her young womanhood in which she had felt the thrill of first love had been the kiss she shared with her friend, Sally. However, she also complains that their moment of intimacy was interrupted by Peter Walsh who had grown jealous of the blossoming friendship between the young women. Peter had become alienated from a relationship he did not understand.

Throughout the first part of the story, Clarissa indulges in memories of her girlhood at Bourton, her volatile friendship with Peter (who has returned from India seeking a divorce in order to marry an Indian girl) and her short-lived affair with Sally, now married with children. She ruminates about her life as a whole and questions her decisions. She worries over her life choices, in particular her choice to marry Richard Dalloway, whom she chose over Peter Walsh. These entanglements have comprised the most fulfilling relationships of her life, but also have compromised her sense of independence. Reclamation of that independence, coupled with the threat to her social life, institute and sustain the story's central tension. Early on, she expresses the wish to live her life over again, to have been more assertive, and thus more like a man. Feeling "invisible, unseen, unknown," Clarissa deeply desires a more meaningful life.[12]

Because of her desire to live a more insightful life, the theme of kinship between mother and child, family members, and friends take center stage in *Mrs. Dalloway*. This broad Darwinian theme implies natural affinities such as mutuality, mirroring, attunement, and social cohesion. The dual theme of kinship/affinity, woven into the plot, is complemented by overlapping thoughts and images that forge a chain of shifting associations. As Clarissa first begins her day, her thoughts return to the past when she was a young woman at Bourton. Immediately following those memories, we go back to the present moment: as Clarissa leaves her house, we enter the mind of her neighbor, Scrope Purvis, who refers to her as "a jay, blue-green, light, vivacious," an image that returns throughout the story.[13] This reflexive structure allows Woolf to tell one story through several points of view. Clarissa Dalloway, the focus of these observations, is on the downward slope of fifty, a virtual survivor of war and a literal survivor of a lengthy illness. We are introduced to Clarissa with no preamble: she rises from her bed as if newly born when she decides to begin seeking after her own Truth, a lofty goal disguised by an ordinary walk to the local florist. It is important that we know little to nothing about her from the outset as it adds to the illusion of reality—we get to know her gradually as we would anyone else in life, through observation.

During the course of the action, an even bigger question emerges concerning how to connect all of the pieces of life, the good, bad and in-between, in the face of chance. Thus, Clarissa and Septimus, both of whom attempt to achieve harmony with the world around them, represent not only two sides of the human coin, but also two sides to Woolf's personality. Clarissa, who both enjoys and loathes company, sleeps in a bed that becomes more narrow with age; Septimus, who sees visions and hears voices, can find no relief from his madness.[14] Virginia Woolf their creator, was intimately acquainted with both worlds.

Diary and Background

The lived circumstance out of which *Mrs. Dalloway* emerged infuses it with a deeper level of significance, especially with regard to this theme of affinity. In October of 1922, Woolf writes that her latest novel would be a "study of insanity & suicide: the world seen by the sane & insane side by side—something like that?"[15] Her struggles with bouts of insanity were a regular part of her life. Starting on a new project would have her "swimming in calm water again."[16] In addition, while she was writing, she was immersed in reading and translating Aeschylus, the influence of which emerges when Septimus hears the birds singing in Greek, as well as Joyce's *Ulysses*, which helps to explain, at least in part, the mythic resonance of *Mrs. Dalloway*. Another crucial influence was her friendship with Vita Sackville-West who had entered her life around this same time. They initiated a relationship which would last for most of the rest of their lives. Her devotion and conflicting feelings for Vita appear as Clarissa's memories of her flirtation with a childhood friend, Sally Seton, who was later married, just as Clarissa would also later marry Richard, mostly out of a sense of duty and decorum. Even though they lost their initial connection after Clarissa left her girlhood home, Woolf leaves open the possibility that her friendship with Sally would resume. The unbroken link between past and present is yet another iteration of affinity.

These plots and subplots concerning friendship and love affairs reveal Woolf's interest in addressing how and why we make certain associations and not others. Issues of connections within and outside of the boundaries of gender and class, in particular, recur throughout her fiction. The characters in each of her novels grapple with this issue again and again: how do we really know another person, and equally important, how do we make ourselves known to others? Her diaries testify to her sarcastic and sometimes acerbic views of society, and of her own ambivalence to being social, and yet, she consistently pushes herself to engage with others, even when she felt uncomfortable. In March of 1923, she says that being social requires fortitude which she sees as one of the advantages, even though she had written just weeks earlier that she enjoyed making social calls on her friends.[17] Her fear of society seems to have been countered by the innate sense of curiosity that made her such a good writer.

In June of 1923, she expresses difficulty in writing the novel and what she perceived as her inability to write realistic fiction.[18] However, in the midst of the difficulty, she says that she also felt a sense of freedom, seeing herself at the full force of her faculties. In this confident state of mind, Woolf says that she was "more of a human being."[19] From this we can infer that storytelling was a creative outlet by which she could understand not only herself but human experience in general. She wanted to know what happened behind the faces, underneath the surface: how can we ever truly know each other? Questions like these seemed to have guided her choice not only of plot, but of narrative style. As she labored over *Mrs. Dalloway*, she began to master a method of characterization she describes as digging out "beautiful caves" behind each one, bringing them together at the end.[20] Mining the thoughts of her characters gave her license to invent her own kind of mythology. Within those caves she discovered a goldmine of character development, a new way of writing fiction that attempted to get at the heart of human experience.[21]

The greatest challenge she faced when writing *Mrs. Dalloway*, however, was not narrative style, but in finding a way to successfully depict madness in the scenes when Septimus hears the voices in his head and birds singing in Greek.[22] The references to inner voices reflect Woolf's own struggles with mental illness and the subsequent disconnection to reality. She had heard voices speaking Greek, as does Septimus; she had also endured the attentions of doctors like Sir William Bradshaw whose advice was isolation and bed rest. Clarissa, at the beginning of the novel, is recovering from an unknown illness, but unlike Septimus, she makes a conscious decision to not give in or give up. The two of them are related in other ways: Septimus and Clarissa express their desire to relate to other people. While Septimus pushes people away, a failure to connect which costs him his life, Clarissa learns to negotiate the various relationships in her life—who to keep close and who to keep at bay—in an effort to strike a healthy balance between solitude and society. Woolf may have written this novel, at least in part, to understand the state of her own mind, painful as it was for her to revisit memories of her illness. As we know, from the previous chapter, she often contemplated the effects which her illness had on her mind and her writing, but at the time she was writing *Mrs. Dalloway*, she had begun to exhibit greater confidence and to feel less restrained by comments from critics, both internal and external ones.

Web of Affinity: Introduction

The innovative narrative structure reflects Clarissa's metaphor of Life as an inclusive mist which spread around her and everyone she knew. The Queen's car passes by and everyone on the street looks in the same direction; the crowd cranes their necks to see the airplane's skywriting: in these moments we glimpse the Darwinian *web of affinities*. Interactions between human beings in *Mrs. Dalloway* run even deeper, however, to the point that the main characters know each other's stories intimately. Those intersections keep them together and keep them from going under.[23] Woolf seems to suggest that if other people know your story, you can never truly die because your story is your life, just as one's memories contain the identity and meaning of their experience. Clarissa's journey through London attaches her to people on the streets of London and in Regent's Park; although she is unaware of it at the time, she becomes attached to Septimus, who also catches a glimpse of the car and the airplane. The caves behind which Woolf so carefully carved her characters suggest the intersections which bind them together, so that structure and imagery sustain the theme of affinity, on both physical and psychological levels.

The porous boundaries between characters reveal how one person's story/life becomes part of someone else's story/life. Not every character in the novel experiences a positive, intimate exchange, however; between Clarissa and Doris Kilman, there is little sympathy, although they share a love for Clarissa's daughter. Woolf suggests that the possibility for relationship exists, even though the characters do not acknowledge it. Mystical interactions between human beings, those aspects of everyday life that seem inexplicable, rise to the surface as characters meet and separate and meet again. Each one is on their own journey, yet each one knows that Death is the unwelcome guest who hovers always in the background. The tale of human survival, of which *Mrs. Dalloway* is one, takes us back to one of the basics of evolution and adaptation. Darwin theorized that this struggle was common to all of life, but "most severe between the individuals of the same species."[24] This insight, although not initially applied by Darwin to human life, frames the intense battle between Clarissa and Kilman over Elizabeth—they both claim her as their daughter. Clarissa and Septimus engage in a life and death battle within themselves: both constantly yearn to understand their lives, to find a way to survive the people and issues that haunt them: Clarissa to understand her decisions and accept her life at middle age, and Septimus to conquer the demons over which he has no control. Through their mental and emotional sufferings, they become forever a part of one another.

The situation which begins the novel reveals through its very *ordinariness* the *extraordinary* power of stories to establish bonds between us. On a simple journey, Clarissa figuratively crosses paths with Septimus and Rezia Smith who are in Regent's Park, as well as with Peter Walsh, who is on his way to see her after being abroad for many years. Scenes between Peter and Clarissa illustrate this point: Peter inhabits Clarissa's thoughts throughout the morning because she knows he is expected sometime in June or July. Further on, he encounters Septimus and Rezia in the park; although they do not speak, they have made contact. The point of view shifts back to Peter when he thinks of Clarissa. He reminisces about their youth and anticipates seeing her once again, creating a bond between them that echoes her memories of him. At that moment, Septimus and Rezia's actions and thoughts overlap with Peter's movements as all three of them hear an old woman singing an unintelligible love song.[25] Her song pulls them into the greater human Story of love, pain, suffering, and joy, showing the fine line between tears and laughter. As they move through the plot, the main characters create unbreakable links which form the structural framework, producing a circular, yet forward-moving momentum. As Woolf understood, our thoughts rarely if ever move in a straight line: rather, for many people, the experience is similar to the old psychologist's game of association: one thought leads to another, to another, and so forth. Our thoughts are recursive, not linear. If we are to regard fiction as being adaptive, we must be willing to accept the premise that it fills a unique and irreplaceable role in human life—its power to connect us to each other has the potential to transform not only the way we see our own lives, but the way we interact in the world. This is crucial to the analysis of fiction, in general, as a product of the human imagination, as well as to this analysis of *Mrs. Dalloway*.

As the characters' stories expand into larger and larger circles, so do their relationships. Approximately halfway through the novel when Septimus and Rezia visit the psychiatrist, Dr. Holmes, another link is made through Sir William Bradshaw who had earlier encountered Septimus when he was referred by Holmes. When Bradshaw attends the dinner party at the end of the novel, the loop is closed. Connections like these occur throughout—in fact they *are* the story. This theme remains always in the front of the reader's mind, reminding us of the underlying affinities between us all. Sometimes, in the novel, just as in real life, chance encounters don't amount to much, but sometimes they do. The structure of *Mrs. Dalloway* emphasizes the idea that these characters are all inextricably bound to each other in a kind of kinship. Points of contact made throughout the day between the main characters come full circle at the end of the novel: Clarissa, Peter, and Sally (whom she has not seen until that evening) converge at the Dalloway house for the party. In the last sentence, Peter Walsh confirms not only Clarissa's existence, "For there she was," but the uncanny effect of her existence on him.[26] He questions his life's choices, reflecting on lost opportunities to be with Clarissa. Further, this last sentence provides a definitive ending, yet it an ending that remains somewhat open, giving the reader a hint that the relationship between Clarissa, Peter, Sally and Richard will continue past the boundaries of the story. This conclusion re-embodies Clarissa who had been absent for most of the day having left her home that morning. In a way, she had become bodiless, floating through the minds of Peter, Kilman, Sally, and even, in a strange way, Septimus. Interesting, however, is that although the novel begins with her words, it does not end with her, but with Peter—up until the very last sentence, she is not in the room with Peter and the other guests, but in a different part of the house. While they are wondering where she is, she gazes out of an upstairs window, considering the news she had just heard of Septimus's death, further establishing their uncanny connection. *Mrs. Dalloway* reflects Woolf's notion of real life in that we begin with one story and end with another. If our lives are our stories, our interactions with each other make us all part of each other: we melt into each other's lives, even into the lives of those with whom we share little to no affinity, losing our hard edges and boundaries.

Affinities and Oppositions

Although Clarissa is the story's central consciousness, the expanding web of relationships begins and ends not with her, as we may have expected, but with that of Peter Walsh of whom she had been thinking that morning as she left to buy flowers. As she remembers her youth at Bourton, she naturally thinks of Peter, who she thinks may or may not have been in love with her. She knows she will see him soon, sometime in June or July as he had said in his letters. Throughout the morning, as she runs her errands, she thinks of him and their conversations, disagreements, arguments, of how she could have married him, of how he teased her about marrying Richard Dalloway. She recalls being angry with him for not fulfilling what she saw as his potential. She also remembers the uncomfortable encounter when she and Sally exchanged a kiss in the garden and he interrupted her with cryptic question, "Stargazing?"[27] Clarissa, however, had a generous, expansive nature, capable of pulling all things into herself and of allowing disparate thoughts to live at peace inside of her mind. She had arrived at an age when she felt good about surviving it all "the ebb and flow of things," and happy to be a part of the life around her, knowing that she, Peter, and all of them lived on inside of each other's thoughts.[28]

Peter is pulled into this network early on, surfacing in Clarissa's thoughts. He visits after returning from India, just as she had predicted he would, connecting Clarissa to her past and to the present moment.[29] Peter all but forces his way into her room, declaring that although she may be busy, or resting, she WILL see him after his five-year absence in India. He finds her mending a dress for her party, and is immediately taken back to their shared life at Bourton. He notes that she had not appeared to change at all in all the time he had known her. Although he remarks that she has grown older, she is the same somehow, that mending a dress is such a *Clarissa* thing to do. As he takes out his pocket-knife, she thinks the same of him—his old habits mark his identity. In this way, the two find their youthful relationship to be intact. As they converse about small, unimportant things, their thoughts betray what is happening beneath the surface: she wonders why she hadn't married Peter after all, and he thinks that marriage to Richard had not been kind to her. As their visit continues, Peter becomes more and more uncomfortable as the past rises up between them; he begins to feel like a failure. They began to challenge each other, as armies face off in a battle. Peter admits that he is in love with a married woman, and presents this fact to Clarissa as an offering or a garland. In the face of this new fact about her old friend, she suddenly feels old, as if all of the good years are behind her—she feels that it's all over for her. At the end of their exchange, Peter grabs her by the shoulders and asks if she is happy—at that moment they are interrupted by the entrance of her daughter, Elizabeth, and he leaves without his answer. In his ears echoes her reminder of the party that evening, and in the next section, Woolf begins with that phrase, connecting Clarissa once again with life in the streets of London. The web of affinity will expand to include not only Peter and Clarissa, but also the old woman in the park, Septimus, and Rezia, relationships that come full circle by the time the story comes to a close.

Between Clarissa and Septimus lies the most crucial affinity. Readers have noted that Septimus is Clarissa's double, or as some have said, her *doppelgänger*. What is the function of this doubling? One possible answer is that Septimus is a kind of child to her. Certainly he is the child of the culture in which they both grew up. "Hail Britannia" is a call to arms that they both heard and responded to in their own ways: he to battle, Clarissa to marriage, both doing their duty for the good of the Empire. Septimus realizes, even in his shocked state of mind, that he was sold a bill of goods, a realization that comes too late to save him. In her own way, Clarissa was also disillusioned about Life. Like him, she expected to have a happy and fulfilled life after marriage. While she has been happy, for the most part, she reflects that her life grows more constricted with age, as symbolized by the narrow bed; her daughter grows away from her, and her husband stands at a distance, preoccupied with his own concerns. Like Septimus, Clarissa seems somewhat shell-shocked as she walks out into the London streets. The world of 1918 was certainly far different than the world of 1922. Within a few short years, the modern world offered conveniences and luxuries she had never dreamed of, but for Septimus and many others, the brutality of human nature had stayed the same. He represents a sort of Everyman of the Modern era. The comparative experiences of Clarissa and Septimus pose a question for us: Who is really equipped to survive the brutalities of war, let alone those of everyday life?

The journeys of these twin souls never physically coincide, and yet as they cross paths with all of the other characters throughout the day, they come into close psychic proximity. A thread forms between them, a correspondence so robust that when Septimus takes his final plunge, Clarissa feels the pull and thinks vividly of what it must have felt like for him to be suddenly free.[30] Lady Bradshaw tells her of his demise as a bit of gossip and as a reason for arriving late to the party, never imagining the impact it would have on Clarissa. As she walks into an adjacent room, thinking to find Lady Bruton and the Prime Minister, she finds instead an empty room, allowing her space to let the news of Septimus's death to sink in. She imagines his fall and the impact of his body on the ground, likening his suicide to tossing a coin into the Serpentine River. She thinks of the company of people under her roof as going on with their lives, yet she admired Septimus for having defied the empty chatter of everyday life.[31] While he could not resist the call to give up his life, Clarissa finds her way back to life through her husband, daughter, and friends, as well as the old woman across the street who had persisted to old age.[32] As Clarissa contemplates what has happened, she recalls a phrase, "Fear no more the heat o' the sun" from Shakespeare's *Cymbeline*. This phrase brings her comfort, even as it underscores the tension between affinity and discord:

> Fear no more the heat o' the sun,
> Nor the furious winter's rages;
> Thou thy worldly task hast done,
> Home art gone, and ta'en thy wages:
> Golden lads and girls all must,
> As chimney-sweepers, come to dust.[33]

Furthermore, the repetition of the first line of this song builds a sense of irony regarding the dilemmas of the two main characters—Septimus who is driven by fear and Clarissa who fights her fear in the face of the inevitable.

The overlapping relations caused by the narrative structure includes not only characters who feel an affinity for each other, but also those who share little or none, such as Clarissa and Doris Kilman. Despite the fact that these women stand in opposition to each other, they share a tenuous affinity through Elizabeth, Clarissa's daughter. Clarissa and Elizabeth have grown apart as Elizabeth has matured: although Elizabeth is Clarissa's biological daughter, we see little evidence of mother-daughter bonding. On the other hand, Kilman sees herself as a surrogate mother to Elizabeth, and tries desperately to bond with her through religious and historical studies in which she tutors the young girl. Mother-child kinship is evident in the scene in which the two take tea together on the afternoon of Clarissa's party. While Kilman has Elizabeth to herself, she jealously guards their time. As these relationships indicate, both the notion of kinship and its opposite, the competition for resources, play a part in human survival. Just as Clarissa would like for Elizabeth to carry on in the Dalloway family tradition—and at the end of the novel, she might be well on her way as she stands next to her father at the party—Kilman would like for her to follow in her own footsteps in the service to the poor and downtrodden.

These two women could not be more different: Clarissa is described as light and pink, while Kilman is described as dark and brown. Clarissa represents wealth, while Kilman represents poverty. Yet Kilman's survival instinct (Clarissa thinks of her as a "prehistoric monster") makes her resilient. She defies Clarissa's maternal position and sets herself up as the *better* of the two mothers, more equipped to teach Elizabeth about what life was really like, not the pampered version that Clarissa would have her believe in. It is difficult to know with 100 percent certainty which version Woolf herself would have agreed with. From what we know of Woolf, she did not believe in God, but we know that she grew up more like Clarissa than she did Kilman. She also exhorted women of all classes to find a "room of their own" and cultivate a voice. In any case, the relationship between Clarissa and Kilman highlights the struggle to survive common to every human. Although Kilman's body and soul seem more battle scarred than Clarissa, for her part, Clarissa is perhaps better at hiding her wounds from the outside world and thus more fit to survive in a community that prizes outward appearances above all. Their connection through Elizabeth is an expression of their desire to survive.

The Affinity of Myth: Human Past, Present and Future

Myth represents a bridge to our common human ancestry, and thus signifies an affinity with our common human fears and desires. With Myth, we dive past our conscious memories and into a subconscious realm which houses a collective Human past. The stories of Myth are so old that we don't know their exact origins. The kind of information that such narratives communicate about human beings continues to intrigue us because they contain a Truth which binds us together. We recognize ourselves in Myth. Karen Armstrong points out that a myth "was an event which, in some sense, had happened once, but which also happened all the time ... mythology is an art form that points beyond history to what is timeless in human existence, helping us to get beyond the chaotic flux of random events, and glimpse into the core of reality."[34] In other words, in telling of a thing that happened but is also always happening, Myth transcends the mundane and everyday world, giving us the power to transform our lives and to find a renewed sense of meaning and direction.[35] Whether that mythic world is recalled from *Cymbeline* as Wyatt asserts, or from the tale of Persephone, which I prefer, Myth is foundational to *Mrs. Dalloway*, connecting the characters and the reader to a shared human past that transcends the physical world.

In alluding to Myth, *Mrs. Dalloway* further reveals the evolutionary power of stories to create connections between people who are unrelated, connections which form at least a loose social cohesion within and across communities. At the center of the novel we find *eternal myth-time*: when Peter Walsh crosses through Regent's Park, he hears a song from an old woman whom we understand to represent Time, History, and the overall plight of Humanity: "the voice of no age or sex, the voice of an ancient spring spouting from the earth."[36] This eternal presence at the center of the book which sings of "love which has lasted a million years" connects Clarissa to Peter, as well as to Septimus and Rezia on the level of their shared Humanity.[37] Her old familiar song of lost love seems to emerge from the very beginnings of human life: "the old bubbling burbling song, soaking through the knotted roots of infinite ages" issues from "a mere hole in the earth."[38] Although it is unintelligible for the most part, this song of love and pain connects Clarissa's story to every story that came before her, as well as to every story that will come after her. Eternal myth-time tells us that what appears to be our journey and ours alone is actually the journey of Everyman and Everywoman. This allusion to Myth builds a deeper level of affinity, both between the characters and between the story and its readers, making it an integral part of the narrative.

Clarissa's story reminds us of who we are, where we came from, what we share as human beings, as well as what is possible to share, once we overcome our fear. The rootedness of Story in our shared human past and our mythology creates the most meaningful connection of all. Because we all share this common ancestry, regardless of all that threatens to separate us from each other, the same themes that captured our attention hundreds of thousands of years ago continue to appeal to us today. Again, Armstrong asserts that "Human beings have always been mythmakers," from the time of the Neanderthals. Because we are "meaning-seeking creatures" who are prone to "fall easily into despair" over a life that sometimes makes no sense at all, "we invented stories that enabled us to place our lives in a larger setting, that revealed an underlying pattern, and gave us a sense that, against all the depressing and chaotic evidence to the contrary, life had meaning and value."[39] One of the ways we gain this sense of meaning is by connecting to other human beings through similar experiences. The Hero story is a well-known archetype: through an act of sacrifice she brings redemption and restores order. This gift to the community reconnects them to each other. The act of a hero is replicated a thousand times a thousand throughout human history. Through Story, we become the heroes of our own lives, all of us on a journey to discover life's meaning. As Joseph Campbell asserts, "the hero has a thousand faces," but they are faces we recognize without fail.

If everyday life represents the earthbound, Myth represents the transcendent—through Myth and the affinities it builds, we gain the occasional glimpse of something beyond our limited perceptions. This belief in the transcendent, whatever form that takes, lifts us out the drudgery and threat of meaninglessness and places us on a higher plane of existence. In *Mrs. Dalloway*, both Clarissa and Septimus long for a transcendent experience, and yet in modern life, transcendence has been declared dead. Both characters are trapped, albeit in different ways, by their bodies, surroundings, relationships, but most importantly, by their own thoughts. They are not allowed to be free. Dreamers are condemned as crazy; middle-aged women are relegated to the parlor and the flower shop. In a modern world bereft of Mythos, the writing in the sky is not a message from the gods, but an advertisement for coffee creamer. Again, turning to Armstrong, we learn that "all mythology speaks of another plane that exists alongside our own world, and that in some sense supports it."[40] Here she speaks of a kind of mystical affinity created by Myth—an affinity between people, time, and the nature of reality, or lived experience. The mythic framework, instead of denying the evolutionary power of Story, reinforces themes of connection, affinity, and social cohesion, and with that reinforcement, the argument that Story could indeed be adaptive for human survival.

The allusion to Myth is not anything new, of course. Virginia Woolf often turned to Greek mythology as the common historical and cultural ground in many of her stories in order to bring to light new, more modern meanings. Like her contemporaries, such as Pound and Eliot, she tapped into the literature of the Western European tradition as a way of grounding her work in common cultural heritage. References to Greek language and Myth are integrated throughout the text, as well as references to ancient British history. We can thus see Clarissa as both heroine and goddess, as indicated early on in this brief scene: after Clarissa returns home from her shopping trip, she hands Lucy her umbrella, which she treated like a "sacred weapon which a Goddess ... sheds" after her battle has been won.[41] In fact, she plays the part of both warrior and victim, maiden ("narrower and narrower would her bed be") and Crone (middle-aged: "She felt very young; at the same time unspeakably aged"), both a seeker of wisdom and an embodiment of that wisdom.⁴² Hers is a journey of reconciliation, with herself, her daughter, her husband—in short, with her life. Her *plunge* takes her, renewed, back into her everyday life.

Septimus, her double, is also a hero-warrior, but unlike Clarissa, he is also a victim. Although still a young man, he has aged before his time due to the ravages of war and so has become wiser than his years in his distrust of doctors and established authority. While Clarissa survives her illness, Septimus' illness overwhelms him to the point that he can find no relief. Instead of comfort he finds judgment and misunderstanding. His wife literally does not speak the same language, and so he is further cut off from human sympathy. While she loves him, she cannot find a way to communicate with him, to bring him back from the edge of the abyss. His is a journey to freedom; desperate to find some relief from the voices in his head, he does the only thing he can and simply flies away.

This brief summary of the two journeys cannot, of course, fully explain the connective power of Myth in the novel. The references are many and they run deep. The intertextual references also abound for those that recognize them. The most important of these is the echo/parody of James Joyce's novel, *Ulysses*, which is his retelling of the journey of Odysseus. Not only does Woolf design a similar mythic structure in her novel, her references reinforce the inextricable nature of Darwin's web of affinities between the two heroes and the community. Clarissa and Septimus are twin souls on hero quests through the city of London: there are obstacles to overcome, monsters to slay, and signs in the sky. While Joyce called on the myth of Odysseus for his structural framework in *Ulysses*, however, I would argue that Woolf (instead of simply following Joyce' plan) could also have had in mind the myth of Persephone, the daughter of the gods who was abducted and swept away to Hades. In Ovid's myth, the Sirens played the role of handmaidens to Persephone to watch over her. When she was taken to the Underworld they were sent to find her, but having failed to bring her back, Demeter transformed them into birds.

As in *The Odyssey*, where Sirens lured sailors to their deaths with their irresistible songs, in *Mrs. Dalloway* the Siren's call is heard in different guises and to different purposes. Throughout, Clarissa/Persephone reasons with those people and forces which issue that call, keeping at bay the temptation to follow them back into the Underworld. Her Sirens come to her in the form of the distractions that she faces—her own doubts about her marriage to Richard, worries about her daughter and Miss Kilman, her difficult relationship with Peter, her buried love for Sally. As she grapples with these problems, they threaten to pull her under. Moreover,

Clarissa's Sirens take the form of various people in her life who do not fully know or understand her, those who would place her in a box in which she does not belong. Ultimately, she hears their call, but chooses to walk away, making a conscious decision to go on with life, despite the fact that she applauds Septimus's decision, saying to herself that she was glad that he had "thrown it away."[43] Although Clarissa is shocked by his death, she ultimately sees it as a victory; he has freed himself, showing her the way to her own kind of freedom. Septimus hears the Sirens call when he imagines the birds in the park singing in Greek, tempting him to end his life: their seductive song promises ease and freedom from fear. "A sparrow perched on the railing opposite chirped ... in Greek words how there is no crime ... there is no death."[44] Significantly, because Clarissa is described as birdlike, this image connects Clarissa to both the Siren's in Ovid's myth as well as to Septimus. The Sirens call to both Septimus and Clarissa, tempting each of them in different ways. Clarissa faces the narrowing bed and the demon of Kilman (Kill Man), while Septimus ultimately loses his fight against the call to self-destruction.

Clarissa embodies a modern-day Persephone, reflecting the nature of her own journey, one that takes her not into the Underworld, but into the World of light and life as she struggles to rejoin humanity. Persephone's tale does not, of course, provide a perfectly aligned framework. I would not suggest that there is a one-to-one correspondence between plot and characters of these narratives. The plot of Woolf's novel is not as predictable, branching off as it does in different directions depending on how the characters meet and interact. The upward trajectory of Clarissa's journey is paralleled by the downward turn of Septimus' path, and the connection they share is a moment of decision: to live or not to live. Thus, the overwhelming reference to Sirens is the call to Death. Septimus answers the call by leaping out of the window, while Clarissa, standing at her own window, walks away from this call, deciding to rejoin her life.

Conclusion

Although further discussion of Myth goes beyond the scope of my book, it is important in closing this section to understand that it adds an important dimension to the argument that Story may have been adaptive for human survival. Although ancient storytelling humans could hardly have dreamed of such an advanced civilization as London in the 1920s, the links between them and their prodigious ancestors were initiated by the stories they told so many thousands of years ago, as Armstrong and others have explained. Seeking explanations for natural phenomena, trying to understand death, or even recognizing the pattern of seasons, all laid the groundwork for human social and cultural advances, enabling them to survive in a harsh environment. Stories that bind communities together are powerful, but those that add ritual to Story are even more so, for good as well as for evil. In *Mrs. Dalloway*, we recognize the basic human impulse to understand the world and to establish meaningful relationships in the face of a loss of meaningful ritual. The words of the old woman singing in the park have become unintelligible to the modern ear, although they once held meaning. In the end, Clarissa chooses to embody her boon of life, while Septimus chose a different path, seeking instead a physical re-embodiment of transcendence.

Lehrer argues that Woolf intuitively understood what many psychologists and neuroscientists know to be true about the way our minds operate—that our "selves" emerge from the "fragments" of daily experience.[45] Her illness informed her literary style, he says, giving us a glimpse not only into the inner workings of the mentally ill individual but, I would add, into human consciousness in general, into the continuous struggle we all experience as we try to navigate everyday reality. "The self," Lehrer states, "emerges from the chaos of consciousness."[46] Woolf's "Self" is laid bare in her writings, and in reading her stories, we are faced with ourselves in the here and now. In the next section of this chapter, we will see this theory come to life when the villagers at the pageant in *Between the Acts* are faced with reflections of themselves before they were prepared to respond. Research reveals the ways in which our brains have evolved to take on more and more complex tasks. The world has become its own Rubik's cube of sorts, a puzzle of numerous knots and endless conundrums. The species that can unravel these increasingly complex knots, as well as create more complex ways of being and moving in the world, will survive. If we can learn to cooperate, our chances of survival will increase exponentially. The reverse is also frighteningly true: the adverse effects of the complex brain are also a huge risk to our survival. We may dream of fabulous ideas for all kinds of innovations in technology and culture, but then become trapped by their outcomes and consequences. *Between the Acts*, written during the beginning of World War II and the bombings of the English coast, presents us with a kaleidoscope of history that takes us from the prehistoric cave to the manor house, from the mammoth and the mastodon to the modern advances of the motor-car and the airplane. With all of our knowledge, we are still asking how to create affinity: How can we achieve peace in the midst of chaos and avoid that Siren call to annihilation?

Between the Acts (1941): Plot and Introduction

With the threat of war on the horizon, the Olivers—Isa, Bart, and Lucy—and a small group of guests gather at Pointz Hall on the eve of the annual village historical pageant where they sit discussing, among other things, the controversial placement of a cesspool on the site of the old Roman road. *Between the Acts* is a story of both family and national history, but more importantly, the story of people yearning for meaningful relationships in an increasingly unstable world. In the intervals between the scenes of the pageant, family drama and romantic intrigue unfold amidst a sense of confusion regarding identity, ownership, and relationship. The plot is fragmented by interruptions and hesitations in the conversations and scenes in the pageant. As this pageant ends, the actors hold up fragmented mirrors to their audience, creating a moment of recognition, encouraging a sense of unity and identification. Unfortunately, the meaning is lost on the audience: the moment of recognition quickly fades, and the characters are "dispersed" back to their own lives. When asked the meaning of the play, no one, not even the village Reverend, has an answer. As the novel concludes, the *stage* is made ready for another *act* in the human drama.

This plot, which concerns a day or two in the lives of a small group of family and friends, was the vehicle by which Woolf could write "anything that comes into my head."[47] In planning her last novel, she wanted to write a new kind of story that brought together "all life, all art."[48] The connections that could create out of an "I" the inclusive "We"—*this* was her subject. She didn't hold out much hope for a future in the late 1930s: the British past, however noble, seems to have dissolved into a literal cesspool. Despite signs of evident progress, war loomed on the horizon and humans still seemed mired down in the same old patterns with the same basic needs they've always had: to eat, sleep, procreate, and dispel bodily waste. From the days of ancient history to the present day, nothing seems to have changed. Most were still fighting, struggling, and dying without having achieved the significant social ties that all humans seek.

The overarching evolutionary theme in the novel, the problem of creating and sustaining affinity, emerges as each character seeks a way to build sympathy in their desire to become part of something larger than themselves. Adding to the complexity, the structure is episodic and fragmented, the content constantly pushing against this fragmentation, seeming at times to mistrust it. The resulting tension between the structure and content encourages the reader to re-evaluate the link between the present moment—the event of the pageant—and the past, represented by the pageant, the land, the ancestral home of the Olivers, and their family history. By telling this story, Woolf reminds herself and her readers of the blessings, as well as the curses, of the attempt to create affinity. As the characters seek meaningful relationships with each other, they suffer disappointment and betrayal time after time. The novel ends with the hope that life will not only go on, but that it might be better than before. Nothing is determined—all is expectant.

In *Between the Acts*, the Darwinian notion of a web of affinities is expressed as a desire for connection on three levels: (1) the personal/individual, as reflected in the lives of the Oliver family, their friends, and the participation of the villagers in the pageant; (2) the historical, based on references to British history in the pageant, and (3) the global, based on references to ancient history. Since a large portion of the novel—the pageant—concerns a critique of history, which implies teleology, it may seem counterintuitive to apply Darwin's theory of evolution which was non-teleological. In his view no pre-ordained goal of progress exists in the natural evolution of species, even though it was interpreted that way early on and sometimes still is: the thinking seems to go "if we evolve, we must evolve towards a goal of the perfected human." The evolutionary process itself does not imply progress towards a goal. Humankind invented Story (and History is one kind of story) to make sense of our experience, to satisfy that need we have for purpose. Further, as a story, history gives the past a necessary structure. As a critique, *Between the Acts* both feeds into and casts doubt on the official history of the British people as a story that everyone can agree on. Not only do the characters wonder about origins and histories, but the narrative structure presents the tension between unity and disconnection, connections that were made and broken from our ancestors to our progeny: for instance, the pageant, the "play-within-a-play," resists the dominance of males over females throughout history.

In fact, the novel as a whole poses questions for us to ponder: is meaningful connection between all human beings even possible? If we achieve such connections, will we increase our chances of survival? In what would be her last novel, Woolf reimagines all of human history, not just British history, as one long quest for survival—through our relationships with each other, the earth, and with ourselves, the human race is on a quest which never ends. The closing words indicate yet another beginning, engendering a belief in a future, but these words also urge us to wonder if that future could be more inclusive and less destructive. The recursive nature of the structure may imply a negative response: the same story of humanity and its struggles will surely begin all over again with every new day, but at the same time, the story hints at hope. Woolf's burning question regarding meaning in human life takes us from an ocean shore to a stage; from a global metaphor, the sea, to a more local one, the English village; from an all-encompassing image to a tightly framed experience, framed both in terms of the plot as well as the proscenium of a stage. It is on the local stage that her final drama of humanity will play out.

Diary and Background

Woolf's last novel communicates her hopes concerning love and community, alongside her deeply held fears of disconnection and isolation, all too common to the human experience. As World War II drew closer to the shores of England, she became even more anxious and depressed. The basics of survival from one day to the next rise to the top of the list of priorities in times of war. But in the remaining months of her life, she and Leonard were relegated to hiding in the bushes as they felt bombs falling all around them. Shocking, but perhaps understandable, was that she, Adrian, and Leonard had made a suicide pact in case Hitler conquered England, once they learned that they were on his list of those to be taken captive. The Woolfs heroically lived day after day in these horrific conditions, with Virginia saying goodbye in the end out of necessity for herself and her love for Leonard. *Between the Acts* brings a small glimmer of hope to the next phase of human life, even though she could not find that last bit of hope for herself. One of the many questions posed by this novel has become even more urgent in the 21st century: What happens when the web of relationships between humans is stretched to its limits?

More poignantly than the previous novels, *Between the Acts* was shaped by the realities of the time at which Woolf was writing. As we read the novel alongside the diaries, another evolutionary theme emerges: her own quest to find meaning in horrific circumstances. The pageant can be interpreted not only as a means for her to explore the ups and downs of human history, but also as a distraction from the looming war. Further, the several fragments of dialogue and snippets of literature and criticism scattered throughout the novel encapsulate not only the idea of a shattered identity, but also refer to what Woolf perceived as the disconnected pieces of daily life in the small village of Rodmell where she ended her days. We must return to the diary to provide the necessary background information in order to fully understand this last novel.

Between the Acts began as *Pointz Hall* in 1937, a novel she planned to be all "dialogue" and "poetry."[49] By the following year, she had envisioned it in its entirety. It was to be a story in which she would weave together all of history, life, art, and literature. The concept grew out of her desire to write a story unlike any other—one that would consist of variations on a theme, as well as a new kind of criticism. Although she had reached a point at which she didn't necessarily want to continue writing fiction, she wanted to compose a narrative that revolved around one theme told from various perspectives: she writes that all of the scenes would "radiate to a centre."[50] Woolf was in her prime as far as her creative abilities: she felt that she had become the "mistress" of her own writing. Her age and experience accounts for this comfort to a certain extent—she had grown, both as a human and as a writer who knew her own mind.[51] She may have intuited that this was to be her swan song, given the evidence in the diary: "I feel oughtn't I to finish off *PH* [*Pointz Hall/Between the Acts*]: oughtn't I to finish something by way of an end? The end gives its vividness, even its gaiety and recklessness to the random daily life. This, I thought yesterday, may be my last walk."[52] On this same date, she complains that the war had broken her feeling of security and that she had lost the sense of an audience, what she refers to as her "echo."[53] The audience which had "thickened [her] identity wall" had disappeared and she had begun to lose her bearings. She expresses fear that she may fall over the edge of "a precipice ... and then? I can't conceive that there will be a 27th June 1941," approximately one year after she wrote these words.[54] And so she had predicted that there was no future for her. The fact that she soldiered on for another nine months after this entry is probably something of a miracle.

Within nine months, she had completed a draft of *Between the Acts*. Had she lived, Leonard says, she would certainly have revised it: this last novel comes to us as a gift. It was important to her to include the English countryside, complete with a traditional English country house, children and their nursemaids.[55] In so doing, she captures forever a moment in the lives of English people on the brink of war. As World War II drew nearer to England, she writes of becoming more fearful, but says that she found more relief by "[diving] into fiction."[56] During these months, the war seeps into her diary more often. In September of 1938, she designates Hitler a "ridiculous little man" who conjures a "housemaid's dream" of "death and war and darkness," remarking that it was all unreal to her.[57] Her frustration with the obsession people had with always wanting news of the war finds its way into *Pointz Hall/Between the Acts* when the audience talks about the war in the intervals between scenes of the pageant. Although Woolf felt the strain of impending battle, she continued writing.[58] In October of 1938, she thought more often of her new idea not primarily as fiction, but as a kind of literary criticism. From her perspective, this novel had become a compendium of poetry, her notes for the *Times Literary Supplement*, comments about and quotations from English literature and all of the work she had been collecting since 1920. It was to be her last word on literature, writing and life.[59] This novel is comparable in structure to a set of nesting dolls, one story fitting inside another and another and another. At the end, the reader is left to ask, along with LaTrobe's audience, what is the central meaning? How does the meaning of this story, or any story, finally become apparent?

The varied and often chaotic voices of the villagers, intermingled with the literature, fill the pages.[60] Woolf simultaneously speaks through Isa Oliver, Miss LaTrobe, Mrs. Manresa, and Lucy Swithin. Her own experience of village life infuses the details of the setting with very real energy: the cows in the background of the pageant are the very cows she sees on her daily walks, imagining them to be her own cavalry.[61] But, given her diary entry on June 9, 1940, in this period of time she suffers greatly from her fear of certain death at the hands of the Germans and their bombs. What she called her writing "I"—her persona as a writer—had disappeared; she no longer had an audience because she hears nothing back when she speaks [writes]. This, she says, is "part of one's death."[62] Throughout 1940, the Woolfs and the villagers of Rodmell were showered with air raids. She wrote virtually of nothing else for months, but in September of 1940, records that she kept writing *Pointz Hall* in spite of her fears. The contrast between peaceful (and sometimes boring) village life and the horror of a war all around them is apparently not lost on her, which is the ultimate irony. She wonders what it would be like to die from being hit by a bomb,[63] her mood vacillating from dread to an almost eerie calm.

Despite her misery of dealing with the war, the fright of bombs, the unsettling nature of life, she claims in November of 1940 to be happy and still writing *Pointz Hall*: "Oh the freedom!"[64] She writes of the landscape under flood waters as being primeval "as it was in the beginning."[65] This same sense of deep history forms the bedrock of *Between the Acts*. On this same day, she describes being happy and excited about the new book, having found her "old hunger for books" once more.[66] For this novel, she explains that she drew on her "human naturalist" notes, which initiated a new kind of rhythm in her writing that freed up her mind. After Christmas, contemplating her life as a writer and as a woman, she once again asserts her identity: "I am I; and must follow that furrow, not copy another."[67] In this way, she speaks through LaTrobe, the author and director of the pageant, who insists, regardless of criticism, of expressing her own vision, of having things her own way. *Pointz Hall* officially became what we know as *Between the Acts* one month before she walked into the river just steps from her home.[68]

Because this novel was published posthumously she was not able to revise the manuscript. This leaves us to wonder whether we even have the story she intended. In 1941, with the war in full swing, Woolf rallies herself to "go down with [her] colours flying."[69] A few days later, she was gone, her mental illness having the last word. Perhaps Woolf knew, even as she was writing, that it would be her last attempt to express what it means to live and love in an often hostile and unforgiving world. Her suicide, just days after completing the novel, throws her work into sharp relief against this question of the role of affinity in human survival. In this, her final novel, Woolf interrogates like never before the meaning of human life and the stories we tell ourselves and each other to explain the obstacles in life, such as disappointment, love, war. What is the message we should be getting from *Between the Acts*? Are we all just savage brutes under the skin? Have human beings changed through thousands of years of history? Will we ever change? Woolf asks us to consider whether love can save us from ourselves.

Ancestors, Prehistory and Mythology

Between the Acts calls attention to the unchanging nature of human behavior across history and the search for social affinity regardless of the cost (or should I say, in spite of the cost) in order to survive. On another level, the story concerns the pageant of events that we call *history*, the kind of events that happen outside of individual, everyday experience. While these events shape our daily lives, they do so at a great distance: it is *between the acts* of national and global dramas that Woolf's idea of real life takes place. She shows us how this process, which we take for granted, works by way of the narrative structure. In the intervals between the scenes of

LaTrobe's pageant we see the tiny details, such as the gramophone, that have gone into the production of the play; in contrast and in complement to this, we overhear the main characters of the novel working through their personal dramas. The large-scale backdrop of English history simultaneously puts us on the mountain top and down in the valley: individual human life is the chief focus, but is also somewhat insignificant in comparison to all of human history, a notion that Woolf embraces as well as problematizes. Communication between characters breaks down to some extent, but their relationships are not irredeemable. For example, when the story ends with Isa and Giles fighting about their infidelities, we are initially led to believe that the marriage may be finished; however, after this argument, they retreat to their bedroom to create a new life, just as it has been since the beginning of time. The evolutionary themes of affinity and kinship are made all the stronger by numerous references to ancient history.

Because it is anchored in the deep past (as well in more recent past for the characters), *Between the Acts* emphasizes the manner in which Story may have become adaptive for human survival. Both the structural and historical themes of the novel reveal the possibility that stories present us with opportunities for forging bonds between the past, present and future, as well as between people who come from different walks of life. Hope for the future, Woolf says, lies in our willingness to reach beyond the boundaries of such categories as gender and class to learn, and to remember, the hard lessons of human history. "We all play our part" in the human drama, a phrase we hear throughout this story, from audience to actor, from the swallows to the cows, from Village Idiot to Queen. If this is true, what then? What kinds of associations can we make through our stories, past and present, my story and your story, *his-stories* and *her-stories*?

Lucy Swithin, Bart Oliver's sister, is keenly interested in prehistoric world history, British history, and her own ancestors who hover as a constant presence in the pictures that hang on the walls of her childhood home. We envision along with her the ancient British landscape populated by the mammoths and cave-dwellers about which she reads. It strikes Lucy that the landscape of the present day has been saturated with blood and bones, accumulated over millions of years to form the soil under the characters' very feet. This historical connection is made clear in the following example: On his way to the refreshment tent to meet Mrs. Manresa, Giles Oliver steps on the snake trying to swallow a toad and gets blood on his boots as a result, recalling the ancient roots of all of life and the close proximity of death that can come from nowhere. Further, the pageant which lies at the center of this novel, spanning prehistory to the novel's present day, is comprised of a set of living portraits, tableaus come to life. This pageant serves as a vehicle, not only for the poetry, literature, criticism, and history Woolf wanted to include, but also as a way for her to wonder if anything has actually changed—how far have humans walked away from the cave? LaTrobe, the writer and director, creates a new world for her audience, a view of life in the present of 1938 in which all are one, all are connected. As the pageant functions as a play-within-a-play, we bear witness to a microcosm of the human experience.

Although references to a common English past recur throughout the story, both the narrator and Lucy speak of an even more distant past, the prehistory of England, reflecting Woolf's own interest in these subjects. The notion that at an earlier point in history there was no English Channel, that the British Isles and the continent had been one, fascinates and intrigues Lucy, leading her to think more philosophically about the nature of human life and our place in Nature as a whole.[70] The notion that the sea and land were once joined leads her to retain some sense of hope for humanity: for Lucy, a connection to the land is a connection to national identity as well as human identity. She wants to believe that we are part of nature, an expression of the earth itself. Within the context of the story, the sea becomes a symbol for the potential chaos of life, both its unity and its discord. Although her brother, Bart, reminds her that Pointz Hall is thirty-five miles from the sea, Lucy observes that one might still hear waves breaking after a storm. This is an idea which brings her a measure of comfort and helps reconnect with her brother and with their heritage.[71] She and Bart are proud of their family heritage because they were in England "before the Conquest," but as Isa observes, in the days when mammoths walked through what was now Piccadilly, they were all "savages."[72] Lucy's imaginative journeys into the past invade her thoughts of the present: in her mind, the housemaid, Grace, becomes confused with a "leather-covered grunting monster" emerging from an ancient forest.[73] Unlike the other characters, Lucy enjoys a boundlessness of mind; she is not tied to the here and now. Although the servants, housemaids, and villagers refer to her as "Batty," she alone seems to be contented with her life. When forced to come back into the here and now, she sinks into her aging body with some feeling of regret, even irritation. She relishes her links to the past. The residents and servants of Pointz Hall even boast of a ghostly lady who drowned herself in the lily pool.[74] When it turns out that the bones at the bottom of the pond were those of a sheep and not of a lady, it makes no difference to the locals because it represents another link to a proud and colorful past.

The novel reimagines the past as both connected to and at odds with the present time. Lucy reminds everyone, though no one is listening, that the Barn in which they took their tea had once been a swamp.[75] Thus, it is a sort of holy ground for her, a sacred space. At an earlier time when there was no English Channel, Lucy imagines that fields of rhododendrons bloomed and "humming birds quivered at the mouths of scarlet trumpets." In the midst of the pageant, the actors sing "the earth is always the same," regardless of the relentless passing of time.[76] The overarching theme of the novel, especially visible in passages that describe ancient history and its relationship to the present, is the mystery of unity—are we all One? Can there be an unbreakable bond between our past, present, and future as human beings? As the spokesperson for the meta-view of family and human history Lucy sees, in her mind's eye, the landscape as it had been before mankind inhabited it.[77] The land, she believes, will be the only thing to survive, just as it had for millions of years. For her, any final meaning of life remains a mystery beyond their grasp. In general, survival of the fittest only means something within a specific context of the history of both people and their land: what are the conditions they are expected to survive?

We are given a hint about the future as the novel closes. Although Isa and Giles are Woolf's representatives of the imperfect human race, they will be the foundation of another generation. Their argument at the end of the day must happen, given all that has gone before: their disagreements, infidelities, and misunderstandings. But out of their mutual affinity they will begin another generation—life will continue as it always has since "the night that dwellers in caves had watched from some high place among the rocks."[78] I would argue that in this way, *Between the Acts* enacts not only mythmaking but world-making on a grand scale. The protagonists' mythic counterparts tie this novel, like the others, into a deep narrative structure that reaches back thousands of years; it is even Biblical in a sense, as Isa and Giles play the parts of the modern Eve and Adam. Recall that Giles kills the snake in the garden, crushing it with his foot. It is too late for these characters to avoid Original Sin, but the mundane horror of his cruel act underscores the carelessness with which he and Isa treat each other, as well as their connection to the first ancestors.

In addition, oblique references to Greek mythology tie this story into deep human history. The remnants of ancient Myth re-emerge in the structure of the hero cycle, but especially in the conceit of the Three Graces: Isa, La Trobe, and Lucy. La Trobe could also be cast as either Thalia, the Muse of comedy, or perhaps Clio, the Muse of history: Lucy praises the pageant, telling LaTrobe that she had touched her in a way she had trouble expressing, but that she had felt like she was a part of the history she had read about, and had a part to play in it herself.[79] In this brief interaction, LaTrobe and Lucy meet in a "common effort to bring a common meaning to birth" but, "they failed."[80] At the very least, Lucy might finally say, the play's director had made her feel a part of things, that she had awakened in her a sense of her own "unacted part" in the play. As creator, artist, and a kind of magician, LaTrobe brings to the stage a "re-created world."[81] She plays the part of master storyteller, the pageant being her attempt to communicate with the villagers the meaning of their common history as English citizens. More than that, the pageant attempts to explain their place in the world as human beings in the face of an impending war. What is the purpose not only of life itself, but of literature and the arts? Can music, even unintelligible music, save us? Can literature help mankind to survive?

Connections of Language: "We Are the Words"

Darwin's notion of affinity becomes key in understanding why this story is arranged in episodes and not in chapters. The fragmented structure, which initially seems to work against this trope, coheres through the repetition of images which mirrors the way we must discover connections in our own lives. An overall pattern emerges from the disjointed pieces of the pageant, audience comments, sounds of the gramophone, and the various panoramas that Nature provides during the intervals. Events seem to exist primarily in the realm of the liminal: the word *unfinished* comes to mind. The narrative is built of circles and semi-circles that enclose and exclude various scenes and characters, circles that intersect and overlap. These circles build in density until the end of the pageant when the audience leaves. The last and most significant circle encloses Isa and Giles in the world-within-a-world of their bedroom.

Embedded within the story is the notion that the words we say to each other have the power to either create or destroy potential relationships. As a writer who pushed the boundaries and limits of fiction, Woolf crafts every piece of dialogue in her stories as unique to each character through imagery, but also through what I refer to as *voicing*, a device that allows her to tease out the tension inherent in language. In this novel, she makes a similar move, but here, the episodic form heightens the effect of misunderstanding and miscommunication. Sometimes the words miss their mark. Sometimes there is nothing left to say—sometimes the words one needs to express a certain feeling are particularly hard to come by. Lucy articulates her dissatisfaction with having no words to express her most intimate feelings, while for Giles, words seem somehow menacing, forcing him to obey and acquiesce.[82] While Giles and Isa seem to struggle for the words to *voice* their feelings, Mrs. Manresa claims not to be able to communicate very well, although she is described as a "chatterbox." Words in this story can be symbolic, meaning more than themselves. Phrases such as "heart of silence" and "dispersed are we" acquire more meaning with each repetition.[83] In addition to repetition, are the numerous contrasts made all the sharper by the sparsity of the language: passion/apathy; unity/division; words/silence; harmony/cacophony. These oppositions operate within a cyclical rhythm built on tension and resolution, even though the narrative discourse, like the pageant itself, is halting and abrupt.

The ellipsis marks that pepper the text indicate not only unfinished thoughts but the possible emptiness of the words. Bits of poetry and song throughout the pageant forge unlikely links between what is happening on the stage and what is happening in the audience, both during the play and during the intervals between scenes. Like the audience, the reader is forced to decipher the meaning of these episodes and snippets and apply that meaning to their lives. Isa speaks to herself in lines of poetry and bits of song, the subjects of which are reflected in the plot intrigue with her husband and Mrs. Manresa. What could have seemed a collection of fragments is unified because of repetition. On the other hand, during the pageant when communication is most crucial, words become lost and disconnected from their meaning—the wind blows them away, the singers are not loud enough to be heard, the gramophone too quiet. Words become lost through misunderstanding, or because they do not suffice to explain a character's feelings.

Regardless of their ability or inability to express themselves, the characters remain connected through their desires, for love and intimacy, for understanding, gratitude, and even death. While repetition brings characters together on the structural level, this same repetition simultaneously calls into question the idea that despite our differences as humans, we find affinity in a mutual desire to be loved. Are we indeed, as Mrs. Manresa declares, all the same, being the same "flesh and blood under the skin?"[84] Although Woolf grounds her philosophy and her fiction in the things and realities of everyday life, the everyday struggles, triumphs and need for love and affection, the fact that she put these words in Mrs. Manresa's mouth make this conclusion tenuous at best. Woolf was certainly skeptical that it was true, especially given the context of the story: World War II, Woolf's increasing anxiety and depression, and her growing isolation. However, Manresa's style of communication is offset by the way in which the other characters interact: hers is not the last word. Woolf seems to contemplate the idea that perhaps we are the same under the skin; if only we could believe that, we would not experience such strife in our lives.

The Pageant: The Story of Human History

Pointz Hall, the setting for the pageant, provides a physical frame for both the living and the dead (ghosts and memories), while the landscape of nature furnishes the proscenium of LaTrobe's stage. Each age of British history is represented by a short scene which includes snatches of poetry, music, and drama. This pageant, which occupies the center of the narrative, contains at least four "plays-within-plays," one of which contains yet another play. The play-within-a-play for the Elizabethan section concerns the concealment of a child in the bushes; the subject of this scene makes little sense, either to the audience or to Isa in particular, who struggles to follow the thoughts. "Did the plot matter?" she wonders.[85] The only reason to have a plot, she decides, is to convey emotions. The next mini-play occurs in the 18th century scene, a domestic drama of romantic intrigue entitled "Where There's a Will, There's a Way." Readers can easily see the relevance of this comedy of manners to the story of romantic intrigue involving Isa, Giles and Manresa. In general, this series of plays within the larger story serve as an ironic commentary on the main plot, further challenging us to consider the notion of progress towards a better world through social affinity.

The themes in the pageant ripple through the plot of the novel like stones tossed in a pond. The pageant seems to function in a similar way to the play-within-a-play in *Hamlet*, echoing themes and/or actions in the primary storyline. The mini-plays do not consist of what we might consider high drama or even particularly good drama—there are no murders, serious political intrigue, or treasonous ideas. In particular, the 18th century comedy of manners provides a commentary on the domestic drama unfolding *between the acts* of the pageant, just as the pageant consists of a commentary on English society in the present day. Each of the plays, nested one inside the other, relate to the action of the primary story. Woolf also manipulates the idea of *play*, adding a further dimension to the notion of the web of affinities: LaTrobe, considering the impact of the pageant before it began, wonders what the audience will make of it: "for another play always lay behind the play she had just written," and confesses that even she does not entirely understand the play.[86] Since her theater was constructed in what she calls Nature's "cathedral," however, she hopes that her audience will be able to see her larger point regarding the relationship between the past and the *present moment*.[87] Why is this kind of intellectual *play* important in terms of the adaptation of fiction for our species? Why do humans need to *play* with language, making our very minds into a *play*ground for ideas? The ability to *play* with the various options for action when we encounter a problem, for instance, is directly related to our need for affinity in the struggle for survival.

Isa's quotations of poetry and music, scattered through the intervals of the pageant, communicate much the same message regarding how to make life meaningful. She contemplates suicide at one point, wishing that her pain would end. In this way, she voices Woolf's own feelings about her sanity, questioning her ability, even her will, to continue to live. As the rain begins to fall, she exclaims "O that our human pain could here have ending!" adding a few sentences later, "O that my life could here have ending."[88] Lines from the pageant, coupled with such thoughts, interact to create almost a third text—the reader is in some ways "writing" this story as she reads, making meaning from the fragile connections Woolf has given birth to. As the author, Woolf plays with the roles of LaTrobe, Isa, and Lucy, their voices intermingling in a plea to finally understand the puzzle of human existence. Are we really meant to be alone? Can we survive alone? These were the riddles Woolf had been pondering throughout her life.

When she came to the end, she still did not have the answers, although she may have searched right up until the day she died. Her frustration is reflected in the puzzled audience at the end of the play who want to know the final message of what they have seen in the pageant. It seems that, in the end, all that are left are bits and pieces.[89] In the village reverend's mouth, questions about meaning sound ironic. Could it be true that we are all just part of one big unified family? He disavows the prescriptive words of the pageant. "I am not here to explain," he says. "I speak only as one of the audience, one of ourselves." If we are truly fragmented as the mirrors show us, "surely, we should unite?"[90] Because his conclusion is framed as an inquiry and not a statement, these last words sound like a plea. As we've seen, the context suggests that Woolf sensed a deep and growing divide in the world, one for which she had no answer. I would argue that although she wanted peace and unity, she doubted it could be true. She may be saying that the final answer lies in the fact that life continues from day to day

("The curtain rises. They speak"). As Isa and the rest of the family consider the meaning of the pageant, she thinks to herself "Surely it was time someone invented a new plot" for a new day.[91]

The Love Connection: Romance and Family

From the main plot of the novel to the brief, one-sentence exclamations of the audience, themes of love and kinship emerge as a central concern. The story of Isa and her family reveal the importance of connecting through family and ancient bloodlines. The Oliver family seem almost tribal in their loyalty to their ancestral home, especially Bart and Lucy. For this reason, Isa almost comes across as an outsider, although she is married to Giles who will inherit Pointz Hall. She even admits that she was not particularly interested in having a child to continue the family line. Isa is unhappy partly because she and her husband seem to have lost their initial spark. She seeks romance in Rupert Haines, the "gentleman farmer," although he never speaks and makes only two brief appearances.[92] Giles shows disinterest in both his wife and his son, more interested in pursuing Mrs. Manresa, who is the target of his illicit sexual desire. She competes with Isa for Giles' attention, yet she leaves the estate grounds after the pageant to return to her own "camp," having felt a bit triumphant that Giles, her "sulky hero," was her protégé for the afternoon.[93] LaTrobe, the writer, seeks kinship with the community through her art, but ends the day alone in a pub, drinking ale and thinking of her next endeavor. Finally, there is the kinship between Bart and Lucy, the brother and sister whose home provides the setting for the pageant: Bart is Giles' father, a crotchety old man who appears to be content with his life to a great degree, but in his dreams, returns to his glory days in India. No one is left in his life who understands him. Lucy, his sister and Giles' aunt, is described as a rather silly old woman who also lives in the past, but not in her own past—not her own, but the past of the ancient world, the caveman and the mammoth. Pointz Hall affords its inhabitants and guests with the roots that connect them to both the land and the community.

Intertwined in the production of the village pageant are the stories of the main characters, those who speak *between the acts*: Isa and Giles Oliver, Bart Oliver, Lucy/Cindy, Mr. and Mrs. Haines, Mrs. Manresa, William Dodge, and Miss LaTrobe. Despite their conflicts, each of them is bound up with the others, but not in obvious ways. One of the oddest kinships forms between William Dodge and Lucy. Dodge had arrived with

Mrs. Manresa, the two of them having stopped when they saw that there was to be a village play. During one of the intervals in the pageant, Lucy takes Dodge on a walking tour of the old house which is on the National Historic Register, right up the stairs and into the very room in which she had been born. Although during this tour she forgets his name, in him she finds a kindred spirit and he in her.[94] As their eyes meet in the mirror in her childhood bedroom, they smile at each other. In that moment, William responds to Lucy's vulnerability and childlike faith, feeling confident enough to reveal his identity to her without fear of judgment.[95] Although their relationship exemplifies an unlikely partnership, it becomes evident as they interact that they are, indeed, authentically kin. Neither one of them quite fit into their communities. Dodge's sexual identity places him in a category apart, and Lucy has already become a ghost, an impression made all the stronger by Woolf's description. She seems mostly made of air, her thoughts wandering from topic to topic somewhat aimlessly.

Between the Acts explores on various levels many of the links and kinks of human interaction: from the love between mother and child, brother and sister, to the love between husbands, wives, and lovers, both heterosexual and homosexual. Woolf sets in motion situations designed to emphasize the ubiquity of love, to question its stability, but also its ability to bring meaning to our lives. While Isa, Giles, and Mrs. Manresa form the primary triangle, others exist in parallel configurations: (1) Isa—Haines—Giles; (2) Giles—Manresa—Dodge; (3) Dodge—Giles—Isa. These various love interests compete with, but also complement, each other. Isa is attracted to Rupert Haines which Giles suspects, but cannot figure out who she is looking for on the day of the pageant. While Giles is angry and almost petulant, Rupert is described as somewhat mysterious and romantic. The triangles comprised of (1) Giles, Manresa, and Dodge, and (2) Dodge, Giles, and Isa are complicated by the fact that Dodge is homosexual. Giles refers to him as a "half-breed," and even Dodge thinks of himself as a "half-man" when he and Lucy are on their house tour.[96] He feels inadequate, and yet he, and not Giles, establishes a friendship with both Lucy and Isa. Giles, who would seem to be at the top of the heap of masculinity, cannot come to terms with his own identity and throughout most of the novel seems lost. Although Dodge is initially attracted to Isa at the tea party in the Barn, as soon as Giles appears, he forgets all about Isa.[97] Further, Dodge is attracted to both Isa and Mrs. Manresa because both women seem nurturing. Mrs. Manresa as the "wild child" will not judge Dodge,[98] while Isa finds in him a kindred spirit, one who appreciates poetry and art.

The romance at the center of it all involves Isa and Giles who, in the opening scene, find themselves in a mid-life crisis of sorts. She remembers having met him on a fishing trip in Scotland where their lines had become entangled.[99] He had, and still has, a roving eye, as does she, although his affairs perhaps are more public. She harbors a secret desire for Rupert Haines, of which Giles is mildly aware.[100] He flaunts his lust for Manresa primarily in order to annoy Isa, and is described as almost a petulant child; however, these flirtations and small affairs lead nowhere, at least not permanently. At the end of the day, the two engage in a quarrel, a scene which Woolf tells us is as old as time and humanity itself.[101] This kind of love, although it seems cold in comparison with the kind of feelings that Manresa engenders in Giles, outlasts the hot passion of the fleeting affair. Out of this kind of tumultuous but lasting partnership, children are born, the race is perpetuated, and the drama continues. It is ironic that sexually, Giles find Manresa more fit, more to his liking. And yet he stays with Isa, who is less sexually robust but is the mother of his child. This pattern is in keeping with what we know of Paleolithic man and the first families. As Schlain has pointed out, the male generally stayed with the female who bore his child.[102]

This kinship of families, especially between mother and child makes for an unbreakable bond between humans, and yet as a mother, Isa behaves in a distant, almost cold manner. She and her son, George, do not seem to interact much at all—he is more of a bother to her than anything else. She does not seem happy to see him at the tea during the pageant's intermission, but she is also puzzled that Giles acts uninterested in his son. Isa does not seem to understand her son, although she quietly defends him against Bart's criticism that he is a "cry baby"; however, she also "loathed the domestic, the possessive; the maternal," phrases that imply that she feels torn with respect to the role of motherhood.[103] Thus her maternal feelings towards her child appear tenuous. Dodge notes that when she sees George approach, she changes from one role to another, just like changing her dress, calling attention to the unnatural relationship between them.[104] Certainly Giles has little to do with his son; he is more interested in a flirtation with Mrs. Manresa. For his part, Giles does not interact with George at all. During the intermission of the play, he hardly notices him and prefers to follow Mrs. Manresa, trying to make an impression on her. Kinship between mother and child is not strictly limited to Isa and her son, George. Miss LaTrobe is portrayed as a mother figure, and the audience members as her children. She teaches them but also chastises them, as many of them mention in their chatter in between the scenes; they whisper after the scene with the mirrors of how she wanted to expose them for what they were.[105]

LaTrobe, as playwright and author, is necessarily also the Mother as Teacher: she desires a connection with her audience and wants them to reflect on the pageant they have witnessed so as to internalize the lessons it presents from history.[106]

The Biology of Affinity: Mirror Neurons

The mirror is perhaps the most compelling image of connection in the novel. Its reflexive properties afford Woolf the opportunity to explore, on literal and figurative levels, the utility of meta-cognition, the ability to *see twice*. The primary function of a mirror, of course, is to reflect what we set in front of it, whether it be ourselves or something else; when it is ourselves, we tend, naturally, to think that the reflection shows us a reality, a solid identity, our *Self*. Further, a mirror reflects with no judgments; we provide those ourselves. What we see in the mirror encourages pure, one-to-one identification—I am who I see that I am—which gives us the illusion that *I* am a whole, although flawed, human being. From neurobiologists, we have learned of brain cells known as *mirror neurons*, mechanisms that apparently facilitate relationships with others. For many years, it has been thought that the mirror neurons in those with autism do not fire properly, thus disrupting their ability to successfully connect with other people. Ben Thomas, in *Scientific American*, reports that "mirror neurons might be involved in feelings of empathy, while others think these cells may play central roles in human abilities like speech."[107] Throughout the story, mirrors operate as tropes of self-identity, but also as a way to identify with the Other.

More specifically concerning the role of mirror neurons in stories, Gottschall points out that they "fire when we're at the movies or reading books or whenever we witness a story character emoting." In fact, those who read fiction tend to have higher levels of empathy and better social skills than those who don't "due in part to the "strengthening of the mirror neuron response."[108] The *mirror* in *Between the Acts* suggests this kind of power—when the mirrors are broken, as they are when the actors hold them up to the audience, affinity is lost and any sort of meaning with it. But the other important aspect of this concept is that understanding and communication is tied to biology—it is a mechanism within our brains that enables us to foster empathy. Although Greg Hickok and other neurobiologists may argue the fine points of what these neurons actually do to aid in understanding (imitation, etc.), I will leave it to scientists to tackle the scientific facts regarding their function.[109] The fact that such mechanisms have discovered them fuels the evidence that we are biologically built for communication, identification with others, and for affinity.

From the outset, mirrors operate as the primary trope for psychological reflection. The morning after the opening scene of the novel, Isa sits before the three-fold mirror in her bedroom considering herself from three different perspectives.[110] As she looks into the glass, she sees reflected in her eyes her attraction for the "gentleman farmer," Haines. As she notices the washstand and her dressing table, she remembers her husband, her "other love." The story of a conventional relationship, characterized by the phrase "the father of my children" is, to her way of thinking, a "fiction," but, ironically, her fantasy about Haines is not. The "inner" and "outer" loves thus compete for her attention.[111] The third fold of this self-reflecting mirror shows her to herself as a mother, represented by the sight of her son in the garden.[112] She seems to wonder which of these selves is her real Self. More to the point for us is how these selves are connected. Woolf teases her readers with the image that, as Isa remarks, books represent the "mirrors of the soul," both the bored soul and the sublime. But what good did books do? What did they reflect back to her or what answers could they give? Isa wonders "What remedy was there for her at her age ... in books?" More than books, her dreams and daydreams act as mirrors because they reflect her deepest, hidden desires.[113] The split between the real self and the dream self can be quite revealing, as it is for Bart Oliver, who dreams of being once more a young man in India, while in the present, he snoozes in his armchair, an old man whose life is nearing its end.

The mirror works as a connective trope as well. Recall that moment when Lucy takes Dodge on a tour of the house. When they smile at their reflections in the mirror, they recognize each other's souls and form a deep kinship. The mirror reveals them—their inner selves—to each other, creating an unusual bond between two people who are, on the surface, dissimilar. Perhaps the most telling example, however, occurs at the end of the pageant when the actors hold up pieces of mirror to the baffled audience, enacting a strong trope of reflection, mutuality, and mirroring. As the actors emerge from behind the stage with shards of mirrors, Woolf represents the surprise of the audience at being caught off guard as a question: "What's the notion?" To be shown themselves as they were before they were given a chance to ready themselves is "unfair" because of the way it distorts reality. "What an awful show-up!" they exclaim, as all of nature and landscape cooperate in the joke.[114] When the fragmented faces and bodies of the audience members are reflected back to them, the division between Man and Beast dissolves. After the audience sees themselves as fragments, this trope of disunity is reinforced when the actors say their lines in a series of fragments. Only Manresa remains unaffected by the flashing shards and takes it as an opportunity to preen. The majority of audience members seem confused by what they see as an "intrusion" into their private faces. They are surprised by the sudden appearance of the mirrors: "What is the meaning of this?" they ask each other: what does she want us to do? Who does she want us to be? As LaTrobe closes the play with her explanation, delivered through a megaphone which expands her voice, the meaning of the mirrors becomes clearer, at least her own intention of its meaning: "we are all the same."[115]

When the actors hold up these mirrors, the reader becomes, by implication, part of that audience and yet also exists apart from it. We are able to see ourselves along with the audience, and yet we are on stage with the actors. In a more direct way than in any of her previous stories, Woolf asks "who are you? Who am I? And how do we connect?" As she grew older, she experienced premonitions of her death and thus had contemplated for years in what way her life was linked to those around her. With the exception of a few close friends, family and her marriage, a sense of having found complete satisfaction in relationships may have eluded her, and yet, here we are, still reading her novels and talking about how we connect with them. The stories that she wrote have found a way into the mainstream of culture on both sides of the pond and around the world. The pageant goes on.

Conclusion

The survival of human beings in a world of misunderstandings, *misleadings*, and worst of all, war, occupies the very heart of this novel. It seems fitting that *Between the Acts* marks the end of her writing career as well as her life. She began in *The Voyage Out* to examine the place of human beings in the world, of our role in creating/destroying civilization, of our purpose in life. With that first novel, she started her search for answers. While she may have discovered some of those answers, she was not afraid to keep asking. *Between the Acts* poses the question of human survival in terms of not only the war that was brewing in Europe, more and more often intruding onto the English coast, but also in terms of friendships, romantic relationships, marriage, and offspring. This novel asks us to consider not only who will survive, but also who will survive in a particular kind of world. The knowledge that the characters have of each other is partial, as it is of necessity for all of us.

In this microcosm, this slice of village life to which Woolf had grown so accustomed in the last years of her life, each of the main characters feels alienated in some ways and puzzled by their lack of fellow feeling. Throughout the novel, they complain of being either too close to each other, or not close enough.[116] Isa feels "prisoned" within her body, but jostled and upset by the closeness of other people's bodies.[117] With this closeness, she does not feel more intimate with others or gain more knowledge of human nature, however—people will remain mostly a mystery that only one day may become clear.[118] Her desire to *know* the Other is echoed when Lucy says, "We haven't the words," that what really mattered was "Behind the eyes," and not "on the lips."[119] The possibility of fully knowing one's fellowman was on Woolf's mind when she was writing this novel, as it had been in her other stories. With *Between the Acts*, Woolf posits yet another iteration of a theory about life: that if we are to survive, live to fight another day, we must come to terms with this conundrum. Knowledge of others, taking the step outside of our own minds—is a hurdle that must be crossed, at great risk and expense, but well worth it.

Between the Acts is Woolf's final word on the powerful potential of Story to connect humans threatened by disconnection from each other, their shared past, present and future. In this interconnected patchwork of history, literature, music, and theater, she tells one last time the story of the search for life's meaning within a group of people very much like herself. LaTrobe, who represents Woolf, re-creates human history in a play and engages the villagers to re-enact it. Through the pageant, she seems to be saying that if only we could understand our context—where we came from, what we have made of ourselves—we would be able to survive this war and have a future. In 1941, the British coast and further inland were being shelled frequently; the war was growing closer, as was Woolf's sense of impending doom. And yet the novel ends on an optimistic note. The play ends, and yet, it does not, even though the hope that is expressed may be muted: life will repeat, over and over again, in a one scene after another. Although we continue, we may not improve, but we can have faith that the curtain will continue to rise. Many of the evolutionary themes of previous stories come through here—love, loss, survival—as well as the question we have grown accustomed to hearing in her fiction: what does it mean to be human?

This novel resounds with familiarity for readers down through the years since its publication. We can relate to it on many levels: as women, as men, as lovers, as children, as grandparents and the aging, as those who have been marginalized and as those who have always known home as the center of life. Especially now, with wars burning around the globe, Woolf's fears of chaos and of her disillusionment with life ring true for us. Throughout the story, Woolf asks "who are you? Who am I? And how do we connect?" in a more direct way than in any of her previous stories. From *Jacob's Room* to *Between the Acts* is a long journey: Jacob is the missing hero, and in LaTrobe's pageant, we are the heroes of our own lives. In between these two novels, we meet Clarissa Dalloway, who takes a journey through one day of her life, reconnecting and rediscovering her reason to live, while Lily, in *To the Lighthouse*, starts at home, goes away for ten years, and returns home, reenacting the age old cycle of the hero. Her boon is what she learned about her life in the intervening years, brought to bear on the circumstances after Mrs. Ramsey's death. It is Lily's insight that we are left with, in the form of a painting, words having been too painful. After writing *To the Lighthouse*, Woolf would indulge in writing a fantasy history in *Orlando*, followed by her most ambitious novel of all, *The Waves*, a meditation on life that could be likened to a three-part invention in words. As we will see in the next chapter, stories not only have the power to comfort us in times of grief and build bonds of affinity, but stories also have the power to strengthen our brains through cognitive play in order to create a better world.

Chapter Four

The Power of Story to Create: *Orlando* and *The Waves*

"The time has come," the Walrus said,
"To talk of many things:
Of shoes—and ships—and sealing wax—
Of cabbages—and kings—
And why the sea is boiling hot—
And whether pigs have wings."—Lewis Carroll, *Alice in Wonderland*

What a phantasmagoria the mind is and meeting-place of *dissemblables*.
—Woolf, *Orlando*

"There is a sense of the break of day.... Yes, this is the eternal renewal, the incessant rise and fall and fall and rise again."—Woolf, *The Waves*

Not only do stories comfort us in our grief and create connections between us through similar experiences, but they have proven to be powerful avenues for cognitive development. Among its many creative functions, stories engage our minds in *cognitive play*: they teach us to solve problems, plan for the future, and imagine a better world. Of the many evolutionary advantages we gain through the kind of cognitive play and cognitive mapping afforded us by stories—duly noted by interdisciplinary scholars such as Gopnik and Dissanyake—cognitive play might be one of the more basic tools in brain development.[1] In *Homoaestheticus*, Dissanyake argues that the arts not only enhance and engender creativity, but also introduces innovation, transformation, curiosity, and foresight into the mix of tools we need to live.[2] It seems that everyone in recent days has been talking about the benefits to the brain that only stories can offer. This surge in interest regarding the power of stories and storytelling has begun to circulate in popular culture, taking the art of stories and applying it to everyday life. Recently, Brené Brown has claimed that stories, through the challenge they present to our brains, have the power to transform the way we think.[3] This change in thinking instigates a paradigm shift—our patterns of thought change, and with them, the trajectory of our lives including, I would argue, the lives of those around us. Courage and creativity beget more of the same. Because stories tap into our brain's capacity for flexibility and innovation, they play an important role in human survival.

In addition to challenging, pleasing, and uplifting us, stories also helps us become better thinkers. Boyd has argued that as a human behavior, Art (a category in which he places fiction) provides the vehicle for playful engagement, training and strengthening the brain and thus the mind, just as physical exercise trains our bodies to be strong and our muscles flexible: "the high concentration of pattern that art delivers repeatedly engages and activates human perceptual, cognitive, and expressive systems, especially in terms of sight, hearing, movement and social cognition."[4] In other words, Art gives our brains a rigorous workout. Furthermore, Boyd argues that because art involves us in social interactions, it "becomes a social and individual system for engendering creativity" which enables us to think beyond our present circumstances.[5] Sealing his argument for cognitive benefits, Boyd reminds us that cognitive play in the Arts amounts to a "zero-sum game"—there are no losers, only winners. Our species, through Story, has discovered a virtual Fountain of Youth.

Cognitive scientists have discovered that a key aspect of successful brain development is the ability to recognize patterns which, in turn, enable us to first organize and then more fully understand the world around us. We know that art, in general, is made possible by a structural design of repeated patterns, but what might not be as widely known is that pattern recognition shapes our ability to make crucial predictions regarding unknown situations. Stories especially excel in this regard because pattern recognition lives at the heart of stories: without the predictability provided by plot, that tension and resolution we crave, there would be no story, just a series of loosely related episodes. As E. M Forster once said, "The king died" implies a series of episodes, but not until we add conflict does a plot, that sense of tension and resolution, enter in: "The king died and then the queen died of grief."[6] This simple statement of Story's formula belies the power of plot development that keeps us reading. Once pattern is coupled with experimentation in fiction, creating a greater opportunity for cognitive play, the positive effects on the brain multiply.

Stories provide the kinds of knowledge about the world that we need to survive, far beyond facts and figures, delivering a powerful one-two punch to our brains: art can, in this way, engage our brains in more than "routine processing of the environment," giving us "a supernormal stimulus, ... a rush of the kinds of patterned information our minds particularly crave." Boyd further argues that this function of art can "fine-tune our minds for rapid response in the information modes that matter most to us." If art *trains us* to be adaptive to different environments and social circumstances, our chances for survival become greater. The benefits are legion: as Boyd explains, through stories we "effortlessly and playfully" learn to "explore possibility as well as actuality," an ability that he claims "makes all the difference."[7] Thus, life becomes somewhat easier for us to navigate because of Story.

Hand in hand with cognitive play is a story's power to facilitate Theory of Mind, a concept which refers to an ability that enables us to "construct and navigate our social environment."[8] This ability is an integral part of who we are as human beings. In fact, our knack for mind-mapping has become vital to our success as a species. In her book, *Why We Read Fiction*, Zunshine theorizes that we are drawn to fiction, at least in part because "works of fiction provide grist for the mills of our mind-mapping adaptations that have evolved to deal with real people."[9] Reading *fiction*, she says, gives us permission to "try on" different selves and practice pretend scenarios, so vital in the *real* world. All of the advantages for the reader also adhere for the writer, perhaps even more because the writer is the creator of these fictional scenarios. Although Zunshine focuses on the reasons we read fiction, the practice of writing fiction has at least an equally significant influence on the author's Theory of Mind, either in helping to create it, or to express it to readers. The benefits of this cognitive play to both writer and reader come into clear focus as we turn our attention to *Orlando* and *The Waves*.

In 1927, Woolf hints that she wanted to compose a new kind of story, a fantasy entitled *The Jessamy Brides*.[10] This brief glint in her eye marks the birth of *Orlando*. She would proceed to write one of the most playful historio-biographies we know of. In this new project she played out her wildest romantic dreams in an irreverent romp through 350 years of British history and culture. This story of a man who falls asleep one day only to awaken as a woman enables readers to explore the evolutionary benefits of cognitive play through both content and structure. Woolf theorized that the strongest mind was unified and creatively powered by expansive and innovative thinking, which could be achieved by bringing together the perspectives of females and males. In her other novels, she displays her keen wit and sense of humor, but in *Orlando*, one of the most elaborate experiments in modern British fiction, she pulls out every stop, striking out in a new direction with her fiction and displaying the nimbleness of her brain. The characters in *Orlando* and in *The Waves* become adept at exploring possibilities and adapting to new circumstances, a theme paralleled by the inventive structure of each novel. In the first part of the chapter, I will explain how *Orlando* challenges our notions of identity, sexuality, and love; in part two, I will explore how the unique structure of *The Waves* engages our minds in cognitive play by pulling us into a deeply rhythmic meditation on the lives of six characters. These two novels invite us to consider the evolutionary advantages of stories to stimulate the kind of creative thinking shown to be a key to human survival. Specifically, I will argue that these stories engage in a kind of cognitive play, and thus challenge us to imagine and enact a better world.

Orlando (1928): Plot and Introduction

Orlando spans roughly 350 years. Beginning in the age of Elizabeth, the plot sweeps through the Renaissance in an ironic description of the Restoration, the Enlightenment, the Romantic period and the Victorian era, finally coming to rest on October 11, 1928. Orlando, a 16-year-old boy when the novel opens, fancies himself a hero, a sort of Adonis or Ares, as we first see him in his father's attic swinging his sword at the head of Moor. Adding to this initial heroic imagery, the narrator builds a portrait of a young adventurer, reporting on Orlando's every move as he makes his way through an often hostile and uncomprehending world. With each new age comes change, some of which is unsettling to Orlando. To find solace for his hurt feelings he escapes into his writing, turning most often to a poem called "The Oak Tree" which he keeps with him always. He wakes one morning midway through his life to find that he has been transformed: he is now a woman, a discovery accompanied by the proclamation "Truth! Truth! Truth!"[11] She does not seem otherwise surprised by this change. After a series of adventures in which she escapes the "gipsies" [sic] to return to her home in England, she marries a sea-captain. When the novel closes, we have arrived at 1928, what the narrator refers to as Present Day.

Although much of her world has changed along with her gender, Orlando has remained much the same, her personhood intact. Even as she recognizes that the longer she is in a female body and becomes more enculturated into the expectations of women during that time in history,[12] what remains crucial to her identity is the way she thinks about life. I would maintain that her *humanness*, not her maleness or femaleness, is at the center of the novel. Orlando is *more human* than most, in fact, because she has experienced the world as both a man and a woman, thus increasing her fitness and chances of survival. *Orlando* is immensely entertaining; it is a fountain of joy from which the reader may drink again and again. It is a story oozing with a sense of abandonment, its *"Joie de vivre!"* ringing out loudly and clearly. More important than its pure entertainment value, however, is that this novel pushes readers to see themselves and the world from a new perspective. Orlando's adventures and misadventures serve as a means to an end: to defy a stifled way of thinking in order to imagine new possibilities for what it means to be human. But I am getting ahead of myself.

From the evolutionary point of view, one of the reasons humans tell stories is to construct social bonds that foster a sense of community and mutual understanding. Any salesman knows that if she wants to score a sale, she will tell her customer a story to ease into his heart. Any father who has a recalcitrant child knows that if he wants that child to go to sleep, he must first tell her a fairy story. For most of us, the familiarity of a story's structure soothes us and awakens in us a sense of fellow-feeling. We might say that Story seduces us and pulls us into the lap of humanity. Because fiction is such a familiar form, we are able to recognize ourselves in the stories we read. We smile to ourselves and wink at our friends and say, "yes, that's me in that novel," or "I can totally see you as such-and-such character." Even though *Orlando* takes us out of familiar territory into uncharted lands, however we ultimately recognize that it is human to love, to have adventures, to live on the edge and to do heroic things in the name of love. As its plot soothes our need for tension and release, its fantastical elements engage our brains in important cognitive exercise. The playfulness of *Orlando* engages readers at the level of a game which upsets, and resets, our preconceived notions of sex and identity. Woolf is telling a Truth, but *telling it slant*, as Emily Dickinson would have said. This sideways-truth-telling gives to stories an unparalleled power to change the way we see the world.

With *Orlando*, Woolf invents yet a playful narrative in which she seeks to grasp the meaning of human life. It is a novel that defies easy classification: *Orlando* simultaneously acts as a satire of society and culture, a romantic fantasy, a fairytale and a biography. Jane de Gay, like other Woolf scholars, emphasizes the story's historical aspects, arguing that the novel is a rewriting of history from the feminist point of view.[13] While I agree that historical context is important, there is more at stake here: this story of the fluctuating perceptions of reality overturns our timeworn ways of knowing and experiencing the world. It is a story that reveals how the passing of time alters not only our sense of self but also our understanding of other people. Further, this novel not only bends the boundaries of time, but also of gender. *Orlando* rollicks through hundreds of years of history and culture, relating events through the eyes of an androgynous hero. In a consistently mischievous tone, the narrator tells a story which tackles issues pertinent to human identity and human experience. When Woolf wrote *Orlando*, she was taking a mental break from the more serious-minded project of writing *To the Lighthouse* (a fact she alludes to in her diary), but even though the tone is light, she addresses serious issues, made even more serious through its contrast with the playful nature of the story: the nature of sexuality, love, and human identity. What is life in the context of the seemingly eternal span of history? How do stories enable us to better understand ourselves and our surroundings and help us navigate the world more effectively? To put it briefly: How does narrative innovation in stories help us adapt?

Background and Structure

With *Orlando*, Woolf plays fast and loose with the genre of fiction. Like Clarissa Dalloway, she goes off on a "lark" and takes a "plunge" into new fictional territory. We learn something of her frame of mind and her overall plan by looking into her diary, the playground for her new ideas. She began writing *Orlando* in 1927 and published it in 1928, only a year after *To the Lighthouse* appeared in print. In October of that year, she explains that she was writing the novel "half in a mock style" but that she wanted to keep a careful balance between "truth & fantasy."[14] This book was to be "an escapade ... the spirit to be satiric, the structure wild."[15] By early March of 1928, she had finished it, of which she says she had written more quickly than any other to date, that "it is all a joke ... a writers [sic] holiday."[16] Clearly, she was writing this novel as a way to have some fun. In doing so, she exercised her brain, and ours, in some very interesting ways. Like the main character, Orlando, who is the master of disguise and subterfuge, the structure disguises itself as many other things in a profusion of styles, bending the boundaries of genre. It proclaims itself to be a 19th-century-style biography, the narrator playing the part of an apologetic biographer who does not possess the necessary facts to write a reliable account of events. The effect is both comedic and quaint. In place of the style she had taken such pains to develop in *Mrs. Dalloway,* in *Orlando,* she writes a rather straightforward, albeit satiric, narrative line through the voice of a limited omniscient narrator. Woolf steps back from the line of experimental novels that precede this one, at least in style and structure. The theme, characters, and plot are perhaps her most experimental, but the structure and form seem to return to an earlier style such as she used in her first novel, *The Voyage Out.*

To make matters even more interesting, this 19th-century-styled story recounts the life of a 350-year-old gender-bending protagonist, a man who finds his true form at last in the shape of a woman who then dresses as a man and roams the city by night. It is evident from the outset that this story is a satire which integrates many genres of literature. In addition to biography and satire, *Orlando* involves readers in an extended romantic fantasy, particularly noticeable in the first half of the story when he encounters a character named Sasha, a Russian princess whom he first mistakes for a man dressed as a woman. At this point, London has been transformed into an icy fairyland, complete with nightly revelries and carnivals. Orlando and Sasha seem made for each other: they have an intense but short-lived affair in this romantic setting. This section of the plot provides an example of the way Woolf creatively manipulates events in an historical timeline, crossing the boundary from novel to fairytale.[17] In this great expanse of narrative, Woolf satirizes both the society and literature of England: women, men upper and lower classes, educated and uneducated—from peasants to poets and even Queen Elizabeth herself. The various levels of society of which Orlando partakes become the prime targets of this light-hearted satire, including all of the characters h/she encounters. Woolf takes a bite out of Society and its expectations concerning its female citizens and their power, or the lack thereof.[18] Even Orlando's choice of a husband is part of this satiric look at sexual identity and gender roles, as each see themselves in the eyes of the other.

Orlando is unique in Woolf's body of work in that it freely mixes fiction with other genres. The genre of biography acts as the perfect metafiction for this tale because a *biographer* would naturally have more latitude than a more ordinary narrator to diverge from the main topic into loosely related philosophical subjects. This would be in keeping with the times: the question of time and change relative to the human mind is one that not only Woolf was concerned with. Her predecessors and contemporaries, such as Nietzsche, Spengler, Pater, Hulme, all philosophers with whom Woolf was familiar, had grappled with similar ideas. As these subjects are part of her satire, *Orlando* becomes a culmination of theories from all of her previous novels, as well as philosophies regarding cultural difference, sex, identity, and the nature of human love.

Why Orlando?

To what end does Woolf tell this particular story, so different in style and subject from what she had previously written? What may have been at stake for her? Most importantly, how does *Orlando* exemplify the evolutionary benefits of cognitive play? With this novel, Woolf takes a rare perspective on some of her most treasured ideas, providing a richly textured and emotionally saturated plot through which she can experiment with narrative form to her heart's content. She reaped the benefits of that cognitive play in more ways than one, and, I would argue, so did her readers. The most ingenuous aspect of the novel is her fictional account of androgyny. From the first page, readers are introduced to a strange new world in which nothing, including gender, is as it seems, and if it is, it doesn't stay that way for long. In this way, Orlando resembles Alice, falling headlong into a topsy-turvy Wonderland where down is up and left is right. In the first chapter the boy, Orlando, is playing the role of warrior; by the time he is in his thirties, he will have transformed into a woman.

If, as I have been arguing, one of the benefits of fiction to both writer and reader is cognitive play and the working out of a Theory of Mind, then *Orlando* gives us fertile ground for this analysis, especially if we take into account a text with which it is intimately connected, A *Room of One's Own*, *Orlando*'s true sister-text. Appearing on the heels of *Orlando*—Woolf was, in fact, composing these two pieces almost simultaneously—it proves useful to view A *Room as One's Own* as a complementary text, each text informing the other. *Room* investigates the main ideas in *Orlando* further, specifically with regard to a woman's position in the world, not just as a writer—although this is Woolf's primary concern in *Room*—but as a human being in relation to other human beings. Throughout this monograph, she poses a series of ideas, scenarios, and fictions designed to ignite a spark in the minds of her audience about this category of human known as *Woman*. She satirizes at great length all of the male writers who have either NOT written about women OR written about them in ridiculous ways: the notion that women were at one time thought to have the brain of a cat is one of her most famous critiques. Her final argument consists of her contemplation of an androgynous mind which both acknowledges and then enacts its male and the female aspects. The interplay of fiction and non-fiction around this subject thus makes it tempting as well as fruitful to consider them together: as each illuminates the other, we gain clearer insight into Woolf' philosophy of fiction as well as her growning interest in cognitive play.

Much of *Orlando* concerns the act of writing, and in this respect consists of self-reflexive story about the composition of a poem entitled "The Oak Tree," begun in the 16th century by the boy, Orlando, completed in 1928 by Orlando as a woman. Orlando wanted her/his poetry to be taken seriously, reflecting Woolf's feelings as a writer, at least early on in her career. As she explains in *Room*, it is important that the female writer not allow her anger at men to overshadow her creative power. Letting go of the anger enables an "incandescent" mind to emerge.[19] In her praise of Jane Austen's work, Woolf argues that because she was not angry with men, her fiction was freer, more creative. Anger, Woolf claims, has a way of stifling creativity. Better, she says, to channel that anger into more fruitful avenues and find a way to work with men rather than against them, starting with our own minds. Men, too, can greatly benefit from embracing the female side of their brains instead of shutting it out or silencing its voice. Shakespeare provides the best example of one who had this kind of mind because he was able to generate characters and situations that seemed to rise above one gender's point of view.

In the culminating chapter of *Room*, Woolf writes of the superior type of mind which *marries* the female side of the brain with the male side. This consummation results in a more enlightened way of thinking, and for Woolf, a more imaginative perspective on the world. Instead of one side having dominance over the other, the two sides would cooperate and co-create. The notion of androgyny has a long history, first stemming from Greek mythology, and then taken up by philosophers and poets such as Plato and Sappho. Invoking this concept in *Room* encouraged female writers to invent their stories from a place of strength and peace rather than from a place of resentment. Because the androgynous mind is the more highly ingenious, it is thus the more highly evolved. In *Orlando*, Woolf puts this theory into practice, her love for Vita Sackville-West acting as the fuel for her fiery fantasy. The beauty of the androgynous mind is that it draws its creative and cognitive strength from both sexes.

We inhabit a real world with very real problems, but this imperfect domain is paralleled by the fruitful realm of our imaginations. We constantly map both, sometimes second-by-second depending on how familiar we are with our surroundings at any given moment. The *real* and the *imaginary* work in tandem to get us through the day. These cognitive maps of truth interact, contract and expand with context, and so must of necessity be elastic and pliable. Fortunately, narrative is a plastic enough framework to enable us to consider how to solve problems within spheres of new possibilities, or, in the case of a story like *Orlando*, psychological possibilities in which the story itself enacts the consummation of the female and male sides of the brain. As Marilyn Farwell has written, of all of the possible meanings of androgyny in *Room*, Woolf most likely meant an interplay or balance rather than a complete fusion in order to provide what she calls a "width of perception"[20] so necessary to good writing. In fact, Woolf's theory even includes specific ideas about the writing styles of men and women. In *Room*, the theory of androgyny includes a "woman's sentence," one that is vastly different than the default mode of male-dominated discourse and goes so far as to suggest that a woman's book "has somehow to be adapted to the body" of a woman, more "concentrated" and "shorter" than a man's.[21]

The framed story of *Room* is Mary Beton's account of her days leading up to the lecture on women and fiction, in which she tells of going to the library for research and having lunch. When she awakens on October 26, 1928, Mary/Woolf declares, after having a kind of epiphany, that no one is really interested in the future of fiction, that there is no connection between people, because they are too worried with their own lives. At an impasse with regard to the impending lecture, she happens to see, through a lucky confluence of events, a woman and a man get into the same taxi. This situation sets her to thinking about what it would be like to have a "unity of the mind," similar to what happens in *Orlando*.[22] Although each chapter in *Room* builds to a climax in which her explanation of her philosophy of the androgynous mind is fully revealed, in *Orlando*, the androgynous mind emerges in the union between Shel and Orlando, in which the philosophy comes to life. Their delight in each other's company is evident in their mutual recognition of the other's gender, "you must be a man!" and "you must be a woman!" If only, Woolf wonders in *Room*, we could think without feeling that we had to hold anything back, then we could let our thoughts flow freely. Her "plan of the soul" was that the female and male sides of the brain would have "intercourse," and in doing so, naturally cooperate with each other.[23]

For another model of this kind of mind she takes note of Samuel Coleridge for whom the androgynous mind was "resonant" and "porous," as well as "naturally creative, incandescent, and undivided."[24] Woolf traces men's anger with women to the fact that they were more "challenged by women in the present age to assert their dominance," finding in men's writing a strident freedom which is lacking in women's writing. She imagines that lying across the page of every man's writing looms the letter "I"—this superior ego, she theorizes, overshadows all else, all other voices, all other perspectives. Male-centered writing is boring, she argues, because nothing can grow from it.[25] She posits a new theory that if instead we read the work of an androgynous mind, such as Coleridge, a poet whose words "explode" in the mind, we would recognize that his ideas are fertile and lead to other ideas, connecting to other minds. *Room* concludes with an exhortation to her female audience to think not as man or as woman, but as "man-womanly" or "woman-manly." Otherwise, she warns, creativity will be squelched. "The whole of the mind," she writes, must be involved in the creative process; the writer "must let his mind celebrate its nuptials in darkness."[26] Woolf's theory of the androgynous mind found its fictional expression in *Orlando*.

Placing *A Room of One's Own* and *Orlando* side by side as sister texts reveals that this ultimate freedom to live and think and write without impediment, represents the ultimate in human development for Woolf. To get beyond the petty differences between the sexes and get at what is most elemental—this kind of thinking, Woolf believed, would result in the perfectly developed human being. The interesting thing here is that not only was Woolf bi-sexual, she was also bipolar. She was painfully aware of what it was like to be of two minds, and while she enjoyed her time with Vita, it could not have been without some pain to know that they could not be together in a real and lasting sense. Vita, by all accounts, did not have Virginia's sensitivity, and more resembles the young man Orlando, or the younger, unmarried woman Orlando in her constant series of love affairs. Woolf's realization regarding her own psyche made her sympathetic in many ways to the plight of women living in a society that paid so little mind to their creative powers, let alone their social and political influence. Once women become empowered, they might begin to change the world in their own way. The phrase "room of one's own" had metaphorical power even in Woolf's day. That metaphor has gained considerable power through the years and become applicable to us in ways that go beyond gender, to include both class and race.

Our imaginations allow us to accompany and inhabit the minds of the characters on their adventure within this fantasy. We wander with Orlando from age to age and sex to sex as she/he discovers that authentic human identity need not be limited to our sexual organs or our cultural training. This is especially true of a writer who must float free of the restraints of thinking either as a man or as a woman. This story tells of a freshly conceived approach to evolutionary adaptation. Those who embrace the androgynous mind are displaying a higher degree of fitness in order to survive in a world of creative imagination and expression. When a common word does not suffice to express a thought, we simply create a new one. If our clothes are ill-fitting, we simply change them. Likewise, Woolf might have argued, if our minds are too narrow, we must expand them and embrace more than one point of view. No doubt that when she imagined the benefits of the androgynous mind, Woolf had thought of not only Coleridge and Shelley, but also certainly of Keats' *negative capability*, a concept he defined as that moment "when man is capable of being in uncertainties. Mysteries, doubts, without any irritable reaching after fact and reason."[27] In *Orlando*, she asks us to hold within our minds two competing ideas without favoring one over the other: the woman and the man, united in body, soul and MIND.

From a Darwinian perspective, stories may well have been adaptive for this very function, to aid us in understanding the way our brains function, as well as to help us expand and build on that capacity through time. We got better at it, in other words, and as we did, we built our own feedback loop. This *expression thing* became not only addictive for humans, but also adaptive. This novel tells us how Story represents both women and men. We draw strength, and a greater creative capacity, from each other than we could ever do alone. The advantage to this particular story is that it makes clear that although fiction is not *factual*, it is *truthful*. As we've seen, more can be said coming at a truth sideways than can be said coming at a truth head on, armed with facts.

Androgyny, Identity and Orlando

The "marriage of two minds" begins almost immediately in the first pages of the novel. A young, male Orlando is described not only in heroic terms but in feminine terms: he is a beautiful boy, especially with respect to his legs, and the joy of his biographer.[28] He is the young hero, in love with life, and yearning to be a writer. Underneath the huge oak tree on his vast property he spends his days writing poetry, dazed and in love with nature. With the coming of the Great Frost, he journeys to London where he falls in love with Sasha. When he sees her for the first time, he does not know whether he is looking at a male or a female because her clothing is sexually ambiguous.[29] His curiosity gets the best of him, however, and the narrator says that regardless of sexuality, he was aroused and began to pursue her. He watches her as she skates across the ice, thinking with admiration on her physical prowess. But when he looks closer, he knows she is a woman.[30]

In the style of a Shakespearian sonnet, the narrator pays tribute to her mouth, breasts, and eyes. In the style of a metaphysical poet, the narrator says Orlando first "turned hot" and then cold, possessed of wild desires. This first love affair is already characterized by androgyny. The sexual ambiguity of Sasha, I would argue, takes the focus away from a strictly contained idea of human sexuality and broadens that idea to include variations which are more inclusive of the whole human experience. The minds of Orlando and Sasha begin to meld. Orlando thinks that they are completely like-minded, two halves of a whole. This relationship did not last, however, as Sasha slipped away in the middle of the night to return to Russia. She left in his mind a lasting impression, however; in the second half of the novel, when Orlando has become a woman, she sees Sasha again, an old woman, and remembers their lost love.

A human being, according to the narrator of *Orlando*, is a "perfect rag-bag of odds and ends," and "lightly stitched together by a single thread."[31] Our outside appearance is misleading: although we are seen as a whole to those who know us on the outside, on the inside we are various and complex beings. ToM is supported by modern psychology and neuroscience. The way we perceive ourselves and the world around us is not a continuous, unified process, but as Woolf had intuited, is pieced together from various stimuli.[32] The thing that holds us together and keeps our identity intact is memory.[33] Thus, as Orlando changes from one age to the next and one sex to the other, his/her memories and identity do not change. Time and change, two of the most challenging aspects of being human, do not change the basic nature of humans. It is only outwardly that our human identity changes. Time passes, but "the mind of man" does not move at the same pace or with the same apparent consistency.[34]

The theme and enactment of androgyny becomes even more layered and complex as Woolf plays with the idea of affinity, a web of relationships which includes the Archduchess/Archduke, Sasha (past and present) and Nick Green (past and present). Woolf's idea of gender is not a fixed category but a space of inquiry regarding the relative stability of identity. In other words, she asks, if I am a woman and someone thinks me a man because of the way I am dressed, is my human identity, the essence of my human spirit, still the same? And what about my identity through time?

Am I the same person I was yesterday, even though events may have transpired which alter my perspective? Woolf composes the perfect story to bring these questions closer to the surface of her own mind, as well as to the conscious level of her readers' minds. Although the novel seems to be all in good fun, it challenges our notions of nature and nurture at a specific point that everyone can relate to: gender, and the roles that our genders seem to necessarily force us to play.

Are those gender roles born in us as humans? *Orlando* seems to argue that they are not, that it is culture that teaches women to be *feminine* and men to be *masculine*. Although those roles may change with the times, there are roles for each gender to play. This seems to argue against my original point—that Woolf's stories are about what is *real*, not about what is *socially constructed*—that there is a basic, true meaning to being human that stories convey. In this instance, however, Woolf tells a story that is a social construct playing off of another social construct, that of gender, essentially describing the tension between internal reality and the externally, imposed system. While one may be born with female genitalia or male genitalia, the roles that come with those organs are imposed by cultural expectations and norms. Instead of gender ending up as a category of no-meaning, Woolf's notion of gender reflects the way *real human beings* experience the real world. The performance of gender on a day to day basis varies with individuals in a very real, down-to-earth manner. Survival in a world of shifting cultural norms and expectations is tricky at best and dangerous at worst. We have all seen what happens when one does not fit into the gender role that society dictates: that person may be shunned because people fear what they do not understand. By couching Orlando's tale in humorous terms, she accomplishes a goal she may not have intended: to open the borders around sexuality and gender, and to demystify and normalize homosexuality. Woolf opens up a provocative space in which readers can imagine with her a world in which gender does not impose a boundary around creative expression.

Although the unconventional novel ends in a rather conventional marriage, it is rescued from the run-of-the-mill by its being situated within a satire. The marriage of Shelmerdine and Orlando remains consistent with the concept of the consummation of two minds and the celebration of nuptials. Shel and Orlando see in each other a reflection of their own genders, which brings them even closer together in a kind of sympathetic union. As Nathaniel Brown argues, "only if the mind could see itself mirrored or reduplicated through the medium of the loved one could the circle of the self be transcended.... The closer the resemblance, the surer the connection."³⁵ One of the ways she achieves this is through the ambiguous clothing the characters wear, from Orlando to Sasha to the Archduke to Shelmerdine. Woolf holds up for inquiry the kinds of creative expressions that are representative of both men *and* women. In *Room*, she comes back to this notion in her famous discussion, mentioned earlier, of the woman's sentence. Toril Moi, Sandra Gilbert, Susan Gubar, Julia Kristeva and many others, have taken up such issues in their scholarly work: is there such a thing as a woman's sentence, a woman's language, a woman's style of expression?³⁶

I would ask, further, if there is such a phenomenon, how would it fit into this analysis of Darwinian themes in Woolf's fiction? Women and men come together, biologically speaking, to procreate, to pass along their genes to the next generation. This basic procreative act is mirrored in Woolf's concept of the "intercourse" between the male and female sides of the brain, which she discusses in *Room*. As a result of this union, memes emerge that neither could have imagined alone. When the mind is thus fertilized, fruitful communication and true ingenuity become possible.

Orlando grows into this notion, almost as if she is a child again, learning to walk: when she awakens as a woman, she realizes the impediments that she, as a man, had placed on women, and now wonders why; even further, she feels anger at men for their strict definitions of womanhood.³⁷ She also realizes at this point that because she had been a man, she knew better than anyone their "secrets" and "weaknesses," as well as her own. Knowing both and belonging to neither, she considered them both a curse and a blessing.³⁸ In this context, the themes of mutuality and kinship become especially interesting. As the child and the mother form a physical, emotional, and psychological bond, the child mirroring her facial expression and gestures as a necessary aspect of development, so the male and female sides of the brain (*Room*) made explicit in *Orlando*, mirror each other and become reciprocal, each finding satisfaction in the other. As she literally reflects on her newly acquired state of being, Orlando looks on herself as a kind of new creature, privy to both male and female states of mind and ways of being and moving in the world. Unfortunately, culture and society had not yet caught up with her/him.³⁹

All humans have a deep need to express themselves, to be understood by others and to know the "Other." Alienation from one's kin causes us to become restless and unhappy. One of the overarching question in all stories, as I have argued, may well be not just "what does it mean to be human?" but also "who are my kin?" Likewise, an urgent desire of all humans may very well be to share their story in order to find a deep and meaningful associations with other people. Kinship, sexual and personal identity: an interconnected tissue wraps itself in and around the entire story, as Orlando finds affinity with both men and women, and with both high and low society. More deeply than that, however, she discovers an affinity within herself, between the male and female side of her mind, soul, and personality. As I've said, even though the novel ends in marriage, Orlando's very unconventional mate is described in an almost feminine way. In this way, Shelmerdine is her perfect mate. In each other, they see the other's reflection, a mirror of the other's desires. Once Orlando becomes accustomed to being a woman, one phrase returns to her: "life and a lover," a phrase that becomes embedded in her mind as her final goal. Like Adam awaking in the Garden of Eden, she realizes she is alone and longs for a mate.[40] Nothing would remedy this situation but that she found one, and so she has a go at a series of lovers, but is left unsatisfied.[41] She wonders if that is all there is to life. However, after she meets Shel, her soul mate, she finds a great deal of satisfaction and turns again to writing—as a way to express of all she had learned and all she felt. Returning to "The Oak Tree," she continues a quest to find the ultimate meaning.[42] At the end of this contemplative period of writing, she asks again "What is life?" In other words, what is this thing we all have but do not understand? The biographer answers "we don't know," providing a sarcastic perspective on Orlando's protracted efforts, as if to say, just live your life![43] In the living of Life, Woolf suggests, we find its meaning.

This novel urges us to consider the ways in which we need each other in order to survive. After Orlando's return to her life at the estate, she finds that it has gone on without her—that she may as well have been dead. But she also realizes that although she could have continued to write in solitude, enjoying her own thoughts, that all of that writing would have no purpose if there were no one to read it. Her poetry needed an audience, just as she needed other human beings in order to be complete. The principle of affinity arises once more in this example—Orlando discovered, in short, that she needed other people in order to find meaning in life. The "human spirit" does not change with time; we just accumulate "more selves ... built up, one on top of another." Orlando describes her awakening in this way: "for everybody can multiply from his own experience the different terms which his different selves have made with him."[44] In the scenes that follow her pronouncement, she describes what she calls the "Captain," "Key," or true self. Near the end of the novel, Orlando searches for this self from which to analyze her long and varied life, and seems to find it in her return to her childhood home.

In addition to acknowledging the importance of this key Self, *Orlando* challenges our notion of identity. While the mutuality between the male and female sides of the mind plays a prominent role, the body in which the mind is housed does not seem important here—Orlando, whether in the form of a man or a woman—remains *Orlando* from beginning to end. In this way, Woolf's novel is one of the most interesting in terms of Darwinian perspective. Human nature, with its basic drives, needs, motivation, behavior, does not change with the sexual organs of the individual. Not only does Woolf challenge notions of Culture, but notions of Body as an expression of a quintessential human nature.

Orlando is also love letter written to Vita Sackville-West. In this fairy-tale of love, Woolf writes her heart out, and tells us in her diary that she has never enjoyed anything more. The novel surfaced from the depths of her mind, like water from an overflowing well, readers with its sheer boldness and playfulness. She creates in *Orlando* a gender-bending, intelligent, beautiful and handsome hero/heroine who simply cannot be stopped, even by Death. As Bernard will exclaim at the end of *The Waves*, "Against you I will fling myself, unvanquished and unyielding, O Death!" Orlando takes up arms against Death and refuses to die. Exactly what human impulse is Woolf writing to in this story? What deep-seated desire does she address? We all would like to live a quality life as long as possible with the people we love, yes? No one wants to die, but no one wants to live a long life all alone or in bad health. Moreover, *Orlando* narrates the androgynous mind at its fullest expression, creating a mythic correlation with Dionysius, as well as Hermaphrodite in that Orlando dies and returns to life not once but twice, the second time as a woman. Throughout the novel, she is celebrated as an androgynous god/goddess, a shape-shifter who finds the world to be a certain way and simply navigates her way through to a successful end. Not only does she renew herself after finding her true form, but she brings renewal to her home, her land, and to her lover/husband. Even the name and title of the novel are androgynous, seeming almost like a palindrome. Beginning with a "O" and ending with an "O," the title of the novel, suggests a story with no beginning and no end—the possibilities are endless. The novel closes on a triumphant note, one that is full of hope for the future.

The mind set free from society's proscribed boundaries: this was Woolf's ideal state of being. With *Orlando*, we begin to approach not only a story, but a structure and an underlying philosophy that could hold such an idea. Meaning in human life, Woolf might have said, is deeply tied to our work, our families, and our communities. *Orlando*, although told from a satirical point of view in a pseudo-biography, demonstrates some of her most deeply held beliefs about love, life, and writing. More important to my argument, however, is that she continues to play with some of the most basic mysteries known to humans about why we exist. In *The Waves*, her most difficult and emotionally draining novel to date, she will reach the peak of her experimental powers as a writer—the themes which occupy her in this novel range from the quotidian to the universal, and back again. In *Between the Acts*, she dives back into history and philosophy, but in so doing, she returns to the domestic setting of her own village of Rodmell where she will end her life. The questions she asks in all of these novels, however, come back again and again to one overarching concern: how do stories help us to imagine and then create new worlds? How can stories help us to face the challenges of the world we live in, successfully navigate those challenges, fight those battles today, and then live to fight another day?

Although *Orlando* and *The Waves* play with the genre of fiction in some very interesting ways, *The Waves* stands at the opposite end of a scale of Woolf's fictional innovations. While *Orlando* sometimes reads like an outlandish romantic fantasy, *The Waves* seems more like a meditation and variation on a theme. Where *Orlando* feels playful, even with the idea of death, *The Waves* takes a more solemn tone. While *Orlando* focuses almost entirely on the life of one character, *The Waves* focuses on six characters whose lives become intimately connected as they mature. Both novels elucidate the evolutionary argument that stories help to develope greater brain power and new ways of understanding the human condition.

The Waves (1931): Plot and Introduction

Bernard, Louis, Neville, Jinny, Susan, and Rhoda begin their childhoods at the seashore. As they pass from childhood into adolescence, they attend boarding school, after which they pursue various career and family paths— some of them marry, others do not; some find successful careers, while others are content with the domestic life. One of their mutual friends, Percival, a school friend whom they had all loved and revered as a hero, dies after being thrown from his horse. His death marks a pivotal moment for the six friends. Their reactions to his death reveal important insights into their identities. Although five of them enjoy relative success in life, Rhoda ultimately commits suicide, never having found her purpose or anyone with whom to share her life. Bernard sums up their experiences in the last chapter, ending their story on a defiant, yet hopeful, note.

The Waves is Woolf's Creation story, built on the four elements of ancient cosmology: earth, air, fire, and water, the traditional building blocks of life.[45] From the opening sentence of the first interlude, we go back in time to the first day of earth's awakening. Woolf's creation did not require a god; rather, human beings create their own world from the basic elements available to them: their homes, families, careers, losses and loves. This novel, like *Orlando*, takes us into a different sort of world than previously. After taking away the convenient notions of narrator, characters, plot, climax, and resolution, Woolf sets out to challenge our notions of what a story should do. In so doing, she asks us think otherwise about what it means to be a human being.

With *The Waves*, Woolf prepared herself to tackle the most difficult fictional experiment of her life. In so doing, she maintained her quest to elucidate in fiction what she had grown to consider in real life to be mysterious as well as contradictory. As we've seen, her stories consistently engage us in revolutionary ideas about the origins as well as the changing function of stories. Through experimentation and cognitive play, Woolf conveys more than a plot; she facilitates a change in the way we think, not just about fiction, but about life. Just as Darwin clearly believed that his findings, coupled with a new kind of psychology, would shed considerable light on man, his origins, and even his future, in writing *The Waves*, Woolf re-imagines and re-creates a world as it begins, evolves, and matures, gradually revealing the inner lives of characters who we recognize as our neighbors, relatives, friends—and ourselves. *The Waves* is the story of humans whose future is, like our own, locked up in the daily dramas of life, such as love, loss, competition, family relationships. Through daily experience, reflections on the past, and dreams of the future, the six characters re-enact the drama of the human condition. Consequently this story illustrates the idea that if we are to adapt, we must reflect on the past; to see the way forward we must look back at where we've been.

The Waves explores the advantages of being flexible in the ways that we think, the ways we must *adapt* and *become adept* at thinking creatively, all skills that Woolf herself struggled to achieve. Her vision of the relationship between humans and nature mirrors a Darwinian view. As Gillian Beer has said in her discussion of Darwin's philosophy in 19th century novels, "The living world is neither entirely open to man's observation, nor related to him," but we continue to seek a relationship to the world, to invent some meaning for our existence through our stories.[46] *The Waves* proposes a change in the human perspective of life: because Woolf slows the passing of time, we see with almost excruciating detail the way each character is shaped by experience and their reactions to this experience, bringing us closer to understanding the way humans think and interact. The six characters, caught in the push and pull of time and circumstance, try to meet life on their own terms, living out their lives in what Woolf referred to as *moments of being*.

In *The Waves*, Woolf continues to tease out the questions that began with *The Voyage Out* and ends with *Between the Acts*: Why are we alive? What is the nature of life? What is a man? What is a woman? What is our purpose in life? What does life look like when it is well-lived? How do stories help us survive in the worst times of life? Such inquiries provide readers with a path, sometimes murky and sometimes clear, to explore their own solutions to the puzzles of life. Her interest in what we could call "life writing" clearly grounds her fiction. It may seem contradictory for me to claim that in writing stories she found a way to survive in light of the fact that she took her own life; however, as I've said before, practicing the craft of fiction gave her a restorative balance, and during the times she was writing, momentarily saved her from the ravages of mental illness. Through a unique combination of structure, rhythm, and poetic language Woolf creates a story that challenges us to not only change the way we think about stories—how they should be written, how they should be read—but also, more importantly, the way in which we see ourselves as human beings.

Diary and Background

As we look into the origins of this novel, we might begin to understand how this kind of fiction helps us to create both a stronger brain and a new way of thinking about our human condition. Like her other works, this one started in her diary. Entries from this period reveal several central themes: the importance of her experiments with fiction; the impact of reading on her writing, and the way the diary provides a space for the creation of new stories. She knew as early as 1919 that daily writing leads to confidence with innovation: "never mind the messes and stumbles."[47] She found a way to put her diary, her record of the mere "loose, drifting material of life" to artistic use in her stories. The diary did not exist as merely a catch all of ideas about characters and a testing ground for writing strategies, but as treasure chest out of which she mined, over and over again, her richest ideas. She hoped she would find one day that this material had "sorted itself and refined itself and coalesced" in order to "reflect the light of our life." Remarkably, her prediction for how her diary would develop strikes readers today as both accurate and insightful. The diary allowed her to engage in complex cognitive play while also enabling her to understand the way her own brain worked. In fact, this need to understand ourselves could have been one of the primary driving forces behind storytelling in humans all along, as Boyd and others have noted.[48] It could be argued that all fiction writers, on some level, tell their stories to understand their own minds, as Boyd says, that all of art is "a playground for the mind."[49]

Without a doubt, one of the functions of fiction from the evolutionary standpoint is that it challenges our thinking, stretching our capacities to imagine new situations, those unscripted moments of real life. Woolf's stories illustrate this notion in that although she may not have known ahead of time the exact form her stories would take, she loved the challenge of experimenting with new ideas and forms. She sometimes expresses boredom with the way her own mind worked, so much so that she was constantly looking for new projects to keep herself engaged. Early in 1929, she writes about her ideas for a new novel she initially entitled *The Moths*. A full-length novel had not even occurred to her at this point, just an impression of "A mind thinking."[50] The month after deciding that she would indeed write *The Moths* (which would eventually become *The Waves*), she decides that it should reflect "great freedom from 'reality,'" a phrase that may seem to contradict the idea that stories somehow train us to live more efficiently and successfully in the real world.[51] However, by this she did not mean that she would not be concerned with "real life" in terms of actual concerns that human beings experience. Instead "freedom from reality" for her meant freedom from the mundane, characterized by the useless details that get in the way of what is most important in life such as love and relationships. She wanted to focus on meaningful moments in contrast to the moments she might have considered as merely sleepwalking through the day.[52] Her primary challenge in *The Waves* was to discover how to convey this new kind of reality in a new form, one that would not only entertain but challenge her readers to think beyond traditional narrative boundaries.

In her notes for *The Waves*, Woolf reveals that she had imagined the plot to concern "states of soul in creating."[53] She declares that this new form would be a "play-poem"—a sort of experiment with the way the mind actually operataes. Thus, this story would be told in a stream of ideas and thought, but also include descriptions of the physical, natural world.[54] In her ruminations about possible subjects for this new novel, she decides to include such vast topics as "the age of the earth" and "the death of humanity," subjects that appear in the stories as themes and concrete images within the interludes and within the characters' monologues. The word "play" in this phrase "play-poem" means two things: "play" as in drama, but also "play" as in freedom from constraint and freedom to experiment. *The Waves* is an intellectual and spiritual puzzle of sorts, including all of the conundrums about life that Woolf had been unable to solve for herself but remained keen to explore: love, both heterosexual and homosexual; patriarchal power and female passiveness/rebellion; loss and death; family relationships; and even the role that Story plays in our lives.

It is ironic that what made this kind of cognitive play possible, and vitally important for Woolf, was her own often fragile mental state. In *Touched with Fire: Manic-depressive Illness and the Artistic Temperament*, Jamison analyzes the link between manic-depression and artistic creativity in the lives of writers such as Woolf, noting that the manic-depressive brain is adaptive for creativity, but not for stable mental health.[55] However, Woolf, like other writers suffering from similar conditions, channeled her mental energies to consistently invent new ways of telling stories, thereby inventing new ways to think about what it means to be human.

If it's true that one of the many motives for storytelling is to design a map of the world outside of the mind, we have a prime example of this map-making in *The Waves*. Objective facts of the everyday veiled the true reality that was represented for Woolf by the inner landscape of the mind. If we understand ourselves better, she might have said, perhaps we could connect to others more easily and find common ground. In "The Narrow Bridge of Art," she explains that instead of merely recording facts, she wanted her fiction to give "the relation of the mind to general ideas and its [the mind's] soliloquy in solitude."[56] She desired to achieve a synthesis of some kind between "general ideas" and the individual mind, to "make concrete a mental state."[57] For this task, she chose a globe, "round, smooth, heavy."[58] The globe symbolizes Woolf's state of mind. This image also forms an interesting symbol for *The Waves*: the globe of the narrator's world encompasses life's "moments of being" in one sphere: no hard edges, no beginning, and no ending.

Although she wanted to gain a firm hold on the essence of life, her stories and diaries are replete with images of sinking, slipping and falling.[59] Woolf harbored fears of losing herself in an emptiness of non-being, but she also knew that this space was inhabited by the what she referred to as the "essential" self that she could recreate in her fiction: it was a truth about life that lay underneath this surface. This subterranean reality was not just a void, an empty place disguised by outward activity; instead, it was a space where actual life happened. If we could understand it, she might have said, we would be better able to survive the vagaries of living. In writing about the intensity of the moment, she intimates that the images that represent such moments should be the focal point in the modern novel, that nothing of this moment should be excluded except what she called "falsity."[60] Thus, she labored over each of her stories with concentrated precision in order to include the details so vital to what she believed was a more creative vision of reality. Woolf explained life first to herself and then to her readers, her stories becoming a way to *show the true light* of human life.

As Woolf developed her craft, moving her further away from traditional narrative forms, she edged closer to capturing the fleeting nature of life. She continued to seek a form into which she could pour fresh insights about human nature because she worried that existing forms did not fit what was in her mind. Her explorations into the possibilities of new fictional structures eventually unchained her mind from the fetters of what she thought of as realistic fiction, the sort she critiqued in "Mr. Bennett and Mrs. Brown."[61] These forays away from conventional structure created a space in which she could test her theories regarding not only an innovative way to write fiction, but also her own mental state. As time went on, she reached what could be seen as an inherently problematic goal, however—to write stories that reflected her own view of reality at the expense of the objective descriptions of material reality. In this new kind of story, the reader would need to do more work in order to piece together the "outside world" from spare tidbits given her by the narrator. Woolf began to realize that she wanted to tell stories that would challenge and invigorate the way her readers viewed *reality*.

In order to accomplish this goal in *The Waves*, she chose to write to a rhythm, a technique which not only provides the structural framework, but serves as a recurring motif which blurs the boundaries between character and setting. Narrative rhythm enabled Woolf to craft an overarching coherence, a sense that it is not in the details alone that a life has meaning, but that life is encompassed by interconnected moments. Images such as a globe, the sound of birds chirping, a beast stamping, and the loose thread of storytelling associated with Bernard connect the characters' journeys from childhood to adulthood. With repetition, these initial images engender a system of recursive significance. Not only does this description of repetition, pattern, and accumulated meaning refer to the sound of waves, but it also comes to suggest the beast of habit to which Louis feels chained. Although the interlocking imagery binds the characters into a tight-knit community on the one hand, this same sense of community becomes compromised by their lack of communication. As the reader discovers, they survive because they are able to adapt to circumstance. Those who do not adapt have not learned to generate new patterns of thought to help them overcome inevitable obstacles.

How does this poetic novel illustrate the way Story may have evolved to be adaptive for survival? How might a story like this create more robust brains, thereby helping us to survive in the modern world? More to the point, how does *The Waves* help us dream of a better world, based on the idea that imaginative experimentation about life is one of the ways in which fiction enables us to adapt? For Woolf, one of the roles of the storyteller is to explain and perhaps restore the sense of Self. She wanted to achieve the expression of a state of pure being through fiction. Thus, Time in her stories has a unique structure, one that is built not of *clock time* but of *self-time*. The narrative tension thus moves differently than most stories. The rhythmic prose structure of the novel represents an altered state of mind, a meditation, a sort of "OM" of the soul or, as we saw earlier, the "soliloquy in solitude." The "usual order" of life cannot achieve anything for what she had termed "states of soul in creating."[62] By enacting this philosophy of life in *The Waves*, Woolf attempts the seemingly impossible: to capture a more *real* reality, one that can rise above the stable and the temporal and to achieve a level of ethereal consciousness. Woolf's interest in *soul creation* resulted in a new way of thinking about reality. Instead of a sterile view of the world presented in a traditional narrative form, Woolf builds her plot on the principal of rhythmic ebb and flow.

Structure and Theme

The novel, comprised of nine interludes and nine chapters, is reminiscent of *To the Lighthouse* which is organized into three sections, each of which represents a different slice of time in the family's history. In *The Waves*, each section represents both a different time of day and a different phase of life for the characters. From sunrise at the beginning of the novel to sunset as the novel closes, the interludes track the passage of time in one day, while the chapters capture the passage of time in one day that also encompasses a lifetime. In the first chapter the characters come into self-conscious awareness and begin to explore the world around them, while in the last chapter Bernard reflects on all that has come before. The ending seems more like another beginning, however, more analogous to the ambiguity of life. This open-ended conclusion suspends the action, creating a tension for which there appears to be no resolution. We are left with questions that continue to haunt us past the boundaries of the text. Like *Between the Acts*, the closing sentences of *The Waves* suggests the possibility of a new beginning. Both its structure and theme push us to further inquire into how this story could be adaptive in terms of creating resilient brains, better suited for and adapted to modern life. Each character represents a specific aspect of human nature, an impression reinforced by multiple phrases and metaphors which envelop the narrative. The arrangement of the soliloquies makes it appear as if the characters speak in isolation as they try to deal with tragedy, triumph, loss, and success. Unlike the intensely personal tone of the characters, the narrator of the interludes speaks from an omniscient and detached point of view. The interludes pull us to the macro level, the broad view of life that appears to have nothing to do with the ground floor plot which involves the characters.

A strong pulse beats at the center of *The Waves*, playing on the reader's expectations of traditional narrative form and posing a challenge to the way we think of Story. This rhythm is not single but multiple. Although Woolf did not identify a musical fugue as one of her inspirations, I will use the description of this musical form to illustrate the rhythmic complexity of the story's structure. Those familiar with the compositions of Bach know that the term "fugue" designates a piece of music based on canonic imitation, as in one voice "chasing another"; the Latin *fuga* is related to both *fugere*: "to flee" and *fugare*: "to chase."[63] Bach wrote fugues for as many as six voices. In a fugue, a melody line establishes an initial *leit motiv* which is echoed in at least one other voice. These melodic voices are layered in a strict pattern which the listener hears in echoes and developments of initial themes. Sometimes we hear the primary melodic line in the upper voices, sometimes in the lower, sometimes in the middle. Harmonies become dissonances when one of the melodic lines runs counter to one or more of the other melodic voices, an interaction known as counterpoint. Such dissonances then resolve as the voices continually interact with each other in a pattern of tension and resolution, common to both music and fiction. At the closing of the fugue, the voices come together into one melodic line and the original theme is repeated one last time. The structure of a fugue exemplifies the form of *The Waves* as a story which explores how all of us are always independent, intertwined, and also interdependent. In other words, just as the voices in a fugue are in counterpoint, so, too, are the six voices in the novel.

A fugue is more than just form, however; it is also metaphor. Timothy Smith offers the following explanation for this phenomenon: "its purpose is to reveal connections between seemingly unlike things. Its method is to develop an idea in never precisely the same way. Its character is to demonstrate relationships, unveiled both in terms of new ideas born of old, but also in counterpoint with old. The fugal essence is experienced in [the] discovery [that] the new [is made of] the same stuff as the old."[64] Each voice speaks, followed by another voice that answers. Thus the literal structure is also figurative, reinforcing the kinds of relationships the characters share and adding a layer of complexity to the storyline. Similar to a musical *leit motiv*, the reader associates particular images with particular characters. Their initial observations of the world identify them through patterns of repeated images, working like motifs in a piece of music: a word or phrase associated with a particular character bring to the reader's mind that character's history—her or his desires, motives, and experiences. Each time one of those images is repeated, everything we associate with that image returns and thus its meaning deepens.

In addition to connecting the characters through images, Woolf links the interludes to the monologues through imagery as well: for instance, as the monologues open, the characters seem to *chirp* in echo of the birds' "blank melody" at the close of the first interlude.[65] These birds return in each interlude as an analogue to the characters' experiences. As Woolf teases out the separate voices in the monologues, rhythm envelops their words in a hushed, background murmur, the sound of the waves in the interludes. The lighthearted tone of *Orlando* has been replaced with what feels like an elegy. The story seems to move along heavily at a slow pace: Louis refers to the sound of the waves hitting the shore as the "stamping … of a great beast"; this thudding sound serves as the backdrop to their words.[66] The blending of the voices in this fugue-like structure challenges our ideas about individual identity, suggesting, as in *Orlando*, that perhaps we need each other to survive: one person going it alone may not survive.

Although *The Waves* is built on a rhythmic meditation that somehow distances us from the concerns of the everyday, this story breathes with life, evidenced by questions like this one she asked in her diary: "Now is life very solid or very shifting?"[67] Woolf's answer to this dilemma about how to think about life was to fashion new ways of asking the question.

Like most of us, she was not satisfied with easy answers. If she had been, we would not have novels like *The Waves*. Her probing inquiries into the nature of life and all of its mysteries played an important part in her decision to build this story on rhythm, an element so intertwined with our identities as humans that it is literally embodied: our individual internal clocks have been set to the beat of our hearts, so that no two of us are exactly alike. Moreover, her decision to set the novel at the seashore comes directly from her childhood: the sound of waves beating the shore was one of her earliest memories.[68] The rhythm of the sea from the opening interlude is echoed in the fugue-like monologues.[69] In this series of statements, the characters establish the pace for the rest of narrative. Rather than writing a story in a relatively straightforward style, Woolf sets the pace to a steady, pulsing rhythm which gives her both a more stringent structure and the freedom to explore the meaning of human life within an innovative narrative space.

Darwin, Ocean Waves and the Creative Energies of Life

The rhythm of ocean waves reverberates throughout the story. In reading *The Waves*, we are reminded that Darwin, in a rearrangement of the elements of the creation myth, substitutes "the ocean for the garden."[70] The image of the ocean in *The Waves* plays a somewhat different role than in her other novels. Here it seems to refer to the first stirrings of life, in keeping with evolution as the the gradual growth of life and its changes over a long period of time. Each character in *The Waves* could have walked right out of the ocean and into the first interlude with no introductions, no history and no context. They simply emerge out of the first interlude to begin observing the world, like the first humans on earth. Out of an entire ocean of humanity, Woolf narrows her focus to six lives. Ironically, humankind does not necessarily take center stage; certainly, there is a pervasive feeling in the novel that we lack control over our circumstances and so engage in an unending search to find that sense of control and order. This ocean metaphor also provides Woolf with an image whereby she can compare the surface meaning of life with that of the more complex depths.

The ocean not only represents the world as it surrounds the individual, but also the perception of reality underlying our surface experience of everyday life. Woolf recognizes that if daily life blinded us to what was really going on, this *essence* must live a rich life in our unconscious minds. This is what interested her about storytelling, pulling up those bits of hidden life like fish on a line. In her non-fiction, including the diaries, she strategized ways to recover the stream of immediate experience, seeing the unconscious as unorganized and chaotic, a typically Freudian view, and in need of a new form by which to organize it. In "Modern Fiction" she contemplates the idea that external stimuli of the world constantly rain down on the mind: we give each new sensation, as it is filtered through, a different emphasis.[71] Such impressions may initially be chaotic, she theorized, until the mind organizes them in a pattern which for most people takes the form of a story. Bernard echoes her philosophy when he recounts his bath from the nurse, Mrs. Constable. As the drops of water fall down his body, he realizes that *real life* is comprised of a series of moments, an accumulation of sensations that together make up a day, "copious, resplendent."[72]

In keeping with ocean imagery, Woolf imagines her characters as "islands in the stream," creating an analogy for human life as continuous and eternal.[73] She represents this notion of eternity with an image of waves "moving, one after another, beneath the surface, following each other, pursuing each other, perpetually."[74] These nameless "islands of light ... life itself going on" planted in the midst of this ocean, separate the purely human from cultural/social biases and influences.[75] As a result, the characters seem almost bodiless. On one level, they are pure sound and rhythm, lines of a melody in polyphonic relationship, while on another level, they each have a name, a history, family, and friends. Working through the challenges of composing a story with this new form, Woolf evokes an image or concept that pulls the narrative together in a meaningful way. In so doing, she mirrors the way that our brains ceaselessly look for patterns that enable us to make sense of the world. She was not alone in her view of human life as a stream, an ocean, or a series of waves. In 1918, for example, Oswald Spengler, envisioned the repetition of the stages of life as the "endless uniform wave-train of the generations." Even though Spengler's description in *The Decline of the West* differs from Woolf's image, the picture of a stream of humanity is similar to Woolf's concept, as is his idea of "wave-cycles." T.E. Hulme, whose philosophical views of human beings and human nature were, like others of the time, challenged after the publication of Darwin's *Descent*, turns to the wave metaphor to describe the fluctuating movements of the human mind struggling to comprehend the world. His explanation indicates how the writer might represent this movement: "It is as if the surface of our mind was a sea in a continual state of motion, that there were so many waves on it, their existence was so transient."[76] Woolf's vision of the sea as a metaphor for the movements within the mind recalls to us the elemental nature of her Creation story: humans exist in, and were made from, earth, air, fire and water.

The unique structure distills human experience to its most concentrated form, bringing together Nature and Humans into a complex, poetic dance. Nature speaks in the interludes, while Humanity responds in the monologues. Adding to the effect of this dialogue between Nature and Humanity, the interludes move to a different time, much slower than that in the human world of the monologues. When the sun rises in that first interlude, its light is cast equally on every living thing; humans have no say in the matter. Waves pound the shore in a never-ending succession because they have no choice but to do so. The world portrayed in the interludes appears to the reader as from a great distance or from a great height. From this great distance and height, the focus narrows so that we see the world as if under a microscope which shows the details of the natural world in minute accuracy. The shifting macro-micro view enables Woolf to place Nature into close proximity with characters who represent humankind. Nature from this perspective, reveals cyclic change, never-ending and unpredictable; sometimes Nature is tumultuous and cruel, but in the end is deadly. The birds seem innocuous enough at first, but then become vicious as they peck and tear at their food. The competition to survive is fierce, "red in tooth and claw."[77] The message comes across and loud and clear: if we aren't flexible and changeable, like the Nature we spring from, we will not survive.

Change is certainly inevitable, but this constant change comes with no pre-ordained purpose, no overall goal of progressive perfection. Life simply IS. Nature is the great teacher—"adapt," or, "cease to exist." Woolf's notion of "the age of the earth" implies that this dynamic between Nature and humanity is eternal. She seems to imply that if we could harness that unceasing power of creativity and renewal, that we may indeed survive the complexities and dramas of life.

Nature sets the stage for the human drama that unfolds, echoing the Creation story in Genesis. The thudding waves on the seashore carry us from the first sentence in the first interlude, when the world had not yet been made ("The sun had not yet risen.") to the last sentence ("The waves broke on the shore.").[78] Bernard, Jinny, Neville, Susan, Louis and Rhoda comprise the contrapuntal voices. We watch these characters grow from childhood to adulthood, each chapter showing a different phase in their lives. The world that they discover is a world that is new and unknown.

Like babies waking up to discover themselves and their surroundings, the six characters take detailed note of each other and the colors, sounds, tastes of the world in which they find themselves. They literally evolve in each other's presence, thus forming a microcosm of humanity. Woolf decouples the omniscient narrator from the limited 3rd person point of view, the result of which is that the characters become narrators of their own stories. Each incident in the novel is narrated by at least two of the characters, each of them seeing things differently. When we read this story, we follow external actions, but more importantly, the innermost thoughts of the characters: thought becomes action.

Seeing life as a series of moments may have been the preferable state of mind for Woolf, but for most of us and for her characters, such moments occur only rarely. The busyness of life overshadows the importance of being fully present in every moment. As she shows us in everyday life demands that we march to the beat of the machine rather than to a more natural rhythm, like the swells and currents of the sea, or even the beat of our own hearts. If we could gain a deeper sense of self in those moments of being, we might then be able to call on that internal strength when we inevitably lose our balance in the grind of daily life. This dynamic works in the interaction between plot, structure, theme, and character. Knowledge of a key Self which characters lose through daily life re-emerges through the repetition of images, such as the globe, which span the entire novel. In their monologues, they ruminate over the events and people in their lives, in an attempt to dive beneath the surface where they might achieve a fuller understanding of their lives. Woolf's narrative structure thus complements her words.

"Life Itself": Rhythm, Not Words

Rhythm becomes its own linguistic system to represent the way the human mind operates—we are fully present one minute and absent-minded the next, connected one day and lost the next. This creative flux, says Woolf, is not only the nature of human thought but the nature of human life. Rhythm provides the meaning that words alone fail to provide. In fact, throughout the narrative, words play a secondary role in the creation of meaning, not primary, a concept borne out by Woolf's writing on the subject. Words alone never sufficed for Woolf: she saw them as obstacles in the way of meaning. In "Craftsmanship," she declares that to "properly" use words, a writer would need to "invent a new language."[79] Writing to a rhythm gave her a way to separate words from a limited one-to-one correspondence with only one meaning, to hint that somehow, the entire suggested meaning lies above, between, or beneath the words. Words alone could not convey her understanding of Soul. Language operates within a natural rhythm, of course, as it communicates practical, purposeful information. Fictional language communicates a different sort of information which occupies a special category, not of fact but of Truth. Emphasizing the rhythmic quality of words makes us conscious of them on another level. In other words, Woolf's stories utilize language to point indirectly and obliquely to the *real* world. In some respects, *The Waves* does more than describe the puzzle of human life; it enacts the possibility of creative emotional experience, paving the way for meaningful relationships with our fellow human beings.

The unified vision of reality shaped by rhythm seems, on one level, to be an illusion, but on another level it creates a picture of the way in which individual identities give way to community. Each of the characters attempts to express their own impressions of reality. Rhoda alone finds herself outside of this unifying level of communication because she can neither find nor recreate her Self. She becomes lost, unable to make contact with those around her, eventually ending her life. As we know, suicide sometimes is an acknowledgment that communication has failed, despite the best efforts of family and friends to reach out in solidarity with the sufferer. While Neville does not end his own life, he fails to communicate in another way: as a poet he recognizes the relationship between words and rhythm in his life, but he does not enact that knowledge in his life.[80] Instead, he sterilizes the power of words, parsing them out into neat categories. Jinny communicates through her body, denying every reality except rhythm, while Louis resembles Rhoda in his brooding contemplations. Unlike Neville and Rhoda, Bernard invents stories out of everything he sees, and wonders at the way words seem to create stories almost on their own.

Ironically, Woolf often expressed the inadequacy of words to explain *real* life that seemed to always be hiding just out of sight. In *The Waves*, her dilemma with language surfaces through Bernard who wrestles throughout his entire life with his inability to express adequately his feelings about life; however, his deep introspection makes the necessary space in which he can make sense of things.[81] As Woolf suspected, based on her own writings, our ruminations become the vehicle by which we conceive of the very story that releases us from introspection so that we can move on to the next challenge with a renewed perspective. Introspection is only one side of the equation: we also need interaction with other people. This tension encapsulates Bernard's final dilemma. Like the other characters, he fears that his inner Self, although intact, may remain isolated and unexpressed without the give and take of relationships. This kind of isolation is tantamount to the death of the human soul. Just as a wave builds far out in the ocean, growing from a tiny ripple into a wave of giant proportions, Bernard's closing monologue builds the emotional and psychological intensity of the story as it explodes into his final declaration.

Unity: Characters and Imagery

An alternate kind of narrative unity results from Woolf's use of rhythm, the type that a traditional, sequential plot could not achieve: coherence comes not through sequence alone, but more through association. Rhythm represses difference, joining all elements into one all-encompassing pulse. In "Letter to a Young Poet," Woolf counseled him to write about life in all of its variety and diversity, to bring "Taxis" together with "daffodils" in a new and exhilarating dance. This new way of storytelling feels formless: although form creates boundaries in the sense of beginnings and endings, once the individual and general perceptions intersect, definitive boundaries between them melt away. What Woolf called the "natural rhythm of the self" organizes the world, bringing together disparate elements to create a community.[82] The rhythm of the prose tends to level out distinctive features of voicing and its modulations such as we might find in a more conventional narrative. Repetition of phrases and the cross repetition between interludes and soliloquies erase individual differences, creating the appearance of a seamless discourse within a community of characters. However, this surface appearance conflicts with the way the characters interact with each other; they do not see the world the same way. Uncertain of themselves and their surroundings, they yearn for a sense of purpose and meaning.

Each character occupies both the position of actor and position of observer, as we all do in everyday life, but we simply suppress our awareness of our dual positions in everyday conversation. Early on Bernard and Neville discuss an incident, and then argue about their perceptions of each other and of the incident.[83] In the process, their wires get crossed: they misunderstand, misread, and misjudge each other. Through such miscommunications, the general human dilemma is represented. In *The Waves*, Woolf brings to life a world in which the characters seem to have no foundation and no anchor; they must then create, with each passing moment, their perspectives and their responses to life as it happens.[84] *The Waves* allows us a space in which to consider that we may think we are grounded in a comfortable, workable philosophy, but all too often we are taken aback by the unscripted moment. This is yet another reason storytelling may be an adaptive function for humans: stories provide a creative way to help us see the pitfalls of human relations and to imagine solutions to various kinds and levels of conflict.

The Waves depicts a view of the self that is capable of rising above circumstance, revealing both the *solid* and the *shifting* aspects of human consciousness. In addition to bringing together the taxis and daffodils, Woolf tells the "Young Poet" that "[Y]our task—to find the relation between things that seem incompatible yet have a mysterious affinity."[85] The "mysterious affinity" refers to the shifting relationship between the world and the individual. With rhythm as her structural framework, Woolf expresses clearly her theory concerning the fluctuating condition of being human. With this story, she unleashes the power of a new way of seeing that could re-create the world as more empathetic, less judgmental, more creative, less deterministic. As Jinny says, "It does not matter what I say. Crowding, like a fluttering bird, one sentence crosses the empty space between us."[86] In other words, perspective is everything. Acknowledging that it "does not matter what I say," Jinny finds her sense of meaning in the regular patterns of living. In such "moments of being," meaning is elusive; it is only upon reflection that meaning begins to crystallize. Although all of the characters wish for their lives to follow a trajectory towards happiness and fulfillment, they realize as they grow older that there never existed a pre-ordained path to success; the path, as they discover, is circuitous at best. Most of the characters discover creative solutions to their unpredictable circumstances. The rhythmic style brings this all-too-familiar struggle into microscopic focus.

Additionally, feelings of isolation threaten their attempts to communicate—they speak of private impressions, unable to break out of their private worlds to connect with each other. When their desires come into conflict with problems in the world, they become alienated, both from the world and from each other. For the most part, they remain unaware that profound connections could grow out of these very struggles. Only Bernard, through his storytelling, seems to understand that a sense of unity with those around him exists as a potential solution to isolation. Each of them yearn for time to stop and contemplate the important moments of their lives, just as Woolf did, but they often feel lost and alone in such moments. Upon closing the book, certain questions continue to trouble the reader: Is progress achievable? Will we survive the bumps and obstacles to achieve a more fulfilled life? Certainly there were those of Woolf's near contemporaries who thought that true communication was impossible. In the "Conclusion" to an essay entitled "The Renaissance," Pater explains that reality is made from flickering moments, and in this way, create our personal meaning. He defined true success in life as a state in which we "burn with a gemlike flame" in isolation, taking in all of the stimuli of life, but not connecting with others because we are trapped in our own personalities.[87] We are, according to Pater, isolated for eternity. However, isolation was not Woolf's ultimate vision. The characters in *The Waves* want to be free from their prisons in order to experience a sense of community so necessary to life.

In the midst of the sadness of isolation and a lack of understanding, they experience a few moments of happiness, such as when Susan goes home during school holidays, or when Jinny dances, feeling the strength of her body. But by far, the most revealing moments come when they face tragedy or loss. In these moments, they confront a basic truth and must make a decision. Woolf challenges readers to grasp the truth that we don't learn much from stasis; only when stasis is disrupted do we successfully respond to whatever problems life throws our way. Early on in the novel, in the first chapter, Rhoda, Jinny, and Susan are at their lessons. Rhoda yearns for the freedom to find her own way, instead of being forced to sit in a classroom in which she clearly does not follow the thread of the teacher's logic. During her math lesson, she becomes disoriented and sinks down into her own world; while the other children can copy what is on the chalk board and make sense of the figures there, she loses her sense of time and meaning. By the end of the first chapter, she is drowning in the waves of her own imagination. As if predicting her fate, by the end of the novel, she has taken her own life, unable to find a way to go on after Percival died. She remains forever "outside the loop" of time and meaning.[88] However, when Bernard, the last man standing, speaks for all of the other characters, he expresses a necessary and staunch defiance in the face of impending death. As he tells relives their story again from the beginning, he reminds himself (and the readers) of the value—the very necessity—of rising up after a fall in order to triumph.[89]

While Rhoda never gains a sense of purpose, Bernard, her opposite, tells stories to make sense of the world that seems to make so little sense most of the time. Early on, Susan describes Bernard as the spinner of tales, which he fully acknowledges and even sees as a fault.[90] He is compelled to tell stories about himself and the others as a way to focus on something outside of time and the inevitable decay of death that it brings. In the last chapter, Bernard remembers his life and ruminates about death. His desire is to "pass beyond life," a phrase which appears to have two meanings: to literally die, but also to die to the details of life that keep him tethered to surface reality. As this moment ends, Bernard hears once more the sounds of the outside world—the ticking of the clock and the honking of car horns—and so he rejoins the world as an integrated, newly created self. Such episodes within the narrative capture Woolf's desire to come to terms with "mystical feelings" that she shares with all human beings to attend to the soul rather than just the appearances of things.[91] Because Bernard has all along been the scribe of the group (in this sense, he represents Woolf), it is fitting that he summarizes what life has been like for the six friends. In the face of his own death, he reaches his epiphany of what life has meant based on the many challenges he has had to overcome. His stories enabled him to successfully navigate those challenges. Although words do not suffice to express all that he feels, his complaint against the insufficiency of words perfectly frame the dilemma of being human: As he declares in the last few pages, "I need a little language such as lovers use.... I need a howl; a cry."[92] At the end of his life, Bernard, who always had a word and a phrase for everything, realizes perhaps what he had known all along—words alone had never been sufficient to communicate his emotional life.

Woolf often pondered the problem of how to manage the emotions that come with any kind of trauma. Early in 1920, she wonders "Why is life so tragic?"[93] Stories that place loss into a context enable us to creatively think our way out of emotional paralysis. After Percival's sudden death, the six friends gather to remember him. Neville is unable to get past the trauma, while Bernard contemplates "what death has done to my world."[94] After hearing of Percival's death, Rhoda wants to alleviate her grief by connecting with another human being, but finding herself alone, tosses her violets into the ocean as an offering to him. She seems to have found a way, at least temporarily, of finding a creative solution for her loss. Rhoda consistently searches for a meaning in her life, someone to whom she can give herself to: "Oh, to whom?" and wanders through life feeling isolated.[95] Each acknowledges in her or his own way that they had lost part of themselves when Percival died, and yet each remains confused as to how to move beyond that loss. Bernard's creative solution is to make that loss his story, to let it be part of what shaped his life. In this manner, his story represents the story as a whole.

Conclusion

Stories naturally open up within us a creative potential which invites us to leave our own bodies and forget, for a while, the daily business of human life, to participate with another mind in making meaning outside of our own limited experience. Further, stories wield a unique power to push us into different ways of knowing, of seeing connections where before we saw none. Our brains become sturdier as a result and we become more resilient. Again, in "Letter to a Young Poet," Woolf suggested that the writer had "to find the right relationship ... between the self that you know and the world outside...."[96] *The self that you know* seems to be a description of both the internal and the external. The *right* relationship between this sovereign self and the *world outside* could possibly be established through contemplation of the "landscape and emotions within." Once the poet, or novelist, has contemplated his or her inner thoughts, he or she must "render [them] visible" to the outside world.[97]

Paying close attention to matters of the spirit enhances our reason for living, thus adding to the likelihood of our survival. By the time the story concludes, Bernard, an elderly man sitting alone in a restaurant, contemplates the meaning of his life from beginning to end and as he does so, the language of the interludes and monologues comes into his soliloquy, pulling together all of the primary images of the novel. He describes himself as a spy, one who is driven to discover the reality that is consistently hidden from him which he perceives as a central mystery he will never fully understand.[98] These elemental images connect and simultaneously separate Bernard from the world around him. His boundaries of Self extend beyond the physical space in which he exists as he to tries to uncover that "mystical" meaning. Only Bernard is able to finally tell the story that frees him from his paralysis. In the closing chapter, he revisits his life, coming to terms with his decisions. At the end of the day, both literally and figuratively, he realizes that through it all has run a common thread of love which he has shared with his family and friends.

Woolf expresses a familiar modernist angst in her work—an expression of a loss of hope that Eliot's *The Waste Land* had so famously expressed—but her stories also often suggest that things could be otherwise, hinting at alternatives to isolation and a loss of hope. Her characters try to find meaning in the face of mortality; by integrating all of the stories into one, Bernard's closing monologue creates a unified vision of hope. Although they grieve in their own way when Percival dies, they not only struggle to come to terms with his sudden death but to find a sense of purpose in it. The novel's lack of closure is analogous to the ambiguity of living—this novel does not give way to the happy ending cliché which usually brings with it a feeling of satisfaction and fulfillment. Instead, the open-ended *denouement* suspends the action, creating an uneasy tension for which there is no resolution, only more questions that continue to haunt the reader past the boundaries of the text. The closing sentence, like that of *Between the Acts*, remains open to a new beginning. Both the form and the subject of *The Waves* help us to further explore why this kind of story could be adaptive as cognitive play.

In *The Waves*, Woolf speaks her truth through six voices; like a light filtering through a prism, each character represents a part of her Self: she is Rhoda, alone and confused, seeking a way out. She is Susan who only feels truly happy in the countryside, reflecting Woolf's love for the farm at Rodmell. She is Neville who wishes to pin language down into neat categories, and Louis, who is the eternal outsider, the one who never fits in. She is Jinny who wishes to remain sexually attractive and alluring, hating the idea of growing old and unattractive. Finally, she is Bernard, who rises at the end to face life head on: "And in me too the wave rises. It swells; it arches its back.... What enemy do we now perceive advancing against us, you whom I ride now, as we stand pawing this stretch of pavement? It is death. Death is the enemy.... Against you I will fling myself, unvanquished and unyielding, O Death!"[99] Although Bernard is "alone" in the last chapter, his community of kindred spirits surround him: they are never far from his thoughts, and I would argue, they give him the strength he needs to face his own mortality.

Immediately following this closing soliloquy, Woolf writes: "The waves broke on the shore." This ending-that-is-not-an-ending is somewhat reminiscent of Joyce's conclusion to *Ulysses* in which Molly Bloom simply repeats the word "yes," an affirmation of life, but also gestures to the story that lies beyond the boundaries of the text. Woolf's ambiguous ending signals another beginning, an acknowledgement that life will continue for yet another generation. The arc of the story reflects the consistency with her belief in the mystical and the power of Story to engender new ways of thinking about the meaning of human life: "We are the words. We are the music. We are the thing itself."[100]

Part Three: The Past, Present and Future of Story

Chapter Five

The Power of Story in Human Survival

> Life is not a series of gig lamps symmetrically arranged but a luminous halo surrounding us from the beginning of consciousness to the end. Is it not the task of the novelist to convey this varying, this unknown and uncircumscribed spirit?—"Modern Fiction" 154

> One story can change a life. One story can change the world.—Luis Ortega, Director and Founder of Storytellers for Change

> I wanted a perfect ending. Now I've learned, the hard way, that some poems don't rhyme, and some stories don't have a clear beginning, middle, and end. Life is about not knowing, having to change, taking the moment and making the best of it, without knowing what's going to happen next.—Gilda Radner, *It's Always Something*

The history of Story is itself a long and colorful tale: from humble beginnings, Story has become an important part of what it means to be human. In fact, the development of Story and the development of the emotional, physical, and psychological aspects of humans seem to be intimately intertwined. In present day, as we've seen, stories can be written with lightning speed on a mobile device and shared instantaneously over the Internet. The audience for Story has gone way beyond the campfire to catch fire across the world. What does the future hold in store for Story? Where do we go from here? What else can Story teach us? How can we use Story to reach beyond our own circles into new and more challenging territory? In previous chapters, I have argued that stories are part of our past, they inform and shape the present, and they help us face the future with more confidence and less fear. Story performs a vital function in our lives, something we can't accomplish any other way: it brings order and meaning to human experience. The organization of Story gives life a sense of direction and purpose, the sense of a beginning, middle and end. In this way, Story has made us human. The more we learn about this phenomenon, the more we add to our growing understanding of that time from long ago when we were beginning to come into our own as human animals.

The perfect happy ending is never guaranteed, although we may always hope for a positive outcome. We should all be so lucky as to "live happily ever after." The *Disneyfication* of the world has made us, if anything, less happy and more cynical, not to mention the fact that children do not learn the original fairytale or folktale, but a watered-down version meant to placate and please, not to challenge. Although it takes growing up to understand this, what is more important than a happy ending is that the story stays true to itself and its teller. If things don't turn out the way we want, does that mean that the story doesn't have a satisfactory ending? What we need from a story more than anything else is authentic human emotion. We need to be able to recognize what is truly human—whether it is heartache or joy, once we recognize it, it becomes part of who we are and we pass on these deeply human feelings to others. What we learn from stories is a bit more about this thing we call life and how best to live it. We learn from other people's mistakes, but we also learn from their triumphs. Truly, a single story can change everything. This is its power.

The human story is ubiquitous and universal in its ability to inspire, to teach, to lead, to shake us up, bring us together, and maybe even change the way we see each other. The third quotation that heads this chapter could have been written by anyone who has faced death or crisis, but it was written by Gilda Radner, famous comedian and star of *Saturday Night Live* who died in the late eighties of cervical cancer. Radner had known both joy and tragedy in her brilliant, but all too short career. In her memoir, *It's Always Something*, she tells of undying optimism in the face of her greatest fear—death. In recounting her story, perhaps she found a way to make sense of what was happening to her—stories, as we know, bring a sense of order to the unpredictability and imperfection of life. Instead of burying her head in the sand or feeling sorry for herself, she decided to share her journey. Like Woolf, Radner had a wry sense of humor about life, revealed in the characters she created for comedy skits, and like Woolf, she faced her illness with wit and bravery up until the very end. The story she left us with is deeply human and beautiful, creating a powerful testament that will never die. Maybe her story helps us make sense of a senseless death. Maybe it just makes our hearts a little bigger. How does this compare to the story of Virginia Woolf's life and work? Do we know her best through her novels, short stories, diary, essays, or letters? Do we see her most clearly in the note she left for her husband? She had written thousands and thousands of pages in her lifetime, all of them in some way a story about Story: did these stories provide a way of working out their power in her own life? Did her stories bring her comfort? Did they help her to connect with other people? Did her stories create another world in which she could dream of things as yet unknown?

I would say that the answer to these questions is a resounding *yes*.

As I have argued throughout this book, life is a puzzle that Story makes less puzzling. Stories teach empathy. Stories teach us how to connect with our fellow humans. Stories create new ideas and thereby new ways of perceiving the world. In fact, I would go so far as to say stories show us ways to build a better world. Virginia Woolf's fiction illustrates why stories play a vital role in our evolution and in the complex development of our consciousness, because (1) as an author, she stood at the crossroads between an old world and a new one; (2) as a woman writer, she helped to blaze new trails for women who needed to speak in their own voices; and (3) while her work is what critics would consider *high literature* and thus worthy of an academic analysis, the subject matter she focused on is common to the human experience. In short, the broad themes we find in Woolf's stories apply to everyone. But I have other reasons for believing this is so, reasons that have more to do with her accessibility as a writer. She left behind copious amounts of supporting material: her diary (the *story* of her everyday life), enables us to see the depths and heights of her feelings and the way she expresses those feelings within the framework of a novel. Because the diary was a constant companion to her fiction they are interdependent. She used it as a testing ground, and within its pages, she posed questions, berated herself, argued with friends and critics, grieved and celebrated. The ideas with which she grappled in those pages often provided fuel for the novels she eventually published. Finally, I chose to write about Woolf's fiction because the scope of her continuing influence is beyond measure, from the hundreds of women she influenced in her time to the countless thousands she influences today, including me.

Because of Woolf, an entire generation of women—women like Gilda Radner—found their voices and their rooms. They found the courage to speak and write, to tell their stories, some of them for the first time. Her influence stretches far and wide across continents and hemispheres to other authors and artists. Two such examples from many thousands include Rosario Castellanos and Nathalie Sarraute. Castellanos, a poet and storyteller from the Chiapas region of Mexico, cited Virginia Woolf, along with four others, as a role model because she was a woman known to live "with lucidity."[1] Castellanos was not only a literary artist in her own right, but she was a revolutionary leader in her efforts to give voice to the indigenous peoples of Chiapas. Across the globe at roughly the same time, Nathalie Sarraute, one of the world's foremost French writers, famous and influential in her own right, also discovered Woolf, finding her work to be challenging, inspiring, and life-changing. In an interview from *The Paris Review*, she said "The traditional novel, with its plot and characters, etcetera, didn't interest me.... I thought *Mrs. Dalloway* was a masterpiece.... In fact, there was a whole literature that I thought changed all that was done before."[2] Woolf's work has even inspired music. Dominick Argento set her diaries to music, in a piece entitled "From the Diary of Virginia Woolf," for which he won the Pulitzer Prize in 1975.[3] More recently, the Indigo Girls released a song entitled "Virginia Woolf." Emily Saliers has said that when she first read Woolf's diary entries it was a revelation: she felt as if she were talking on the telephone with "a long-lost friend," and that Woolf's diary spoke to her as "a letter to her soul."[4] This song may best illustrate the idea that Woolf's stories live beyond the boundaries of her life: in the last part of the song, the lyricist/narrator responds to Woolf's concerns about her critics and her place in literary history. When Saliers discovered that she and Woolf shared a love of language, she wrote a song that expands, once more, Woolf's influence. Her stories have truly passed beyond the boundaries of her own life to live in the hearts and minds of contemporary readers.

We live through our stories and as we go through life, we add the stories of others to our own. It is how we spend our time both intentionally and unintentionally: it is our habit of mind. As Dutton and others have observed, telling, reading and/or writing stories account for an inordinate amount of our time.[5] When we aren't reading a story, we are watching one on television in our dens, or at a movie theater. We listen to stories as an audio book on our iPhones, or tell them to our co-workers as we describe what happened the previous weekend over a cup of coffee. Our lives become a continuous narrative about who we are from moment to moment, complete with a cast of characters and a soundtrack unique to our personalities—protagonists and antagonists, obstacles to overcome and a quest we must complete to be happy. Woolf determined early in her life that this was one of the most important things she could do with her time. She encouraged aspiring writers to pursue their goals, even while she competed with her contemporaries, such as James Joyce and Katherine Mansfield.

Five. The Power of Story in Human Survival

If we stop and think, the relationship between life and writing stories seems obvious: they inform and shape each other. Life is distilled in Story, and those stories live on in our lives.

Virginia Woolf's novels provide an intriguing perspective regarding why we tell stories. When we read them, we experience Story as it evolved in the life of one writer over many years, a writer who struggled with mental illness, and a woman who had experienced a great deal of personal trauma and loss. Her insights into human nature, coupled with the determination to invent new narrative forms, resulted in a body of work that sheds considerable light on the hypothesis that Story may have an adaptive function for humans. We learn through reading Woolf's work that stories help us to heal because, in telling a story, we impose a structure onto the chaos of the unscripted moment when we are called on to be and do more than we thought. The greater the crisis, it seems, the more we need to understand it and place it into a larger pattern of meaning. Stories, our preferred vehicle, help us to do this. In addition, Woolf's stories reflect many of the evolutionary themes that we infer from Darwin's *Origins* as he describes those primal drives that mark us as descendants of ancient humans.

Woolf's stories tap into basic human dilemmas, thereby appealing to our shared needs as humans: to be loved; to be safe and secure; to win and to be more powerful than our fellow humans. Because she shaped her stories in innovative ways, her work stands out as an example of the creative spark that binds humans together. Woolf's fiction, particularly the six novels that I have focused on in this book, tests the limits and boundaries of the genre of narrative prose, giving a new form of expression to the same problems that our ancient ancestors dealt with, problems that living in this world presents us with every day: death, war, disappointment, love, competition, difficult parent-child relationships, just to name a few. From a Darwinian perspective, Woolf's stories appeal to us as sophisticated cognitive play: readers must work at understanding her stories. Stories generally exercise our brains in ways that other genres cannot do, but Woolf's stories engage in this kind of exercise to a greater degree than most. As evidence of this, we have examined the way she used her stories as a testing ground for new narrative theories such as her philosophy of the androgynous mind, worked out in her diary, in *Orlando*, and in *A Room of One's Own*.

In writing this book, I have learned a great deal about the origins of Story and the role that stories play in our lives. From the historian's point of view, the very earliest periods of human existence may seem hazy at best. Much of what we know about whether stories are indeed adaptive for human survival is based on speculation regarding the habits of early humans in the time before we had writing, as well as on what we have been able to piece together regarding the psychology of early humans. Although Literary Darwinism has been maligned by some as inaccurate and even misleading, this field has revolutionized the way we can understand storytelling not just as an art form, but also as fundamental to human behavior. Sometimes the conclusions I and others have drawn about the role and function of the arts in the evolution of humans have been based on analogy to the developments in other species—the decorative nests of bower birds, for instance, may tell us much about the functionality of art in finding a mate. In the final analysis, I have found Literary Darwinism an invaluable resource and tool for investigating why humans tell stories, but more importantly, how they make us human. My research makes clear the idea that if we take Darwin as our starting point, we can begin to understand how humans are like all other animals, as well as the ways the we differ—we mate; we fight; we forage for food, and we eat; we all, in some form or other, compete for various resources in order to stay alive and pass along our genes for the survival of our various species. All animals feel emotions and use their imaginations and ingenuity to solve problems, but human animals alone express their imaginations through stories and other art forms. Over hundreds of thousands of years, we have made the "behavior" of storytelling an integral part of what it means to be fully human.

It is interesting to note that many creatures seem to exhibit what looks like logical thought, such as insects like small black ants that seem to have the ability to think through a problem. In a recent film entitled "Microkosmos," the creative filmmakers used a minuscule camera to catch the behavior of some of the smallest of these insects—from tiny spiders to praying mantises. In one particularly gripping sequence of the film, a dung beetle struggles with a clod of dirt and dung, rolling it down a path with its head. At one point, this earthy clod becomes lodged on the end of a stick. For several minutes, the beetle works at trying to move the clod off of the stick. All at once, he changes tactics, using his back legs to maneuver the ball of dirt. It pops easily off the stick, and away he goes, whistling, no doubt. Apparently even a dung beetle can use its small, dung beetle brain in order to solve its pint-sized problem.[6] So much for human exceptionalism, you might say! Mr. Dung Beetle's children were probably greatly amused at this adventure. In all seriousness, though, Darwin would not dismiss human ingenuity on this basis. He might say that such incidents provide evidence to suggest an intimate connection to the earth from which we sprang.

This deep association to the earth may be the biological sorcerer's stone: once we fully understand this *secret*, the magic and power of stories become fully unleashed. While insects may not mourn the loss of one of their fellows—as Robert Frost's poem "Departmental" says, "Ants are a curious race"—further evidence emerges every day in the news and on social media that many animals have been known to mourn the loss of loved ones. We have heard stories of elephants grieving over the loss of one of their herd; we've seen baby elephants, in particular, grieve deeply over the loss of their mothers, similar to the way in which a human child would mourn the same loss. Some animals want power and dominion; others just want security. Animals feel rejection and pain, as well as joy. In the recent news is the account of a baby ape who, born into captivity in a zoo, was rejected by its mother. Eventually, it was "adopted" by another female to be nurtured. Even more compelling evidence of the depth of emotion in animals comes from a recent report of Shirley and Jenny, a pair of elephants who were reunited after 20 years—their joy was captured on video, which went viral on the social media. Something about this story captured the imagination of thousands of people. What might this tell us about the evolutionary power of Story for *human survival*?

Our longings for love did not originate in society and culture, but from our "human-ness," our biologically-based need for companionship and society. Boyd, in particular, cites these two needs as underlying reasons for the speculation that fiction is adaptive for humans. Moreover, Harold Fromm, in *The Nature of Being Human*, argues that the "new Darwinism in the humanities" can help us to counter the trend of assigning our "longings, fantasies, and productions entirely to social imprints on a blank and somehow 'free' slate instead of acknowledging their mortal and finite provenance in earth-generated flesh."[7] Stories arise out of this "earth-generated flesh." Our connection with nature and other animals is exposed through our shared struggle to survive. Moreover, the common traits that humans share with the animal kingdom place us not at the top of a hierarchy, but as players right in the middle of this drama of evolution. The biological basis of human nature grounds us in the reality of the everyday. Of course, we are very different from all other animals in numberless ways, chiefly in that our bigger brains have enabled us, over thousands of years, to invent and use new technologies; to engineer not only machines but societies, as well as to solve the ever more complex problems of math and science so necessary to our continuing existence. My emphasis in this book has been on our ability to tell stories of imaginary places, people, and times, an ability that has proven to be not only immensely entertaining and satisfying, but also useful in ways that we are just beginning to understand.

The stories that Woolf tells, which express sorrow and attempt to ameliorate grief, are of particular interest to me because the relationship between body and mind become stronger when we experience illness. We are returned to the basics of living in the here and now. As we saw in Chapter Two, Frank's description of "illness narratives" reminds us of one of the more basic functions of stories: to alleviate stress, anxiety, and grief, a point also made by Austin. Each illness story serves a set of specific purposes for their authors, as well as their readers or listeners. Telling stories about our illnesses restores balance in our lives, giving us the ability to rebound and survive our most traumatic experiences. Remember that in *Jacob's Room*, Woolf is, at least in part, coming to terms with Thoby's death from typhoid at the early age of twenty-six. Although I emphasized the power of affinity in *Mrs. Dalloway*, this novel serves another function as well: Woolf questions the value of the "talking cure" for Septimus, yet writing *Mrs. Dalloway* was her own cure. In *To the Lighthouse*, she tells the story of her mother and father, and in the telling she finds a sense of relief. As I have been arguing, the human compulsion to understand life through stories may have been crucial to our survival, thus qualifying Story as an adaptive trait. Not only does the Darwinian perspective on Woolf's fiction elucidate the ways in which Story functions in everyday life to make our lives fulfilling, but also sheds light on the ways we can change the story we tell at any time—*we have agency*.

The narrative brain is more powerful than we know, becoming even more powerful when it feeds on Story. The acts of both telling and reading stories pull synaptic energy from every part of the brain to build structures that help us make sense of the reality in which we live. In many ways this is similar to the way we create meaningful patterns from sounds and rhythm in music. Much of what I have learned during my research leads me to believe that stories do not stop at merely providing enjoyment, which they surely do (and which may also play a large role in our ability to survive—resilience in the face of trauma is a powerful tool), but they enable us to learn and apply new concepts to new circumstances within a safe environment. This is a skill that could very well have helped humans to survive from day to day as we navigated dangerous, challenging situations.

My research has also made me realize the extent to which the stories we tell shape not only who we are but how we think and relate to others.

I've learned that stories help us to develop a Theory of Mind, which entails the ability to mirror the behavior of others in our species, leading to greater socialization. Finally, as I have discussed at length, children who enjoy fairy tales or who play pretend games are learning how to navigate the real world and its very real problems, a point made so clearly by Gopnik in *The Philosophical Baby*, as well as by Gottschall in *The Storytelling Animal*. Why else are complex spiritual theologies, for instance, best captured in story form? For instance, the Bible portrays Jesus speaking in parables: why might this be? As you will recall, Turner has shown that parables combine "story with projection," creating what he calls a "classic combination ... for constructing meaning."[8] "Parable" did not arise by accident, nor was its purpose literary, but "follows inevitably from the nature of our conceptual systems." In short, it suits the way we have evolved to think. Why do scientists like Neil de Grasse Tyson turn to stories as a way to explain the complex phenomena of the universe in his popular television series? Not only does Tyson make complex ideas accessible to non-scientists, but even more importantly, he understands that if the everyday person is to grasp the concepts of cosmology, he must make use of what he knows about how the human brain works. Story enables us to make sense of our world on every level: logical, emotional, and spiritual.

How Does Story Shape Human Experience?

As a way of reminding us of where we're heading in this argument, let's remember where we've already been: we first analyzed how *Jacob's Room* focuses on the problem of how to manage trauma and grief over the loss of a loved one. In writing this novel, Woolf tackles the loss of her brother, Thoby, but also, I would argue, her own innocence. By the time she had written this novel, she had lost her mother, her step-sister, her father, and her brother. Each of these losses took their toll on her, and as we know from reading her diaries, she struggled to come to terms with these losses throughout her life. While *Mrs. Dalloway* also reflects similar themes, it further develops the Darwinian notion of the web of affinities because it interrogates the connections between human beings, exploring the notion that we all share the basic dilemmas of life: finding the right person with whom to share one's life; letting go of our children to live their own lives; marital problems, aging, misunderstandings with our friends. Death, of course, is the ever-looming reality for all of us, and in

Mrs. Dalloway, Woolf shows, through the narrative style of free indirect discourse and stream of consciousness, the fact that we share this inevitable end. In *To the Lighthouse*, which builds on many of these themes, mother-child mutuality becomes the focal point, at the center of which are the idealized mother-child portrait of Mrs. Ramsey and James. However, as I have argued, Mrs. Ramsey has taken on another child, namely Lily. The relationship between the two takes center stage almost from the beginning, as Lily tries to understand Mrs. Ramsey's influence in her life. While in some regard, Mrs. Ramsey plays the part of the quintessential "Angel in the House" (about which Woolf wrote in "Professions for Women"), Lily knows that she could learn much from Mrs. Ramsey about how to be a strong woman, if only they had the time to spend together. Mrs. Ramsey, the fictionalized Julia Stephen, is preoccupied with everyone and everything, but especially with her husband, the fictionalized Leslie Stephen. As Jane Lilienfield has suggested, Woolf's anger at not being able to spend significant time with her mother comes through loud and clear in this novel.[9] The bond that Lily finally forges with her surrogate mother (and by proxy Woolf), is a spiritual one, embodied in the painting which Lily completes at the end of the story.

Recall that with the creation of *Orlando*, Woolf continues to build on previous ideas—kinship, mutuality, sexual competition, and survival. However, the predominant theme seems to be cognitive play/mapping, the purpose of which is to explode the boundaries not only of fiction, but of our way of understanding human experience. *Orlando* reflects the evolutionary themes of sexual attraction and competition, as well as the theme of survival in a different direction for Woolf. Here she tests not only the boundaries of sexuality and love, but also the boundaries of fiction by creating a pseudo-biography which spans 350 years. She plays with time, narrative structure, and tone in this novel, once again asking "what does it all mean?" *The Waves* takes up each of these previous themes, adding to them a predominant theme of the basic struggle to survive and find meaning in life. The main plot spans the lifetimes of six characters set against a backdrop of the rhythm of the sea. By structuring the novel in this way, she communicates both the brevity of individual life and the eternal nature of the life of the human species. *Survival of the fittest* as a theme emerges in that one character survives to sum up the stories of six lives, and to rise up to future challenges. Finally, in *Between the Acts*, the most predominant evolutionary theme is affinity/kinship which surfaces through the various relationships between characters—both negative and positive—some of whom feel pulled towards each other (Dodge and Lucy), while others are repelled (Isa and Mrs. Manresa). The most significant scene in which kinship emerges as the primary evolutionary theme, however, occurs in the last scene of the pageant. As the actors hold their mirrors up to the audience, they signify not only that *the present moment* in history has come to fruition, but that regardless of the great variety and the fact that every human life is fragmented, all humans are related and connected.

While each novel explores a different facet of Woolf's personal journey, the arc of a larger story begins with *Jacob's Room*. By the time she started this novel she had matured in the kinds of risks she was willing to take in fiction, finding freedom in fresh ways of expression. What had not changed was her interest in finding answers to her countless questions, such as "How does one survive and live to tell the tale?" These stories provide various answers, but together, they tell one Story which asks one key question: What does it mean to be fully human? From *Jacob's Room* to *Between the Acts*, Woolf's characters give voice to this question. As she wrote these stories, she discovered nuggets of truth about her own life along the way. What she learned in the course of her struggles both frustrated and sustained her for many years. Through it all, the phenomenon of Story fed both her mind and her soul. Woolf wrestled with words just as the biblical character, Jacob, wrestled with his angel for a blessing—even though she wielded words as tools to craft her sense of Self, a problem which brings to light yet another facet of the adaptive function of fiction: the creation of the Self and the world in which this Self moves, breathes, and has its being. If we have no Story of Self, we have no Self.

In each of the six novels we have been concerned with here, Woolf crafted a series of characters whose quests for meaning and stability are unique in perspective, as well as in narrative technique. Read in the order of their publication (not by theme), these six novels form the arc of a unique meta-story. In my view Woolf's investigations into the nature of life, whether stated or implied, would seem to show that the stories we tell have a larger purpose than we can understand on a conscious level. We all want to be understood, loved, respected, desired; we all want to feel safe from harm; we all want to have the freedom to express ourselves in the ways that are true to who we are—all of the things, in short, that human beings have always, and will always, want. As Woolf shows in *Between the Acts*, the disparate pieces of life, whether throughout history or throughout one day, must make sense in the end. The alternative would too horrible to consider: dissolution, total destruction, or even worse, apathy. As the following discussion will explain, this meta-story reveals the multi-faceted Self of Virginia Woolf.

Meta-Story: Culmination of Woolf's Novels

Jacob's Room begins the meta-story with an ominous symbol—a sheep's skull in the hands of a young boy, Jacob. The novel ends with his death. *Jacob's Room* could be seen as the perfect modern story because it seems to sum up the bewildering emptiness of the war years in England, even as the war itself provides a shadowy background to the action of the story. This novel provides the exposition that sets the stage: the hero is a young man on a journey to discover what his life will be. He leaves his family to pursue his education at university where he discovers a love of Greek and loose women. As an educated young man of a certain class, he is expected to travel the world, and he does so—traveling to Greece where he finally falls in love, though the object of his affection is a married woman. Jacob never seems to find his path, however: he appears to be unsettled and unsure through most of the story. When he goes off to join the fighting in World War I, it happens offstage. Mrs. Flanders worries about her sons off fighting in the war. He also dies offstage. We learn of his death in the last chapter as we see his mother and Bonamy, his friend, standing in his empty room, going through his belongings. The exposition should tell the reader about the characters, the setting, the themes to be explored as the story unfolds—in other words, the exposition sets the stage for what will transpire in the plot. In many instances, the exposition forecasts the events of the plot, leaving open the possible twists and turns for the rising action, climax, and falling action. In this exposition, we have all of these elements: Jacob is a kind of Everyman who begins his journey rather ignominiously, and dies in relative obscurity. His death is as "empty" as his shoes and his room. Woolf has left the answers to her questions open with this ending, implying that the search will continue with her next novel, *Mrs. Dalloway*.

If the exposition in *Jacob's Room* leaves us on the cusp of rising action wondering what will happen next, *Mrs. Dalloway* begins the next step of the journey with a "lark" and a "plunge" into an adventure through London. In essence, Clarissa could be the next iteration of Jacob. While he had found no stable position in his life, always wandering and chasing butterflies (figuratively and otherwise), Clarissa marries, settling down early in life with Richard Dalloway, a respected member of the government. Although she had been thought of, at least by Peter Walsh, as somewhat flighty in her younger days, her decision to marry Dalloway shocked even Peter. Her marriage to Dalloway seemed to establish her in a solid, substantial life and settled her within a particular class in London society.

She seemingly had it all—a husband, a nice home, enough money and material things to meet not only her needs but her desires, a beautiful daughter. Still, she wonders what could be the meaning of it all: is it as simple as a formula—get married, have a family and live happily ever after? Apparently, all is not as it seems. The plot does not follow a formula or end with these simple life choices for Clarissa, the Everywoman in this tale. Complicating her journey along the way are her conflicting memories of Peter, Sally, and her reflections on the other possible paths she could have followed into now unknown worlds which seem forever separated from her. Further, a "twin soul," Septimus Smith, shadows her throughout. He stands as the opposite of Clarissa in nearly every way except that he, too, questions choices that have taken him to this point in time—a point that finds him losing his mind and his will to live. He struggles every day to continue to wake up and find a reason to keep going. Their lives intertwine at the end of the novel, when his doctor attends the party, bringing news of his suicide with him. While Clarissa is saddened by this news and even a little put off—his death has interrupted her party, after all—she also seems to respect his decision to end it all, to "throw it away." In the first part of the rising action, then, the search for ultimate meaning continues. Is it in marriage? Family? Sexual conquest (Peter)? Financial stability (Bradshaw and Lady Bruton)? Job security and position in society (Richard)? Or is it in religion or history (Miss Kilman)? Can meaning be found in a world in which the atrocities of war happen in the middle of cocktail parties? The action of the meta-story rises in intensity as the stakes become higher.

The action begins to rise to an even more fevered pitch with the next novel, *To the Lighthouse*. Complicating the plot of the rising action is the dilemma of one character in particular, Lily Briscoe, who tries to understand not only the meaning of her own life, especially in light of Mrs. Ramsey's death, but also to find a way forward. Unlike the first two novels, in which we learn of Jacob and Septimus's death in the last chapters, Mrs. Ramsey dies in the middle of the action, leaving Lily to grieve as she tries to find a resolution to her pain. It is interesting that Mr. Ramsey does not seem to go through the same kind of angst as Lily. Taking the children, James and Cam, to the lighthouse with supplies for the lighthouse keeper and his family, he fulfills a promise to his wife, and therefore achieves a kind of closure. Lily, meanwhile, stays on shore, putting the finishing touches to her painting of Mrs. Ramsey and James. She arrives at her own kind of lighthouse through a spiritual connection with the ghost of her dead friend. When she declares "It is finished," she means not only that her pain has resolved itself in this work of art, or that Ramsey had completed his journey to the lighthouse, or even that she had completed her painting, but that her own goal had come to conclusion. The line she places down the center of the painting brings everything into balance and completion, which is the most she, or anyone, can hope to accomplish, given that death is an inevitability. She does not care that her work may not survive; it is enough for her that she completes what she started. The meaning for Lily (and I would suspect for Woolf) is found in the act of creating.

With *Orlando*, the rising action takes a different and more complex turn. Just as in *To the Lighthouse*, Death does not mark the end in this novel, but another beginning. Orlando, the hero of the novel, is also its heroine. The consummation of the two kinds of mind, female and male, of which Woolf would write from a more philosophical point of view in *A Room of One's Own*, is fictionalized in the novel. With the ending of *To the Lighthouse*, Lily had sensed that her vision, her search for meaning, was complete. In *Orlando*, Woolf seems to be saying "Not so fast: here is another way of asking: What does life mean if death loses its power? What if death does not finish, but begin us?" In *Orlando*, Woolf engages in mythmaking, creating a new world, one with limitless possibilities, in which we can see beyond the sleep of death into something more. If Death has no ultimate hold over us, she wonders, and if our sexuality is no longer a limitation, what kinds of doors can we open into that search for what it means to be human? What if it means that creation is a more powerful force than destruction? What if the play can go on and on, ad infinitum, and that life is less personal than we fear? What if life is not about us after all? What if there is something greater than the story of one human being going on here? This forward-thinking philosophy certainly loosens the gripping fear of Death and opens up the idea that human life means what it means only in a larger, universal sense. Life has meaning only in the company and community of others. Purpose in life, in other words, cannot be found inside our own minds, limited to our own perspective. Life for humans has meaning when we can go beyond the limitations of what we see in front of us.

This aspect of storytelling—this ability to free us from the here and now—has been widely noted, most recently by Boyd.[10] Rarely have I heard it explained so well, however, as Denys Finch-Hatton in the film *Out of Africa* with his tale of Masai tribesmen. If imprisoned, he tells the Baroness, they would die, even though their imprisonment may only last a few hours or a few days because they could not see past the bars. These tribesmen, so accustomed to their complete freedom, become convinced that their imprisonment is permanent.[11] Stories give us the ability we so desperately need to *see past the bars*, the limitations of time, space, and identity. In short, *Orlando* inspires us to look past the bars. We encounter characters that seem to be one thing and turn out to be something else: Sasha, the Lady who turns out to be a Lord, and Orlando himself/herself. While Orlando had seen the estate as a kind of prison of solitude early in his life, it becomes a place of celebration as she and Shel return as husband and wife to her ancestral home. Woolf takes her characters on a journey of 350 years to a new "present day" of 1928, and no one and nothing is the same. This novel's answer to the question "what does it mean to be human?" seems to be that if you survive life's ups and downs, you can live to tell the tale, and what's more, live to celebrate the very day you are alive, reading this very book.

We come off the high of reading *Orlando* to find ourselves in *The Waves*, a dark and brooding place. I would argue, however, that this signals the climax of the plot: this is the point at which the conflicts are at their highest. *Orlando*, although it seems to end on a high note, has not completely dispelled the fears and concerns of the human story—as the narrator says, "The cold breeze of the present brushed her [Orlando's] face with its little breath of fear."[12] The triumph of both the homecoming and the completion of her journey are not without reservations. However, that fear does not prevail. As *Orlando* ends on a note of celebration, *The Waves* begins with a solemn, meditative tone, conveying the evolutionary theme of the survival of the fittest through cognitive play. Woven into this overall theme are other Darwinian themes, such as kinship, competition, mirroring, and mutuality, as well as the web of affinities. The opening monologues of the six characters introduce us to their "voices" and to the images with which they will be associated. As the climax, *The Waves* develops most intensely the human struggle to survive. The height of the tension in the meta-story comes with Bernard's declaration to survive in the face of Death, the enemy. Having lost everything else dear to him, he declares at the end that he will keep striving. His will to survive in spite of the chaos around him takes us into the denouement, *Between the Acts*.

Woolf's final novel provides the closing portion of this meta-story, an interesting commentary on all that came before. From *Jacob's Room*, she brings the sense of how the past lays on the present and shapes our view of the future; from *Mrs. Dalloway*, she pulls us into a web of relationships through which each of the characters is connected to the others; from *To the Lighthouse*, she recreates the artist as creator of meaning when

Lily remerges as LaTrobe, the playwright who attempts to bring order to chaos and meaning to the present moment; from *Orlando*, she brings the search light to bear on the inner workings of male and female minds; and from *The Waves*, the sense that the rhythm of life is our constant companion, urging us on to continue living. While the predominant themes of the previous novels also appear in between the acts, the two that are most predominant in *Between the Acts* are mirroring and mutuality. Although one critic has noted that this novel was the longest suicide note in all of British literature, I would argue the opposite. In terms of Woolf's over-arching question about the meaning of human life, I would argue that the denouement to the meta-story ends on an optimistic note. Isa says not once, but twice, that she wishes the pain to stop, but then she chooses not to end her life but to give birth to a new one. The curtain will rise again and the play—however disjointed, fragmented or chaotic—will have another, and another, and yet another act.

Between the Acts, written in a chaotic and disturbing time in Woolf's life, seems to insist that the meaning of human life is in its living, whatever shape that life may take in its time. For Isa and Giles, meaning is ultimately found in the coming back together after their arguments, disagreements and infidelities. Their strength lies in the bonds they share. The ending of *Between the Acts* is highly symbolic, and yet it remains firmly grounded in the earth, in the thousands of years of human history that had preceded this story of the "ordinary mind[s] on an ordinary day." As we stand with the narrator outside of the house and look in at the shadows that are cast on the curtains, the play begins again.

The meta-story which emerges from my reading of these six novels enables us to take a step back from the details and take in the larger sense of Woolf's quest to understand what life was all about. Human life, of course, is a kaleidoscope of diverse experiences—no two people can be said to see things the same way. The limits which our bodies place on us make it impossible to truly know what another person thinks or feels about anything. And yet, we find comfort, connection, and a sense of creative power from stories. We understand each other through this medium of stories, a medium of humanity that communicates our identity. Contrary to the postmodern view that denies the possibility of a shared, human experience, literary Darwinists insist that there IS indeed an experience that is cardinal to what is means to be human, and that stories are the powerful conveyor of that experience.

As we have seen through a wide variety of examples, the notion of a basic human nature in Story cuts a large swath through both culture and history. It must: if there were no shared perception of what it is like to be human, we would not be able to understand each other across cultures. Of course there are cultural differences, as well as dangerous disconnections and misunderstandings. To claim otherwise would be both naïve and untrue. But it is also untrue to claim that culture is all—that biology plays only a small part in the creation and proliferation of the arts, particularly Story as an art form. As Steven Pinker has pointed out, along with others, the "blank slate" notion of the brain is little more than hogwash and perhaps a bit of wishful thinking on the part of some. If our minds arose out of nothing, humans would be infinitely malleable. The basis for all political, industrial, scientific, and humanistic achievements would have all emerged from thin air, apparently. Planting the arts firmly in the ground of our biology gives us the best opportunity to see how Story is vital to understanding what it means to be human; if there *is* a chance to improve ourselves, we must understand this basic part of who we are. When all is said and done, humans share basic desires that are rooted in our common biological and evolutionary history.

I asked at the beginning of this book if you could imagine a world in which there were no stories, a world in which all language was used for one purpose only—to communicate facts and information needed to complete a task or work for a job. This kind of language, while useful for information-based situations—like how to tie your shoes, how to put together a bicycle, or how to cook a steak, is not connected to a world colored by emotions that are driven by desires which are sometimes thwarted and frustrated. For this kind of world, we needed to create another kind of language, the language of Story. Marilyn Charles has said that poetry is the vehicle we use for the "expression of primary experience" of the kind I am talking about here. I would argue that if poetry provides such a vehicle, certainly stories do as well. Charles cites the novels of Virginia Woolf as her central example because of Woolf's poetic prose style, and concludes that "Through her writing, she plumbs the depths of human experience."[13] Poetic language suits the Story of the human soul.

Although I did not set out to prove with absolute certainty that fiction is an adaptive function for survival, the evidence indicates that Story has always provided humans with evolutionary benefits, aspects of our mutual history on this planet that we are just beginning to comprehend, and that it continues to do so today. As I have indicated, at the very base of Story exists a pattern that gives meaning to events—this pattern, when repeated, replicates the rhythm of our heartbeats—tension, release; tension, release.

Over thousands of years, Story has become our default mode for explaining things we don't understand—to ourselves and others. Stories follow a predictable pattern that we find pleasing. Stories are social and interactive—they bring people of all cultures together. However, I would argue, with Carroll, that stories do more than that: they challenge us intellectually—they stimulate our more complex brain through cognitive play and cognitive mapping. While I agree that this is the case, I would disagree with Carroll in assuming that it is only classics such as Jane Austen's novels or Shakespeare's plays that can achieve this kind of stimulation. Even a child's fairytale has power: a simple fairy tale can achieve the same thing in the mind of a child as well as that of an adult. I would argue that an adult reading a child's story understands that power even more deeply. *The Hunger Games* carries all of the same weight of Myth that *The Lord of the Rings* carries; perhaps Collins' prose may not be judged as well-crafted as that of Tolkien, but the pattern of Story is similarly grounded in mythology and the elemental desires of our species. Although I have focused on the fiction of a literary artist, I would maintain that this theoretical approach can be applied to any story from any time or culture to explain how stories make us human: Boyd even applied this theory to Dr. Seuss's book *Horton Hears a Who*.[14] In addition, I would say that some readers, those unfamiliar with Woolf, or who have found her work to be obscure, may find that when viewed through an evolutionary lens, her stories take on a whole new meaning. They are, after all, relatable as stories of human beings who want to understand their lives.

Does fiction play an adaptive role in the evolution of the human species? I believe that it does. It is important that we see fiction as adaptive in human life now—to understand that stories can, and do, help human beings accomplish a variety of things that they could not otherwise do—such as imagining a future time, reflecting on past actions, or, in Woolf's case, putting into words what a moment in time looks and feels like. The meaning of a life will differ from person to person, obviously, but the ways in which we make sense of the world will always be intimately tied to Story. Perhaps humans could have gotten along just fine without stories—but they didn't. Stories filled a need for hundreds of thousands of years, and they are filling those same needs now: to help us find our way through the quagmires of modern life and to find the answers to the most basic of all questions: What does it mean to be human? Stories tell us that it means to talk and be heard. It means that although we are sometimes filled with loneliness and grief, through stories we find healing. It means that each of us crave connections with fellow humans, knowing that only together will we survive. And it means that we can become strong and creative thinkers who will ultimately make the world a better place to live. Instead of dismissing art and fiction as by-products of an over-active imagination, why not become part of the "once upon a time" of the oldest of stories?

Why not believe in the power of stories to change the world?

Epilogue

The Story of Our Future

Life is, soberly and accurately, the oddest affair.—Diary III, September 30, 1926

Laura reads the moment as it passes. Here it is, she thinks; there it goes. The page is about to turn.—CUNNINGHAM, *The Hours*

When we reflect on this struggle [to survive], we must console ourselves with the full belief, that the war of nature is not incessant, that no fear is felt, that death is generally prompt, and that the vigorous, the healthy, and the happy survive and multiply.—DARWIN, *Origin*, 66

Stories live on: Virginia Woolf's stories did not die with her, but have continued to influence and shape the thoughts, ideas, and stories of the generations that have followed, stories that have faithfully captured life in all of its oddity, peculiarity, and mystery. One of the many thousands of writers whose work was shaped by Woolf's fiction is Michael Cunningham, author of *The Hours*. In writing this novel, Cunningham told not only his own story of the quest for meaning, but also what we *could* call the most recent installment in Woolf's meta-story. If we see the denouement of *Between the Acts* as a cliff-hanger, this last installment picks up where that novel left off. In *The Hours*, we encounter characters like those in Woolf's novels, women whose daily lives seem to hide the *real life* that is going on underneath the surface. Cunningham captures each of them in their "moments of being" as they grapple with problems all too familiar to the human condition. In these moments, their lives are illuminated, their humanity shining forth.

With the raising of the figurative curtain of time and space, readers are introduced in *The Hours* to three women from three different time periods: one of them is Virginia Woolf herself, writing *Mrs. Dalloway*; the second is Clarissa Vaughan, a bi-sexual who is caring for her homosexual artist friend; and the third is Laura Brown, the disillusioned wife of a World War II veteran, pregnant and coming to terms with the life she has chosen. These women are modern iterations of every Woolf character who has engaged in the search for the answer to these two big questions: "What does it mean to be human?" and "What is the meaning of life?" The novel's structure maintains the spirit of Woolf's experimental fiction as well—the three women "cross paths" through their common dilemmas across time and space, through reading *Mrs. Dalloway* and through their similar dreams. Cunningham places Clarissa Vaughan in the position of the modern Clarissa, based on Woolf's novel. The cognitive play in which Cunningham engages our imaginations further connects his work to Woolf's. His novel not only appeals to readers as cleverly conceived, but also teaches us something about the state of modern grief, the power of stories to intimately connect us, and to create in us the desire for new possibilities and new lives. As Cunningham's Clarissa is buying flowers for Richard's party, we learn that "she loves the world.... [she wonders] Why else do we struggle to go on living, no matter how compromised, no matter how harmed."[1] Although Cunningham had originally thought of ending his novel with Woolf's suicide, he decided against it, noting that "the novel knew about her death in order to return her to life."[2] Instead of ending with a death, *The Hours* ends on a note of hope, continuing past the last page, faithful to the spirit of the original. Significantly, all of Woolf's novels open outward as they conclude, implying that the story does not stop but regenerates itself with each fresh reading.

 The intersecting stories of three women living in different cities and at different time periods and the significant people in their lives—husbands, lovers, and children—form an intricate pattern of connections within and between separate stories. As we read this novel, we hear the yearning of the characters trying to understand what it all means. The uncertainty of life's ultimate meaning comes at us in various forms. All three women express the desire to understand that their lives as they know them and live them *are enough*—that the present moment is *enough* to keep each of them living through all of the remaining hours of their lives, even though each lives at a different time in history and in vastly dissimilar circumstances. In this novel, we sense some of the basic evolutionary themes we noted in Virginia Woolf's stories: sexual drive and competition, kinship, mutuality between mother and child, the struggle to survive, and the adaptive function of cognitive play, the themes that seem common to most stories. Time in *The Hours* is layered, true to Woolf's own experiments in narrative time and plot structure. The first layer is comprised of Virginia Woolf as she is writing *Mrs. Dalloway*, beginning on a day in June 1923. The second layer emerges in the story of Laura Brown, a mother and wife in Wisconsin, who has begun to read the novel; her story also begins on a day in June 1949. The third layer concerns the story of Clarissa Vaughan and her lover, Sally, on a day in June "at the end of the twentieth century."[3] As a character in Cunningham's story, Virginia becomes part of the fiction, which is only fitting. Portraying Woolf as a character in her own story poses ates an interesting dilemma and dimension: this story, framed by Woolf's actual life, establishes yet another layer of meaning through the link between each of the women: as Virginia is beginning to write *Mrs. Dalloway*, Laura is reading it, and Clarissa is "living" it as the modern day incarnation of Clarissa Dalloway. In yet another twist, Laura is the mother of Clarissa Vaughan's gay friend, Richard who jumps from the window of his five-story apartment building, having decided that he, like Septimus Smith, has suffered long enough. Like Septimus, Richard had begun to hallucinate and hear voices speaking in Greek.

The quantum entanglements between *Mrs. Dalloway* and *The Hours* do not end there. In Clarissa Vaughan's tale, we meet Sally, her lesbian lover and partner, and Julia, her stubborn teenage daughter who is enamored of Mary Krall, a lesbian activist, who parallels Doris Kilman in *Mrs. Dalloway*. In addition to Richard, who I spoke of earlier, we meet Louis, a former lover of both Richard and Clarissa, who parallels Peter Walsh in Woolf's novel. The plots of the two novels also run parallel: in Woolf's novel, Clarissa prepares for a party: within Cunningham's novel in Virginia's narrative, she prepares to serve tea to her sister; in Laura's story, she bakes a cake for her husband's birthday party, while Clarissa Vaughan goes out to buy flowers for a party for Richard who will be receiving an award for his poetry. The women share an illicit kiss in each of their stories: Virginia shares a kiss with Vanessa; Laura with Kitty, her friend from down the street; and Clarissa's thinks of kissing Richard and Louis. Further, the *hours* of the title refer not only to the original title of *Mrs. Dalloway*, but to the hours of the characters' lives and to the choices that they make to continue living from one hour to the next. Laura Brown is Richard's mother, but we only learn this at the end of the novel after Richard has stepped out of his window, falling to his death—at that moment, the three narratives intersect and the story comes full circle. Virginia, having written about Clarissa Dalloway, who hears of the suicide of Septimus Smith only after he jumped out of his window, is connected to Laura who has read *Mrs. Dalloway* and contemplated suicide. Laura is brought together with Sally and Clarissa after Sally's son commits suicide. Added to these details is the fact that Richard refers to Clarissa Vaughan as "Mrs. D." or "Mrs. Dalloway."

At the heart of *The Hours* we find familiar themes regarding the meaning of life and human experience: kinship, sexual attraction and competition, reciprocal altruism, the web of affinities, as well as mutuality (mother-child bonding) and mirroring. Cunningham's story further demonstrates the continuing function of stories as adaptive because of their explanatory power, as well as the way in which they reflect a ToM through cognitive play. In addition, *The Hours* illustrates the concept that Story frees us from the here and now.[4] Virginia's section, layered on Laura's, which is also layered on Clarissa's, takes the reader out of ordinary time and place and into a more speculative, imaginative space. As I have tried to show, stories train us to imagine scenarios that may aid in our survival—if we can imagine such scenes and play them out in our minds, we can learn how to cope. We literally create new ways to think about the world as well as new worlds in which to think these new thoughts. Just because we are not faced with imminent death from dangerous animals while out hunting every day does not mean that we don't have other dangers to navigate in the modern world. Stories help us with this imprecise science of life's navigation. Just as Woolf tested theories of narrative, as well as theories regarding human relationships in her stories, Cunningham's interrelated stories place his characters in various situations which they must traverse in order to reach a particular goal. A happy ending is not the end game, of course. Perhaps happy endings are overrated. The power of stories in the evolution of human life is that *we create our own happy endings*.

Story as a pattern of explanation for the situations that we face in the world varies from person to person and from story to story. The primary values of stories is that they teach us to be flexible and open-minded, to not be satisfied with easy answers when life throws us a curve, but to seek alternative paths. Storytellers have a gift of immortality in that their words live on long past their lives, entertaining us, teaching us, and bringing us comfort when we most need it. In writing *The Hours*, Cunningham extends the life of Virginia Woolf through her words, ideas, and characters, as well as through her philosophies concerning homosexuality and androgyny. With Richard dead and Louis gone, four women are left at the end to grieve their loss and to make sense of what has happened. Like Woolf, they seem to believe that stories make us who we are.

Stories not only bring us together, but they help us grieve, they help us learn how to love, and they give us an identity. We will, no doubt, continue to invent stories in the years to come. It is possible to connect with others through just a look or a gesture. Imagine the power of the well-placed word. Perhaps stories can allow us to see beyond the borders of our homes, towns, and countries into the human soul. Whether we whisper them to our best friends, write them in blogposts, or film them with our iPhones, stories must continue to be an integral part of the human search for comfort, connection, and the creation of meaning.

* * *

And now we have come to the end of the story about the power of Story. One question still remains: Just what does it mean to be human? In *Jacob's Room*, it means to be born and to die. In *Mrs. Dalloway*, it means to grow old and be misunderstood. In *To the Lighthouse*, it means to outlive those you love the most. In *Orlando*, it means to want the fantasy more than the reality, and to be okay with that. In *The Waves*, it means to wake up every day and put your feet on the floor and say "I will live today despite all the odds against me!" In *Between the Acts*, it means that in spite of our best efforts, we make all kinds of mistakes—we hurt each other in innumerable ways, but at the end of the day, we are all we've got. Finally, it means that when the curtain rises tomorrow, the Story will begin again. How that Story unfolds and how it ends is up to us.

Chapter Notes

Introduction

1. Steven Pinker, *How the Mind Works* (New York: W.W. Norton, 1997), 524–525; see also David Barash, *Homo Mysterious: Evolutionary Puzzles of Human Nature* (Oxford : Oxford University Press, 2012), 141–165.

2. Stephen Jay Gould, "Evolution: The Pleasures of Pluralism," *New York Review of Books*, June 26, 1997; see also Daniel C. Dennett's discussion of skyhooks and cranes in *Darwin's Dangerous Idea* (New York: Simon & Schuster, 1995).

3. Brené Brown, "Physics of Vulnerability." http://www.dumbofeather.com/brene-brown-on-the-physics-of-vulnerability/.

4. Virginia Woolf, *The Captain's Death Bed* (New York, NY: Harcourt Brace Jovanovich, 1950), 96–97.

5. S.P. Rosenbaum, *The Bloomsbury Group* (Toronto: University of Toronto Press, 1975), 32–43.

6. Ellen Spolsky, "Why and How to Take the Fruit and Leave the Chaff, " *SubStance* 30., No. 1, 2001, 178–179.

7. Charles Darwin, *On the Origin of Species by Means of Natural Selection* (New York: Signet Classics, 2003), 451.

8. Virginia Woolf, and Jeanne Schulkind, *Moments of Being: Unpublished Autobiographical Writings* (New York: Harcourt Brace Jovanovich, 197), 95.

9. Kay Redfield Jamison, *Touched with Fire: Manic-Depressive Illness and the Artistic Temperament* (New York: The Free Press, 1993), 2–6.

10. Arthur Frank, *The Wounded Storyteller: Body, Illness, and Ethics* (Chicago: University of Chicago Press, 1995).

11. Woolf and Schulkind, *Moments of Being*, 73.

12. Ibid.

13. Ibid.

14. Diary III, November 28, 1928.

15. Woolf and Schulkind, 81.

16. Ibid., 142.

17. Mitchell Alexander Leaska, *Granite and Rainbow: The Hidden Life of Virginia Woolf* (New York: Cooper Square Press, 2000), 122.

18. Darwin, *The Origin of Species*, 191.

19. Diary II, March 1, 1921.

20. Diary II, October 14, 1922.

21. Diary III, September 30, 1926.

22. Diary V, August 6, 1937.

23. Diary V, October 19, 1937.

24. See "Art as Cognitive Play" in Boyd's *On the Origin of Stories*, 80–98.

25. Diary III, May 28, 1939.

26. Joseph Carroll, "Literature and Evolution," in *Human Nature, Fact and Fiction*, ed. Robin Headlam Wells and John Joe McFadden (London UK: Continuum, 2006), 69–70.

27. Virginia Woolf, *Granite and Rainbow: Essays* (New York: Harcourt Brace Jovanovich, 1958), 431–432.

28. Virginia Woolf, *Orlando* (New York: Harcourt Brace Jovanovich, 1956)160.

29. *Hamlet* V.ii. 219–224.

Chapter One

1. Alison Gopnik, *The Philosophical Baby: What Children's Minds Tell Us about Truth, Love and the Meaning of Life* (New York: Farrar, Straus and Giroux, 2009), 49.

2. Judith Rich Harris, *No Two Alike: Human Nature and Human Individuality* (New York: W.W. Norton, 2006), 157.

3. Jonathan Gottschall, *The Storytelling Animal: How Stories Make Us Human* (Boston: Houghton Mifflin Harcourt, 2012), 69.

4. David DiSalvo, "What is Literary Darwinism: An Interview with Joseph Carroll." https://neuronarrative.wordpress.com/2009/02/27/what-is-literary-darwinism-an-interview-with-joseph-carroll/

5. Normimitsu Onishi, "Thumbs Race as Japan's Best Sellers Go Cellular," *New York Times*, January 20, 2008.

6. Lisa Zunshine, *Why We Read Fiction: Theory of Mind and the Novel* (Columbus OH: Ohio State University Press, 2006), 6–10.

7. Simon Baron-Cohen, "The biology of the imagination: how the brain can both play with truth and survive a predator," in *Human Nature: Fact and Fiction*, ed. Robin Headlam Wells and John Joe McFadden (London: Continuum, 2006), 103.

8. I suggest reading versions of these texts that are accompanied by commentary, such as *Darwin: A Norton Critical Edition*, ed. Philip Appleman, 2001, before tackling the original texts.

9. Janet Browne, *Darwin's Origin of Species: A Biography* (New York: Grove Press, 2006), 49.

10. See the article by Ernst Mayr "Darwin's Influence on Modern Thought" in *Scientific American*, 2009.

11. Darwin, *The Origin of Species*, 61.

12. Gottschall, *The Storytelling Animal*, 121.

13. DiSalvo, "Interview with Joseph Carroll."

14. Randall Hood, *The Genetic Function and Nature of Literature* (Cal Poly, San Luis Obispo, 197), np.

15. Gillian Beer, *Darwin's Plots: Evolutionary Narrative in Darwin, George Eliot and Nineteenth-Century Fiction* (1st ed. London UK: Routledge & Kegan Paul, 1983), 4.

16. Darwin, *On The Origin of Species*, 451.

17. George Lewis Levine, *Darwin and the Novelists: Patterns of Science in Victorian Fiction* (Cambridge, Mass.: Harvard University Press, 1988), 23.

18. Brian Boyd, *On the Origin of Stories: Evolution, Cognition, and Fiction* (Cambridge, Mass: Belknap Press of Harvard University Press, 2010), np.

19. Darwin, *Descent of Man*, 95–96.

20. Boyd, *On the Origin of Stories*, 159.

21. Ibid., 162–163.

22. Ibid., 167.

23. Michael Austin, *Useful Fictions: Evolution, Anxiety, and the Origins of Literature* (Lincoln: University of Nebraska Press, 2010), 39.

24. Zunshine, *Why we Read Fiction*, 6.

25. Darwin, *On the Origin of Species*, 76–77.

26. Denis Dutton, *The Art Instinct* (New York: Bloomsbury Press, 2009), 105.

27. Jared Diamond, *The Third Chimpanzee: The Evolution and Future of the Human Animal* (New York: Harper Perennial, 2006), 32–33; 54–57.

28. Leonard Schlain, *Sex, Time and Power* (New York: Penguin, 2003), 12–21; 269–273.

29. Ibid., 201.

30. Gottschall, *The Storytelling Animal*, 7.

31. Derrida http://projectlamar.com/media/Derrida-Differance.pdf.

32. Ellen Spolsky, *The Contracts of Fiction: Cognition, Culture, Community*, (Oxford: Oxford University Press, 2015), xxix.

33. Mark Turner, *The Literary Mind: The Origins of Thought and Language* (Oxford UK: Oxford University Press, 1998), 5.

34. Joseph Carroll, *Evolution and Literary Theory* (Columbia MO: University of Missouri Press, 1995), 50–56.

35. Carroll Abstract for *Evolution and Literary Theory*, http://cogweb.ucla.edu/Abstracts/Carroll_95.html

36. Carroll, *Evolution and Literary Theory*, 104–105.

37. Austin, *Useful Fictions*, 16.

38. Robert Storey, *Mimesis and the Human Animal: On the Biogenetic Foundations of Literary Representations*, 1st ed.

(Evanston: Northwestern University Press, 1996) 115–116.

39. Carroll, *Evolution and Literary Theory*, 4–5; 50–54.

40. Ellen Spolsky, "Darwin and Derrida: Cognitive Literary Theory as a Species of Post-Structuralism" In *Introduction to Cognitive Cultural Studies*, Ed. Lisa Zunshine (Baltimore: Johns Hopkins 2010), 292.

41. Carroll, *Evolution and Literary Theory*, 1.

42. Ibid.

43. Gottschall, *The Storytelling Animal*, np.

44. Boyd, *On the Origin of Stories*, np.

Chapter Two

1. Woolf and Schulkind, *Moments of Being*, 71.

2. This scene recalls a similar passage in *The Waves*, when Rhoda is faced with crossing a small puddle (*The Waves* 64). She, too, felt paralyzed: "Identity failed me" (64).

3. Kubler-Ross, Elisabeth. *On Grief and Grieving* (New York: Scribner's, 2005), 8–24.

4. See Jamison: *Touched by Fire* and *The Unquiet Mind*.

5. See Frank, *The Wounded Storyteller*.

6. Frank, *The Wounded Storyteller*, 75–137.

7. Ibid.

8. Boyd, *On the Origins of Story*, 98–112.

9. Charles Darwin, *The Descent of Man* (Amherst, NY: Prometheus Books, 1998), 130.

10. Diary II, November 14, 1921.

11. Kate Flint, "Revising Jacob's Room: Virginia Woolf, Women, and Language," *The Review of English Studies* 42.167 (1991), 362.

12. Virginia Woolf, *Jacob's Room* (New York: Harcourt, Brace and World, 1950), 176.

13. Ibid., 14.

14. Woolf and Schulkind, 146.

15. Ibid., 140.

16. Diary III, December 18, 1928.

17. Diary II, June 23, 1922.

18. Diary II, July 26, 1922.

19. Francesca Kazan, "Description and the Pictorial in *Jacob's Room*," *ELH* 55.3 (1988), 701.

20. Woolf, *Jacob's Room*, 9.

21. Ibid., 11.

22. Ibid., 8–9.

23. Ibid., 10.

24. Ibid., 14.

25. Ibid., 7.

26. Ibid.

27. This image of the young god will reappear in *Mrs. Dalloway* (Septimus) as well as in *The Waves* (Percival), and in *Between the Acts* (Giles as the "sulky hero"), the hero motif that further connects these stories, reinforcing the theme and plot of the meta-story.

28. Woolf, *Jacob's Room*, 143.

29. Ibid., 146.

30. Ibid., 151.

31. Ibid., 160.

32. Ibid., 36.

33. Kami Hancock, "Deviant Snapshots: Revisiting *Jacob's Room*," *Virginia Woolf Miscellany*, 70 (2006), 10.

34. Lambrotheodoros Koulouris, "'Love Unconquered in Battle' and Other Lies: 'Virginia Woolf' and (Greek) 'Love,'" *Interdisciplinary Literary Studies* 8.2 (2007), 37–53.

35. Woolf, *Jacob's Room*, 173, 175.

36. Ibid., 176.

37. Ibid., 173.

38. Frank, *The Wounded Storyteller*, 115.

39. Ibid., 137.

40. Ibid., 115.

41. Ibid., 138.

42. Virginia Woolf, *To the Lighthouse* (New York: Harcourt Brace Jovanovich, 1955), 209.

43. Diary III, November, 28, 1928.

44. Diary III, January 6, 1925.

45. Diary III, May 14, 1925.

46. Diary III, June 27, 1925.

47. Diary I, May 5, 1919.

48. Woolf and Schulkind, 13.

49. Diary III, November 28, 1928.

50. Diary III, May 16, 1927.

51. Diary III, July 20, 1925.

52. Diary III, February 23, 1926.

53. Diary III, July 22, 1926.

54. Diary III, September 5, 1926.

55. Diary III, September 13, 1926.

56. Woolf, *To the Lighthouse*, 128.

57. Ibid., 63.

58. Ibid., 58–59.
59. Ibid., 79–81.
60. Ibid., 8–9.
61. Ibid., 32–39.
62. Woolf and Schulkind, 28–59.
63. Oxford Reference defines it as "The double-mirroring effect created by placing an image within an image and so on, repeating infinitely (infinite regression)."
64. Woolf, *To the Lighthouse* 49, 50; 29; 14.
65. Ibid., 51.
66. Ibid., 48.
67. Chantal LaCourarie, "Painting and Writing: A Symbiotic Relation in Virginia Woolf's Works," *Interdisciplinary Literary Studies* 3.2 (2002), 68.
68. Woolf, *The Captain's Death Bed*, 192, 198.
69. Jane Dunn, *A Very Close Conspiracy* (London: Pimlico, 1990), 152–153; 158.
70. LaCourarie, "Painting and Writing," 69.
71. Woolf, *To the Lighthouse*, 19.
72. Ibid., 49.
73. Ibid., 53.
74. Ibid., 86.
75. Woolf, *The Moment and Other Essays*, 3–8.
76. Woolf, *To the Lighthouse*, 157.
77. Ibid., 193.
78. Ibid., 145.
79. Ibid., 161.
80. Ibid., 222.
81. Ibid., 223.
82. Ibid., 209.
83. Boyd, *On the Origin of Stories*, np.
84. Frank, *The Wounded Storyteller*, 150–151.

Chapter Three

1. Joseph Campbell, *The Hero with a Thousand Faces*, 14th ed. (New York: Pantheon, 1949).
2. Jean Wyatt, "*Mrs. Dalloway*: Literary Allusion as Structural Metaphor," *PMLA* 88.3 (1973), 440.
3. Darwin, *Descent*, 122.
4. Ibid., 86–87.
5. Ibid., 95.
6. Darwin, *On the Origin of Species*, 451–452.
7. Beer, *Darwin's Plots*, 23.
8. Darwin, *On the Origin of Species*, 53.
9. Virginia Woolf, *Mrs. Dalloway* (New York: Harcourt, Brace and World, 1953), 3.
10. Ibid.
11. See Lauren Artress, *Walking a Sacred Path*, for the definitions of labyrinth and maze: 50–52. While a labyrinth is unicursal (one path in, one path out), the maze is multi-cursal (many paths in, dead-ends, puzzles, and tricks). The structure of *Mrs. Dalloway* could be considered either a labyrinth or a maze, depending on one's point of view.
12. Woolf, *Mrs. Dalloway*, 10–11.
13. Ibid., 4.
14. Ibid., 31; 24–25.
15. Diary II, October 14, 1922.
16. Diary II, October 14, 1922.
17. Diary II, March 17, 1923; D II, March 6, 1923.
18. Diary II, June 19, 1923.
19. Diary II, June 19, 1923.
20. Diary II, August 30, 1923.
21. Diary II, February 9, 1924.
22. Diary II, November 3, 1923.
23. Woolf, *Mrs. Dalloway*, 19–20.
24. Darwin, *On the Origin of Species*, 63.
25. Woolf, *Mrs. Dalloway*, 82.
26. Ibid., 194.
27. Ibid., 36.
28. Ibid., 8–9.
29. Ibid., 40–48.
30. Ibid., 182–184.
31. Ibid., 184.
32. Ibid., 186.
33. *Cymbeline* IV ii, 258–263.
34. Karen Armstrong, *A Short History of Myth* (Edinburgh: Canongate, 2005), 7.
35. Ibid., 10.
36. Woolf, *Mrs. Dalloway*, 80.
37. Ibid., 81.
38. Ibid., 81.
39. Armstrong, *A Short History of Myth*, 1–2.
40. Ibid., 4.
41. Woolf, *Mrs. Dalloway*, 30.
42. Ibid., 8, 31.
43. Ibid., 186.
44. Ibid., 24–25.
45. Jonah Lehrer, *Proust was a Neuroscientist* (Boston: Houghton Mifflin Company, 2007), 169.

46. Ibid., 175.
47. Diary V, April, 26, 1938.
48. Diary V, April, 26, 1938. [The novel began as Poyntzet Hall, Poyntz Hall, or Pointz Hall, later entitled *Between the Acts*.]
49. Diary V, August 6, 1937.
50. Diary III, October 19, 1927.
51. Diary V, May 20, 1938 and November 22, 1938.
52. Diary V, June 22, 1940.
53. Diary V, June 22, 1940.
54. Diary V, June 27, 1940.
55. Diary V, April 26, 1938.
56. Diary V, August 28, 1938.
57. Diary V, September 5, 1938.
58. Diary V, September 20, 1938.
59. Diary V, October 14, 1938.
60. Diary V, May 31, 1940.
61. Diary V, May 30, 1940.
62. Diary V, June 9, 1940.
63. Diary V, October 2, 1940.
64. Diary V, November 3, 1940.
65. Diary V, November 5, 1940.
66. Diary V, November 5, 1940.
67. Diary V, December 29, 1940.
68. Diary V, February 26, 1941.
69. Diary V, March 8, 1941.
70. Virginia Woolf, *Between the Acts* (New York, NY: Harcourt Brace Jovanovich, 1969), 8–9.
71. Ibid., 29.
72. Ibid., 30, 31.
73. Ibid., 9.
74. Ibid., 44.
75. Ibid., 103.
76. Ibid., 125.
77. Ibid., 53.
78. Ibid., 219.
79. Ibid., 153.
80. Ibid., 152.
81. Ibid., 153.
82. Ibid., 55, 59.
83. Ibid., 61, 71, 50, 95–97.
84. Ibid., 39.
85. Ibid., 90.
86. Ibid., 63.
87. Ibid., 65.
88. Ibid., 181.
89. Ibid., 215.
90. Ibid., 192.
91. Ibid., 215.
92. Ibid., 3.
93. Ibid., 45, 107.
94. Ibid., 68–74.
95. Ibid., 70–71.
96. Ibid., 49–73.
97. Ibid., 106.
98. Ibid., 44.
99. Ibid., 48.
100. Ibid., 111.
101. Ibid., 217–219.
102. Leonard Schlain, *Sex, Time and Power* (New York: Penguin, 2003), 48–49.
103. Woolf, *Between the Acts*, 19.
104. Ibid., 105.
105. Ibid., 199.
106. Ibid., 198–201.
107. Ben Thomas, "What's So Special about Mirror Neurons?," *Scientific American*, November 26, 2014.
108. Jill Suttie, "The Storytelling Animal: a new book explores how stories make us human." *Greater Good: The Science of Meaningful Life*. June 13, 2012. http://greatergood.berkeley.edu/article/item/the_storytelling_animal
109. See Greg Hickok's book *The Myth of Mirror Neurons*.
110. Woolf, *Between the Acts*, 13.
111. Ibid., 14.
112. Ibid.
113. Ibid., 16, 17, 19.
114. Ibid., 184.
115. Ibid., 185–187.
116. Ibid., 61, 65.
117. Ibid., 66.
118. Ibid., 61.
119. Ibid., 55.

Chapter Four

1. For a detailed discussion, see Gopnik's book *The Philosophical Baby*, 19–73.
2. Dissanyake, *Homo Aestheticus*, 10.
3. Brené Brown, *Rising Strong* (New York: Spiegel & Grau, 2015), np.
4. Boyd, *On the Origin of Stories*, 85–86.
5. Ibid., 86–87.
6. E.M. Forster, *Aspects of the Novel* (London: Harcourt Brace Jovanovich, 1955), 86.
7. Boyd, *On the Origin of Stories*, 94; 188.
8. Zunshine, *Why We Read Fiction*, 16–17.
9. Ibid.
10. Diary III, March 14, 1927.

11. Woolf, *Orlando,* 137.
12. Ibid., 187–189.
13. Jane De Gay, "Virginia Woolf's Feminist Historiography in Orlando," *Critical Survey* 19.1 (2007), 62–72.
14. Diary III, October 22, 1927.
15. Diary III, December 20, 1927.
16. Diary III, March 18, 1928.
17. Woolf, *Orlando,* 33.
18. Ibid., 139–153.
19. Virginia Woolf, *A Room of One's Own* (New York: Harcourt Brace Jovanovich, 1981), 56.
20. Marilyn Farwell, "Virginia Woolf and Androgyny," *Contemporary Literature,* 16.4 (1975), 435.
21. Woolf, *A Room of One's Own,* 76–78.
22. Ibid., 97; Woolf, *Orlando,* 189–190.
23. *A Room of One's Own* 98.
24. Ibid., 98.
25. Ibid., 100.
26. Ibid., 104.
27. "Letter to George and Tom Keats, December 21–27, 1817."
28. Woolf, *Orlando,* 14–15.
29. Ibid., 37.
30. Ibid., 38.
31. Ibid., 78.
32. Lehrer, *Proust was a Neuroscientist,* 170, 172.
33. Woolf, *Orlando,* 78.
34. Ibid., 98–100.
35. Brown, *Rising Strong,* 198.
36. For more information on these issues, see Moi, *Sexual/Textual Politics;* Kristeva, *Revolution in Poetic Language;* and Gilbert and Gubar, *Madwoman in the Attic.*
37. Woolf, *Orlando* 158.
38. Ibid., 159.
39. Ibid., 163.
40. Ibid., 184.
41. Ibid., 195.
42. Ibid., 267–271.
43. Ibid., 271.
44. Ibid., 308–309.
45. See Tillyard, E.M.W. *The Elizabethan World Picture* (New York: Macmillan, 1944).
46. Beer, *Darwin's Plots* 22.
47. Diary I, April 20, 1919.
48. Boyd, *On the Origin of Stories,* 11.
49. Ibid.
50. Diary III, May 28, 1929.
51. Diary III, June 23, 1929.
52. Woolf and Schulkind, *Moments of Being,* 70.
53. Diary III, September 10, 1929.
54. Diary III, June 18, 1927.
55. Jamison, *Touched with Fire* (References to Woolf: 29–30, 118, 126–128, 224–227, etc.).
56. Woolf, *Granite and Rainbow,* 19.
57. Ibid., 121.
58. Diary III, November 28, 1928.
59. Diary III, June 23, 1929.
60. Virginia Woolf, *The Common Reader* (New York, NY: Harcourt, Brace and World, 1953), 155.
61. Woolf, *The Captain's Death Bed,* 94–119.
62. Diary III, September 16, 1929.
63. Oxford Dictionary of Music online.
64. Timothy A. Smith, "Anatomy of a Fugue," http://www2.nau.edu/tas3/fugueanatomy.html.
65. Virginia Woolf, *The Waves* (New York: Harcourt Brace Jovanovich, 1978), 8.
66. Ibid., 9.
67. Diary III, January 4, 1929.
68. Woolf and Schulkind, 64.
69. Woolf, *The Waves,* 9–11.
70. Beer, *Darwin's Plots,* 9.
71. Woolf, *The Common Reader,* 155.
72. Woolf, *The Waves,* 26–27; 239.
73. Diary III, May 28, 1929.
74. Woolf, *The Waves,* 7.
75. Diary III, May 28, 1929.
76. Schwartz, Sanford, *The Matrix of Modernism: Pound, Eliot, & Early 20th Century Thought* (Princeton: Princeton University Press, 1985), 56.
77. Tennyson, "In Memoriam."
78. Woolf, *The Waves,* 7, 297.
79. Virginia Woolf, *The Death of the Moth and Other Essays* (New York: Harcourt Brace Jovanovich, 1970), 204.
80. Woolf, *The Waves,* 82.
81. Ibid., 287.
82. Woolf, *Death of the Moth,* 208–226.
83. Woolf, *The Waves,* 81–90.
84. Ibid., 77.
85. Woolf, *The Death of the Moth,* 220.
86. Woolf, *The Waves,* 104.
87. Walter Pater, *The Renaissance. Studies in Art and Poetry* (London: Macmillan & Co., 1910).
88. Woolf, *The Waves,* 189, 193, 21.

89. Ibid., 297.
90. Ibid., 186.
91. Diary III, November 7, 1928.
92. Woolf, *The Waves*, 295.
93. Diary II, October 25, 1920.
94. Woolf, *The Waves*, 153.
95. Ibid., 57.
96. Woolf, *The Death of the Moth*, 219.
97. Ibid., 219–220.
98. Woolf, *The Waves*, 291–292.
99. Ibid., 297.
100. Woolf and Schulkind, 72.

Chapter Five

1. Joanna O'Connell, *Prospero's Daughter: The Prose of Rosario Castellanos* (Austin: University of Austin Press, 1995), 223.
2. Shusha Guppy, and Jason Weiss. "Nathalie Sarraute and The Art of Fiction No. 115," interview, 1990: http://www.theparisreview.org/interviews/2341/the-artof-fiction-no-115-nathalie-sarraute.
3. Dominick Argento, et al. *From the Diary of Virginia Woolf*, 1975.
4. Michelle Lee, "Journals Spanning Time: Virginia Woolf, the Indigo Girls, Me," *WILLA*, 5 (1996).
5. Denis Dutton, "Pleasures of Fiction" http://denisdutton.com/carroll_review.htm.
6. *Microkosmos*, Directors, Claude Nuridsany and Marie Pérennou. DVD 2005.
7. Harold Fromm, *The Nature of being Human: from Environmentalism to Consciousness* (Baltimore, MD: Johns Hopkins, 2009), 169.
8. Mark Turner, *The Literary Mind: The Origins of Thought and Language* (Oxford UK: Oxford University Press, 1998), 5.
9. Jane Lilienfield, "'The Deception of Beauty': Mother Love and Mother Hate in *To the Lighthouse*," *Twentieth Century Literature*, 23: 3, October 1977, 346.
10. Boyd, *On the Origin of Stories*, 86–87.
11. *Out of Africa*, 1985 (film).
12. Woolf, *Orlando*, 328.
13. Marilyn Charles, "Epiphany: The Poet's Art, the Analyst's Instrument. Formal Structure as a Vehicle for the Expression of Primary Experience," *Psychoanalytic Review*, 97.3 (2010), 451 457.
14. Boyd, *On the* Origin of Stories, 321–333.

Epilogue

1. Cunningham, *The Hours*, 15.
2. Mullan "Interview with Cunningham."
3. Cunningham, 3.
4. This is an idea Brian Boyd discusses at length in *On the Origin of Stories*.

Bibliography

Albright, Daniel. "Virginia Woolf as Autobiographer." *The Kenyon Review* 6.4 (1984): 1–17. Web.

Alcock, John. "Unpunctuated Equilibrium in the Natural History Essays of Stephen Jay Gould." Evolution and Human Behavior 19 (1998), 321–336. Web.

Argento, Dominick, et al. *From the diary of Virginia Woolf.* 1975.

Armstrong, Karen. *A Short History of Myth.* Edinburgh: Canongate, 2005. Print.

Artress, Lauren. *Walking a Sacred Path: Rediscovering the Labyrinth as a Spiritual Tool.* New York: Riverhead Books, 1995. Print.

Austin, Michael. *Useful Fictions: Evolution, Anxiety, and the Origins of Literature.* Lincoln: University of Nebraska Press, 2010. Print.

Banfield, Ann. *The Phantom Table.* Cambridge: Cambridge University Press, 2000. Print.

Barash, David. *Homo Mysterious: Evolutionary Puzzles of Human Nature.* Oxford: Oxford University Press, 2012. Print.

———. *Madame Bovary's Ovaries: A Darwinian Look at Literature.* 1st ed. New York: Delacorte Press, 2005. Print.

Barkow, Jerome H., Leda Cosmides, and John Tooby. *The Adapted Mind: Evolutionary Psychology and the Generation of Culture.* Oxford: Oxford University Press, 1992.

Baron-Cohen, Simon. "The Biology of the Imagination: How the Brain Can Both Play with Truth and Survive a Predator." *Human Nature: Fact and Fiction.* Ed. Robin Headlam Wells and JohnJoe McFadden. London: Continuum, 2006. Print.

Baumeister, Roy F. *The Cultural Animal: Human Nature, Meaning, and Social Life.* 1st ed. Oxford UK: Oxford University Press, 2005. Print.

Beer, Gillian. *Darwin's Plots: Evolutionary Narrative in Darwin, George Eliot and Nineteenth-Century Fiction.* 1st ed. London UK: Routledge & Kegan Paul, 1983. Print.

———, Helen Small, and Trudi Tate. *Literature, Science, Psychoanalysis, 1830–1970: Essays in Honour of Gillian Beer.* Oxford; New York: Oxford University Press, 2003. Web.

Berthoud, Ella, and Susan Elderkin. *The Novel Cure: From Abandonment to Zestlessness: 751 Books to Cure What Ails You.* New York: Penguin, 2013. Print.

Bishop, E.L. "The Shaping of Jacob's Room: Woolf's Manuscript Revisions." *Twentieth Century Literature* 32.1 (1986): 115. Web.

Bishop, Edward. *Virginia Woolf's Jacob's Room: The Holograph Draft: Based on the Holograph Manuscript in the Henry W. and Albert A. Berg Collection of English and American Literature at the New York Public Library.* New York, NY: Pace University Press, 1998. Web.

Blodgett, Harriet. "From Jacob's Room to

Passage to India: A Note." *ANQ* 12.4 (1999): 23. Web.

Boyd, Brian. "Art as Adaptation: A Challenge." *Style* 42.2 and 3 (2008): 138. Print.

_____. *On the Origin of Stories: Evolution, Cognition, and Fiction*. Cambridge, Mass: Belknap Press of Harvard University Press, 2010.

_____, Joseph Carroll, and Jonathan Gottschall. *Evolution, Literature and Film*. New York: Columbia University Press, 2010. Print.

Briggs, Julia. *Virginia Woolf: An Inner Life*. Orlando, Fla.: Harcourt, Inc., 2005. Web.

Brown, Brené. "Physics of Vulnerability." http://www.dumbofeather.com/brene-brown-on-thephysics-of-vulnerability/. Web.

_____. *Rising Strong*. New York: Spiegel & Grau, 2015. Print.

Brown, Nathaniel. "The 'Double Soul': Virginia Woolf, Shelley, and Androgyny." *Keats Shelley Journal* 33 (1984): 182–204. Print.

Browne, Janet. *Darwin's Origin of Species: A Biography*. New York: Grove Press, 2006. Print.

Bucknell, Brad. "The Sound of Silence in Two of Jacob's Rooms." *Modernism/Modernity* 15.4 (2008): 761–81. Web.

Burghardt, Gordon. "Evolution and Paradigms in the Study of Literature." *Style* 42.2 and 3 (2008): 144. Print.

Burns, Christy L. "Re-Dressing Feminist Identities: Tensions between Essential and Constructed Selves in Virginia Woolf's Orlando." *Twentieth Century Literature* 40.3 (1994): 342–64. Print.

Campbell, Joseph. *The Hero with a Thousand Faces*. 14th ed. New York: Pantheon, 1949. Print.

Caramagno, Thomas C. *The Flight of the Mind: Virginia Woolf's Art and Manic-Depressive Illness*. Berkeley: University of California Press, 1992. Print.

Carroll, Joseph. Abstract for *Evolution and Literary Theory*. http://cogweb.ucla.edu/Abstracts/Carroll_95.html. Web.

_____. *Evolution and Literary Theory*. Columbia MO: University of Missouri Press, 1995. Print.

_____. "An Evolutionary Paradigm for Literary Study." *Style* 42.2 and 3 (2008): 103. Print.

_____. *Graphing Jane Austen: The Evolutionary Basis of Literary Meaning*. New York: Palgrave Macmillan, 2012. Print.

_____. *Literary Darwinism: Evolution, Human Nature, and Literature*. New York: Routledge, 2012. Print.

_____. "Literature and Evolution." In *Human Nature, Fact and Fiction*, R.H. Wells and JohnJoe McFadden, Eds. London UK: Continuum, 2006. Print

_____. *Reading Human Nature: Literary Darwinism in Theory and Practice*. New York: SUNY Press, 2011. Print.

_____. "Steven Pinker's Cheesecake for the Mind." *Philosophy and Literature*. 22: 2 (1998). Web.

Charles, Marilyn. "Epiphany: The Poet's Art, the Analyst's Instrument. Formal Structure as a Vehicle for the Expression of Primary Experience." *Psychoanalytic Review* 97.3 (2010): 451. Print.

Childs, Donald J. *Modernism and Eugenics: Woolf, Eliot, Yeats, and the Culture of Degeneration*. Cambridge: Cambridge University Press, 2001. Web.

Clements, Elicia. "Transforming Musical Sounds into Words: Narrative Method in Virginia Woolf's *The Waves*." *Narrative* 13.2 (2005): 160. Web.

Collins, Michael. "On Literary Darwinism." *Alluvium*: 1.1 (2012). Web.

Cooke, Brett. "Compliments and Complements." *Style* 42.2 and 3 (2008) Print.

Corbalis, Michael C. *The Recursive Mind: The Origins of Human Language, Thought, and Civilization*. Princeton: Princeton University Press, 2011. Print.

Crapoulet, Emilie. "Beyond the Boundaries of Language: Music in Virginia Woolf's 'the String Quartet.'" *Journal of the Short Story in English* 50 (2008): 2. Print.

Cunningham, Michael. *The Hours*. New York, NY: Farrar, Straus, Giroux, 1998. Print.

Dalgarno, Emily. *Virginia Woolf and the Visible World*. Cambridge; New York: Cambridge University Press, 2001. Web.

_____. "Virginia Woolf: Translation and 'Iterability.'" *The Yearbook of English Studies* 36.1, Translation (2006): 145–56. Web.

Darwin, Charles. *The Descent of Man*. Amherst, NY: Prometheus Books, 1998. Print.

_____. *The Expression of the Emotions in Man and Animals*. Chicago, IL: University of Chicago Press, 1965. Print.

_____. *The Origin of Species by Means of Natural Selection*. New York: Signet Classics, 2003. Print.

De Gay, Jane. "Virginia Woolf's Feminist Historiography in Orlando." *Critical Survey* 19.1 (2007): 62–72. Print.

_____. *Virginia Woolf's Novels and the Literary Past*. Edinburgh: Edinburgh University Press, 2006. Print.

Degler, Carl N. *In Search of Human Nature: The Decline and Revival of Darwinism in American Social Thought*. Oxford: Oxford University Press, 1991. Print.

Dennett, Daniel C. *Darwin's Dangerous Idea: Evolution and the Meanings of Life*. New York: Simon & Schuster, 1995.

_____. *Kinds of Minds: Toward an Understanding of Consciousness*. New York: Harper-Collins, 1996. Print.

Diamond, Jared. *The Third Chimpanzee: The Evolution and Future of the Human Animal*. New York: Harper Perennial, 2006. Print.

Dieman, Werner. "History, Pattern, and Continuity in Virginia Woolf." *Contemporary Literature* 15.1 (1974): 49–66. Print.

DiSalvo, David. "What Is Literary Darwinism: An Interview with Joseph Carroll." https://neuronarrative.wordpress.com/2009/02/27/what-is-literary-darwinism-an-interview-with-joseph-carroll/ Web.

Dissanayake, Ellen. *Art and Intimacy*. Seattle: University of Washington Press, 2000.

_____. *Homo Aestheticus: Where Art Comes from and Why*. New York: The Free Press, Macmillan, 1992. Print.

Dunn, Jane. *A Very Close Conspiracy*. London: Pimlico, 1990. Print.

Dutton, Denis. *The Art Instinct*. New York: Bloomsbury Press, 2009. Print.

_____. "The Pleasures of Fiction." http://denisdutton.com/carroll_review.htm. Web.

Ender, Evelyne. *Architexts of Memory: Literature, Science, and Autobiography*. Ann Arbor: University of Michigan Press, 2005. Web.

Ettinger, Ian. "Relativity and Quantum Theory in Virginia Woolf's *The Waves*." *Zeteo:* *The Journal of Interdisciplinary Writing*. http://zeteojournal.com/wp-content/uploads/2012/04/Ettinger-FINAL-formatted-NEW.pdf. Web.

Farwell, Marilyn. "Virginia Woolf and Androgyny." *Contemporary Literature* 16.4 (1975): 433–451. Print.

Flesch, William. *Comeuppance: Costly Signaling, Altruistic Punishment, and Other Biological Components of Fiction*. Cambridge, MA: Harvard University Press, 2007. Print.

Fletcher, Angus. "Another Literary Darwinism." *Critical Inquiry* 40.2 (2014): 450. Print.

Flint, Kate. "Revising Jacob's Room: Virginia Woolf, Women, and Language." *The Review of English Studies* 42.167 (1991): 361–79. Web.

Fodor, Jerry, and Massimo Piattelli-Palmarini. *What Darwin Got Wrong*. New York: Farrar, Straus and Giroux, 2011. Print.

Forster, E.M. *Aspects of the Novel*. London: Harcourt Brace Jovanovich, 1955. Print.

Frank, Arthur. *The Wounded Storyteller: Body, Illness, and Ethics*. Chicago: University of Chicago Press, 1995. Print.

Frazer, James G. *The Golden Bough*. 7th ed. New York: Macmillan, 1960. Print.

Freedman, Ralph. *Virginia Woolf: Revaluation and Continuity: A Collection of Essays*. Berkeley, CA: University of California Press, 1980. Print.

Fromm, Harold. *The Nature of being Human: from Environmentalism to Consciousness*. Baltimore, MD: Johns Hopkins, 2009. Print.

Garvey, Johanna. "Difference and Continuity: The Voices of *Mrs. Dalloway*." *College English* 53.1 (1991): 59–76. Print.

Gilbert, Sandra M., and Susan Gubar. *The Madwoman in the Attic: The Woman Writer and the Nineteenth-Century Literary Imagination*. New Haven: Yale University Press, 2000. Print.

Gillen, Francis. "'I Am This, I Am That'" Shifting Distance and Movement in *Mrs. Dalloway*." *Studies in the Novel* 4.3 (1972): 484–93. Print.

Goldhaber, Dale. The Nature-Nurture Debates: Bridging the Gap. Cambridge, MA: Cambridge University Press, 2012. Print.

Goodheart, Eugene. *Darwinian Misadventures in the Humanities*. New Brunswick: Transaction Publishers, 2007. Print.

Gopnik, Alison. *The Philosophical Baby: What Children's Minds Tell Us about Truth, Love and the Meaning of Life*. New York: Farrar, Straus and Giroux, 2009. Print.

Gordon, Craig A. *Literary Modernism, Bioscience & Community in Early 20th Century Britain*. New York: Palgrave Macmillan, 2007. Web.

Gottschall, Jonathan. *Literature, Science, and a New Humanities*. 1st ed. New York: Palgrave/Macmillan, 2008. Print.

———. *The Storytelling Animal: How Stories Make Us Human*. Boston: Houghton Mifflin Harcourt, 2012. Print.

———, and David S. Wilson, eds. *The Literary Animal*. Evanston: Northwestern University Press, 2005. Print.

Gould, Stephen Jay. "Evolution: The Pleasures of Pluralism." *New York Review of Books*, June 26, 1997. Web.

———. *Full House: The Spread of Excellence from Plato to Darwin*. New York: Three Rivers Press, 1996. Print.

———. *The Hedgehog, the Fox, and the Magister's Pox: Mending and Minding the Misconceived Gap between Science and the Humanities*. London: Jonathan Cape, 2003. Print.

———. *The Mismeasure of Man*. New York: W.W. Norton, 1996. Print.

———. *The Panda's Thumb: More Reflections on Natural History*. New York: W.W. Norton, 1980. Print.

———. *Punctuated Equilibrium*. Cambridge, MA: Harvard University Press, 2007. Print.

Guppy, Shusha, and Jason Weiss. "Nathalie Sarraute and the Art of Fiction No. 115." Interview, 1990. http://www.theparisreview.org/interviews/2341/the-art-of-fiction-no-115-nathalie-sarraute. Web.

Hague, Angela. *Fiction, Intuition, & Creativity: Studies in Brontë, James, Woolf, and Lessing*. Washington, D.C.: Catholic University of America Press, 2003. Web.

Hancock, Kami. "Deviant Snapshots: Revisiting *Jacob's Room*." *Virginia Woolf Miscellany*. 70 (2006), 10–11. Web.

Hanson, Clare. *Women Writers: Virginia Woolf*. New York: St. Martin's Press, 1994. Print.

Harris, Judith Rich. *No Two Alike: Human Nature and Human Individuality*. New York: W.W. Norton, 2006. Print.

Harris, Susan C. "The Ethics of Indecency: Censorship, Sexuality, and the Voice of the Academy in the Narration of *Jacob's Room*." *Twentieth Century Literature* 43.4 (1997): 420–38. Web.

Henkin, Leo Justin. *Darwinism in the English Novel, 1860–1910; the Impact of Evolution on Victorian Fiction*. New York City: Corporate Press, Inc., 1940. Web.

Heider-Simmel. *The Heider-Simmel Illusion, 1944*. YouTube. Web.

Henrich, Joe. "A Cultural Species: How Culture Drove Human Evolution." *American Psychological Association*. 2014. Web. http://www.apa.org/science/about/psa/2011/11/human-evolution.aspx. Web.

Henry, Holly. *Virginia Woolf and the Discourse of Science: The Aesthetics of Astronomy*. Cambridge; New York: Cambridge University Press, 2003. Web.

Hogan, Patrick. *Cognitive Science, Literature, and the Arts*. New York: Routledge, 2003. Print.

Hoff, Molly. "The Pseudo-Homeric World of *Mrs. Dalloway*." *Twentieth Century Literature* 45.2 (1999): 186–209. Print.

Hoffman, Michael. "'Whose Books Once Influenced Mine': The Relationship Between E.M. Forster's *Howards End* and Virginia Woolf's *The Waves*." *Twentieth Century Literature* 45.1 (199): 46. *JSTOR*. Web.

Hoffman, Charles G. ""From Lunch to Dinner": Virginia Woolf's Apprenticeship." *Texas Studies in Literature and Language* 10.4 (1969): 609–27. Web.

Hogan, Patrick Colm. *Cognitive Science, Literature, and the Arts*. London: Routledge, 2003. Print.

Hollander, Rachel. "Novel Ethics: Alterity and Form in *Jacob's Room*. *Twentieth Century Literature* 53.1 (2007): 40–66. Web.

Hood, Bruce. *The Self Illusion: How the Brain Creates Identity*. Oxford: Oxford University Press, 2012. Print.

Hood, Randall. *The Genetic Function and Nature of Literature*. Cal Poly, San Luis Obispo, 1979. Kindle Text.

Howe, Irving. "Mr. Bennett and Mrs. Woolf." *New Republic* 202.23 (1990): 26–8. Web.

Hussey, Mark. *Virginia Woolf and War: Fiction, Reality, and Myth*. Syracuse, N.Y.: Syracuse University Press, 1991. Web.

Ippolito, Maria F., and Ryan D. Tweney. "The Journey to *Jacob's Room*: The Network of Enterprise of Virginia Woolf's First Experimental Novel." *Creativity Research Journal* 15.1 (2003): 25–43. Web.

Jamison, Kay Redfield. *Touched with Fire: Manic-Depressive Illness and the Artistic Temperament*. New York: The Free Press, 1993. Print.

———. *An Unquiet Mind: A Memoir of Moods and Madness*. New York: Vintage, 1995. Print.

Kane, Julie. "Varieties of Mystical Experience in the Writings of Virginia Woolf." *Twentieth Century Literature* 41.4 (1995): 328. Web.

Katz, Ruth, and Ruth HaCohen. *Tuning the Mind: Connecting Aesthetics to Cognitive Science*. New Brunswick: Transaction Publishers, 2003. Print.

Kazan, Francesca. "Description and the Pictorial in *Jacob's Room*." *ELH* 55.3 (1988): 701–719. Web.

Keats, John. "Letter to George and Tom Keats, December 21–27, 1817." *English Romantic Writers*. New York: Harcourt, 1995.

Knapp, John. "Brief Introduction to Joseph Carroll Article." *Style* 42.2 and 3 (2008): Print.

Knight, Christopher. "'The God of Love Is Full of Tricks': Virginia Woolf's Vexed Relation to the Tradition of Christianity." *Religion and Literature* 39.1 (2007): 27. Print.

Koulouris, Lambrotheodoros. "'Love Unconquered in Battle' and Other Lies: 'Virginia Woolf' and (Greek) 'Love.'" *Interdisciplinary Literary Studies* 8.2 (2007): 37–53. Web.

Kramnick, Jonathan. "Against Literary Darwinism." *Critical Inquiry* 37 (2011): 315–47. Print.

Kristeva, Julia. *Revolution in Poetic Language*. New York: Columbia University Press, 1984. Print.

Kronenberger, Louis. "Poetic Brilliance in the New Novel by Mrs. Woolf: *The Waves* Carries Experimental Technique in Fiction almost to the Jumping-Off Place.'" *New York Times*, sec. Book Reviews: Oct. 25, 1931. Print.

Lacourarie, Chantal. "Painting and Writing: A Symbiotic Relation in Virginia Woolf's Works." *Interdisciplinary Literary Studies* 3.2 (2002): 66–81. Print.

Lambert, Elizabeth. "'and Darwin Says they are Nearer the Cow': Evolutionary Discourse in *Melymbrosia* and *The Voyage Out*." *Twentieth Century Literature* 37.1 (1991). Print.

Laurence, Patricia O. *The Reading of Silence: Virginia Woolf in The English Tradition*. Stanford: Stanford University Press, 1991. Print.

Leaska, Mitchell Alexander. *Granite and Rainbow: The Hidden Life of Virginia Woolf*. New York: Cooper Square Press, 2000.

Lee, Hermione. *The Novels of Virginia Woolf*. New York: Holmes and Meier Publishers, 1977. Print.

———. *Virginia Woolf: A Biography*. New York: A.A. Knopf, 1997. Print.

Lee, Michelle. "Journals Spanning Time: Virginia Woolf, the Indigo Girls, Me." *WILLA*, 5 (1996), 21–22. Web.

Le Guin, Ursula. *Language of the Night: Essays on Fantasy and Science Fiction*. New York: Harper-Collins, 1992.

Lehrer, Jonah. *Proust Was a Neuroscientist*. Boston: Houghton Mifflin Company, 2007. 168. Print.

Lennox, James G. "Darwin Was a Teleologist." *Biology and Philosophy* 8 (1993): 409–21. Print.

Lestienne, Solenne. "Communication in the Waves and between the Acts by Virginia Woolf." *Otherness: Essays and Studies* 3.2 http://www.otherness.dk/file admin/www.othernessandthearts.org/ Publications/Journal_Otherness/Otherness_Essays_and_Studies_3.2/Communication_in_the_Waves_and_Between_the_Acts_-_Solenne_Lestienne.pdf. Web.

Levine, George Lewis. *Darwin and the Novelists: Patterns of Science in Victorian Fiction*. Cambridge, Mass.: Harvard University Press, 1988. Web.

Levi-Strauss, Claude. *Myth and Meaning*. New York: Schocken Books, 1979. Print.

Lilienfield, Jane. "'The Deception of Beauty': Mother Love and Mother Hate in *To the Lighthouse*." *Twentieth Century Literature*. 23: 3 (Oct. 1977), 345–376. Print.

Lokke, Kari Elise. "Orlando and Incandescence: Virginia Woolf's Comic Sublime." *Modern Fiction Studies* 38.1 (1992): 235–52. Print.

Lucenti, Lisa Marie. "Virginia Woolf's *The Waves*: To Defer That "Appalling Moment ."* Criticism* 40.1 (1998). Print.

Mackay, Marina. "The Lunacy of Men, the Idiocy of Women: Woolf, West, and War." *NWSA Journal* 15.3 (2003): 124–44. Web.

Maior, Petru. "Inner World and Language in Virginia Woolf's *The Waves*." http://www.upm.ro/cci/volCCI_II/Pages%20from%20Volum_texteCCI2-75.pdf. Web.

Malle, Bertram F., and Sara D. Hodges. *Other Minds: How Humans Bridge the Divide between Self and Others*. New York: The Guilford Press, 2005. Print.

Mayr, Ernst. "Darwin's Influence on Modern Thought." *Scientific American*, November 24, 2009. http://www.scientificamerican.com/article/darwins-influence-on-modern-thought/ Web.

McAdams, Dan P. *The Stories We Live by: Personal Myths and the Making of the Self*. New York: Guilford, 1993. Print.

McEwan, Ian. "Literature, Science and Human Nature." *Human Nature: Fact and Fiction*. Ed. R.H. Wells and JohnJoe McFadden. London: Continuum, 2006. 40–60. Print.

McGavran, James. "'Alone Seeking the Visible World' the Wordsworths, Virginia Woolf, and *The Waves*." *Modern Language Quarterly* 42 (1981): 265. Print.

McIntire, Gabrielle. "Heteroglossia, Monologism, and Fascism: Bernard Reads *The Waves*." *Narrative* 13.1 (2005): 30. Web.

"Microkosmos." Directors, Claude Nuridsany and Marie Pérennou. DVD 2005.

Moi, Toril. *Sexual/Textual Politics*. London: Methuen, 1985. Print.

Monson, Tamlyn. ""A Trick of the Mind": Alterity, Ontology, and Representation in Virginia Woolf's *The Waves*." *Modern Fiction Studies* 50.1 (2004): 173. Print.

Montashery, Iraj. "Rhoda's Non-Identity in Virginia Woolf's *The Waves*." *Advances in Asian Social Science* 4.2 (2013): 806. Print.

Mulas, Francesco. "Virginia Woolf's *The Waves*: A Novel of Silence." http://eprints.Uniss.it/973/1/Mulas_F_Articolo_2005_Virginia.pdf. Web.

Mullan, John. "*The Hours* by Michael Cunningham." http://www.theguardian.com/books/2011/jul/08/the-hours-michael-cunningham-bookclub. Web.

Naremore, James. *The World Without a Self: Virginia Woolf and the Novel*. New Haven: Yale University Press, 1973. Print.

Nicolson, Nigel. *Portrait of a Marriage*. Great Britain: MacDonald Futura, 1973. Print.

_____. *Virginia Woolf*. New York: Viking, 2000. Print.

O'Connell, Joanna. *Prospero's Daughter: The Prose of Rosario Castellanos*. Austin: University of Austin Press, 1995. Print.

Ogden, Daryl. *The Language of the Eyes: Science, Sexuality, and Female Vision in English Literature and Culture, 1690–1927*. New York: State University of New York Press, 2005. Web.

Ohmann, Carol. "Culture and Anarchy in *Jacob's Room*." *Contemporary Literature* 18.2 (1977): 160–72. Web.

Olson, Liesl M. "Virginia Woolf's 'Cotton Wool of Daily Life.'" *Journal of Modern Literature* 26.2, Virginia Woolf and Others (2003): 42–65. Web.

Onishi, Normimitsu. "Thumbs Race as Japan's Best Sellers Go Cellular." *New York Times*, Jan. 20, 2008.

Palmer, Alan. *Fictional Minds*. Lincoln: University of Nebraska. 2004. Print.

Parsons, Deborah L. *Theorists of the Modernist Novel: James Joyce, Dorothy Richardson, Virginia Woolf*. New York: Routledge, 2007. Print.

Pater, Walter. *The Renaissance. Studies in Art and Poetry*. London: Macmillan & Co., 1910. Print.

Peterson, Britt. "Darwin to the Rescue." *The Chronicle of Higher Education*, sec. Volume 54, Issue 57: B7. 2008. Print.

Pinker, Steven. *The Blank Slate: The Modern Denial of Human Nature*. New York: Penguin, 2002. Print.

_____. *How the Mind Works*. New York: W.W. Norton, 1997. Print.

———. *The Stuff of Thought: Language as a Window into Human Nature.* New York: Viking, 2007. Print.

———. "Toward a Consilient Study of Literature." *Philosophy and Literature* 31 (2007): 161–77. Print.

Pinkerton, Steve. "Linguistic and Erotic Innocence in Virginia Woolf's *The Waves*." *Explicator* (2009): 76. Print.

Poster, Jem. "A Combination of Interest: Virginia Woolf's *To the Lighthouse*." *Critical Survey* 8.2, Anglo-Irish studies: new developments (1996): 210–5. Web.

Prinz, Jesse. *Beyond Human Nature: How Culture and Experience Shape our Lives.* London UK: Allen Lane, 2012. Print.

Radner, Gilda. *It's Always Something.* New York: Simon & Schuster, 1989.

Reese, Judy S. *Recasting Social Values in the Work of Virginia Woolf.* London: Susquehanna University Press, 1996. Print.

Richardson, Alan, and Ellen Spolsky. *The Work of Fiction: Cognition, Culture, and Complexity.* Burlington, VT: Ashgate. Print.

Richerson, Peter J., and Robert Boyd. *Not by Genes Alone: How Culture Transformed Human Evolution.* 2nd ed. Chicago: University of Chicago Press, 2006. Print.

Richter, Harvena. "New Ways of Looking at Virginia Woolf." *Studies in the Novel* 20.4 (1988): 417–22. Web.

———. "The 'Ulysses' Connection: Clarissa Dalloway's Bloomsday." *Studies in the Novel* 21.3 (1989): 305–19. Print.

Richter, Virginia. *Literature After Darwin: Human Beasts in Western Fiction, 1859–1939.* New York: Palgrave/Macmillan, 2011. Print.

Rose, Hillary, and Steven Rose. *Alas, Poor Darwin: Arguments Against Evolutionary Psychology.* New York: Harmony Books, 2000. Print.

Rosenbaum, S.P. *The Bloomsbury Group.* Toronto: University of Toronto Press, 1975. Print.

Rudikoff, Sonya. *Ancestral Houses: Virginia Woolf and the Aristocracy.* Palo Alto, Calif.: Society for the Promotion of Science and Scholarship, 1999. Web.

Ryan, Derek. *Virginia Woolf and the Materiality of Theory: Sex, Animal, Life.* Edinburgh University Press, 2013. Web.

Salzani, Carlo. "Review of *Reading Human Nature and Literature After Darwin*." *Bryn Mawr Review of Comparative Literature* 9.2 (2011) Print.

Schlain, Leonard. *Sex, Time and Power.* New York: Penguin, 2003. Print.

Schulze, Robin. "Design in Motion: Words, Music, and the Search for Coherence in the Works of Virginia Woolf and Arnold Schoenberg." *Studies in the Literary Imagination* 25.2 (1992): 5. Print.

Schwartz, Barry. *The Battle for Human Nature: Science, Morality, and Modern Life.* New York: W.W. Norton, 1986. Print.

Schwartz, Sanford. *The Matrix of Modernism: Pound, Eliot, & Early 20th Century Thought.* Princeton: Princeton University Press, 1985. Print.

Schwenger, Peter. "The Obbligato Effect." *New Literary History* 42 (2011): 115. Print.

Scott, Bonnie Kime. "In the Hollow of the Wave: Virginia Woolf and Modernist Uses of Nature." 2012.Web.

Seamon, Roger. "Literary Darwinism as Science and Myth." *Style* 42: 2&3 (2008): 261–5. Print.

Shakespeare, William. *Hamlet. The Riverside Shakespeare.* New York: Houghton-Mifflin, 1997. Print.

Shettleworth, Sara J. *Fundamentals of Comparative Cognition.* Oxford: Oxford University Press, 2013.

Smith, Susan Bennett. "Reinventing Grief Work: Virginia Woolf's Feminist Representations of Mourning in *Mrs. Dalloway* and *To the Lighthouse*." *Twentieth Century Literature* 41.4 (1995): 310–27. Print.

Smith, Timothy A. "Anatomy of a Fugue." http://www2.nau.edu/tas3/fugueanatomy.html.

Smythe, Karen. "Virginia Woolf's Elegiac Enterprise." *NOVEL: A Forum on Fiction* 26.1 (1992): 64–79. Web.

Solso, Robert L. *The Psychology of Art and the Evolution of the Conscious Brain.* Cambridge, MA: MIT Press, 2003. Print.

Spolsky, Ellen. *The Contracts of Fiction: Cognition, Culture, Community.* Oxford: Oxford University Press, 2015. Print.

———. "Darwin and Derrida: Cognitive Literary Theory as a Species of Post-Structuralism." In *Introduction to Cognitive Cultural Studies.* Ed. Lisa Zunshine. Baltimore: Johns Hopkins 2010. 292–310. Print.

———. "Why and How to Take the Fruit and Leave the Chaff." *SubStance 30.*, No. 1 (2001): 177–98. Web.

Stansky, Peter. *On or About December 1910: Early Bloomsbury and Its Intimate World.* Cambridge, MA: Harvard University Press, 1996. Print.

Stelmach, Kathryn. "From Text to Tableau: Ekphrastic Enchantment in *Mrs. Dalloway* and *To the Lighthouse*." *Studies in the Novel* 38.3 (2006): 304–26. Print.

Storey, Robert. *Mimesis and the Human Animal: On the Biogenetic Foundations of Literary Representations.* 1st ed. Evanston: Northwestern University Press, 1996. Print.

Strenski, Ivan. *Malinowski and the Work of Myth.* Princeton, New Jersey: Princeton University Press, 1992. Print.

Suttie, Jill. "The Storytelling Animal: a new book explores how stories make us human."
Greater Good: The Science of Meaningful Life. June 13, 2012. http://greatergood.berkeley.edu/article/item/the_storytelling_animal Web.

Taylor, Chloe. "Kristevan Themes in Virginia Woolf's *the Waves*." *Journal of Modern Literature.* 29.3 (2006): 58. Print.

Tillyard, E.M.W. *The Elizabethan World Picture.* New York: Vintage Books, 1960.

Thomas, Ben. "What's So Special about Mirror Neurons?" *Scientific American*, November 26, 2014.

Thomson, Jean. "Virginia Woolf and the Case of Septimus Smith." *The San Francisco Jung Institute Library Journal* 23.3 (2004): 55–71. Print.

Topping, Nancy Bazin. *Virginia Woolf and the Androgynous Vision.* New Brunswick, NJ: Rutgers University Press, 1973. Print.

Transue, Pamela J. *Virginia Woolf and the Politics of Style.* Albany: State University of New York Press, 1986. Web.

Tucker, Lauryl. "Seeking the Grail, Piercing the Veil: *The Waves* as Parodic Critique of Eliot's Waste Land." *Literature Interpretation Theory* 21 (2010): 285. Print.

Turner, Mark. *The Literary Mind: The Origins of Thought and Language.* Oxford UK: Oxford University Press, 1998. Print.

Urquhart, Nicole. "Moments of being in Virginia Woolf's Fiction." http://writing.colostate.edu/gallery/matrix/urquhart.htm. Web.

Vandivere, Julie. "Waves and Fragments: Linguistic Construction as Subject Formation in Virginia Woolf." *Twentieth Century Literature*: 221. Web.

Viola, Andre. "'Buds on the Tree of Life': A Recurrent Mythological Image in Virginia Woolf's *Mrs. Dalloway*." *Journal of Modern Literature* 20.2 (1996): 239–47. Print.

Wainwright, Michael. *Darwin and Faulkner's Novels: Evolution and Southern Fiction.* New York: Palgrave/Macmillan, 2008. Print.

Wall, Kathleen. "Significant Form in *Jacob's Room*: Ekphrasis and the Elegy." *Texas Studies In Literature & Language* 44.3 (2002): 302. Web.

Watkins, Renee. "Survival in Discontinuity: Virginia Woolf's *Between the Acts*." *The Massachusetts Review* 10.2 (1969): 356–76. Print.

Wells, R.H., and JohnJoe McFadden. *Human Nature: Fact and Fiction.* London UK: Continuum, 2006. Print.

Westling, Louise. "Darwin in Arcadia: Brute being and the Human Animal Dance from Gilgamesh to Virginia Woolf." *Anglia Anglia: Zeitschrift für Englische Philologie* 124.1 (2006): 11–43. Web.

Weston, Elizabeth A. "Narrating Grief in Virginia Woolf's *Jacob's Room* and John Banville's *The Sea*." *PsyArt* (2010). Web.

Weston, Jesse. *From Ritual to Romance.* Cambridge UK: Cambridge University Press, 1983. Print.

Whitworth, Michael H. *Einstein's Wake: Relativity, Metaphor, and Modernist Literature.* Oxford: Oxford University Press, 2001. Web.

Wilson, E.O. *Consilience: The Unity of Knowledge.* New York: Vintage, 1999. Print.

———. *The Meaning of Human Existence.* New York: W.W. Norton, 2014. Print.

Wirth-Nersher, Hana. "Final Curtain on the War: Figure and Ground in Virginia Woolf's *Between the Acts*." *Style* 28.2 (1994). Print.

Wisker, Gina. "Places, People and Time Passing: Virginia Woolf's Haunted Houses." *Hecate* 37.1 (2011): 4–26. Web.

Woodnal, Johnny. "Virginia Woolf's Communist Manifesto for the Soul." http://www2.cortland.edu/dotAsset/123946.pdf. Web.

Woolf, Virginia. *Between the Acts*. New York, NY: Harcourt Brace Jovanovich, 1969. Print.

———. *The Captain's Death Bed*. New York, NY: Harcourt Brace Jovanovich, 1950. Print.

———. *The Common Reader*. New York, NY: Harcourt, Brace and World, 1953. Print.

———. *Contemporary Writers*. New York, NY: Harcourt Brace Jovanovich, 1965. Print.

———. *The Death of the Moth and Other Essays*. New York: Harcourt Brace Jovanovich, 1970. Print.

———. *The Diaries of Virginia Woolf Volumes I–V*. ed. Anne Bell. New York: Harcourt Brace Jovanovich, 1982. (In the book, referred to as D I, II, III, IV, or V) Print.

———. *Granite and Rainbow: Essays*. New York: Harcourt Brace Jovanovich, 1958. Print.

———. *A Haunted House*. New York, NY: Harcourt, Brace and World, 1972. Print.

———. *Hyde Park Gate News: The Stephen Family Newspaper*. London: Hesperus Press, 2005. Print.

———. *Jacob's Room*. New York: Harcourt, Brace and World, 1950. Print.

———. *The Letters of Virginia Woolf*, ed. Nigel Nicolson. New York: Harcourt Brace Jovanovich, 1977. (Volumes I—V) Print.

———. *The Moment and Other Essays*. New York: Harcourt Brace Jovanovich, 1948. Print.

———. *Mrs. Dalloway*. New York: Harcourt, Brace and World, 1953. Print.

———. *Night and Day*. New York: Harcourt Brace Jovanovich, 1948. Print.

———. *Orlando*. New York: Harcourt Brace Jovanovich, 1956. Print.

———. *A Room of One's Own*. New York: Harcourt Brace Jovanovich, 1981. Print.

———. *The Second Common Reader*. New York: Harcourt, Brace & World, 1953. Print.

———. *Three Guineas*. New York: Harcourt, Brace and World, 1966. Print.

———. *To the Lighthouse*. New York: Harcourt Brace Jovanovich, 1955. Print.

———. *The Voyage Out*. New York: Harcourt Brace Jovanovich, 1948. Print.

———. *The Waves*. New York: Harcourt Brace Jovanovich, 1978.

———. *The Years*. New York: Harcourt Brace Jovanovich, 1965. Print.

———, and Jeanne Schulkind. *Moments of Being: Unpublished Autobiographical Writings*. New York: Harcourt Brace Jovanovich, 1976.

———, and Mitchell Alexander Leaska. *A Passionate Apprentice: The Early Journals, 1897–1909*. San Diego: Harcourt Brace Jovanovich, 1990.

Wyatt, Jean. "*Mrs. Dalloway*: Literary Allusion as Structural Metaphor." *PMLA* 88.3 (1973): 440–51. Print.

Yang, Sharon R. "Subversion of "the Prelude" in *Jacob's Room*, Or the Woolf Who Cried Wordsworth." *Midwest Quarterly* 45.4 (2004): 331–53. Web.

Young, Dennis. "The Mythological Element in Virginia Woolf's *The Waves*: Bernard's Vision." *Iowa Journal of Literary Studies* (1986). Print.

Zak, Paul. "Why Inspiring Stories Make Us React: The Neuroscience of Narrative." http://pauljzak.com/. Web.

Zhang, Dora. "Naming the Indescribable: Woolf, Russell, James, and the Limits of Description." *New Literary History* 45.1 (2014). Print.

Zunshine, Lisa. *Introduction to Cognitive Cultural Studies*. Baltimore, MD: Johns Hopkins University Press, 2010. Print.

———. *Why we Read Fiction: Theory of Mind and the Novel*. Columbus OH: Ohio State University Press, 2006. Print.

Zwerdling, Alex. "*Jacob's Room*: Woolf's Satiric Elegy." *ELH* 48.4 (1981): 894–913. Web.

———. *Virginia Woolf and the Real World*. Berkeley: University of California Press, 1986. Web.

Index

adaptative 3–4, 9–10, 13, 16, 18–19, 27, 30, 32, 35, 38–39, 41–43, 45–46, 50, 52–53, 55, 57, 59, 71, 102, 109, 111, 119, 125, 136–137, 139, 143, 145, 152, 155, 157–158, 162, 166, 170, 175–178, 181, 188, 192, 194
affinity 11, 28, 42, 91, 95–99, 101, 103, 105–109, 112–114, 118–119, 121–125, 129–130, 133, 146, 149, 166, 178, 180; *see also* web of affinity
Albee, Edward 7
Alice in Wonderland 141
androgyny 23–24, 26, 97, 139, 141–146, 150, 175, 194
archetype 27, 57, 92, 108
Argento, Dominick 174
Armstrong, Karen 107–109, 112
art 3, 13, 22, 29, 32, 35–36, 42–44, 50, 59, 63, 77, 79, 84–88, 126, 134, 135–136, 154, 176, 184, 187, 189
attunement 59–60, 84, 87–88, 98
Austen, Jane 24, 40, 142, 188
Austin, Michael 38, 41, 48, 178

Baron-Cohen, Simon 34
Beer, Gillian 39–40, 65, 94, 152
Bernard 12, 25–26, 150–152, 161–162, 164–170, 185
Between the Acts 10–11, 18–20, 22–23, 26, 89, 91, 94–96, 112–119, 121, 124, 126–127, 129, 131–133, 151, 153, 158, 170, 180–181, 185–186, 191, 195
biography 7, 24, 138–140, 151, 180
biology 34, 44, 47–48, 129, 187

Bloomsbury Group 5, 25
Bonamy, Dick 71, 182
Boyd, Brian 11, 18, 38–41, 52, 59, 135–136, 154, 177, 184, 188
brain 3, 11, 16, 18, 30, 32, 35, 41–44, 46–47, 52–53, 84–86, 112, 129, 133–139, 142–143, 145, 148, 151, 153–155, 157–158, 161, 169, 175–179
Briscoe, Lily 12, 20–21, 73, 75–77, 79–80, 85, 183
Brown, Brené 4, 135
Brown, Nathaniel 147
Browne, Janet 36

Campbell, Joseph 57–74, 91, 109
Carroll, Joseph 11, 19, 32, 38–40, 46–49, 50, 52, 188
Castellanos, Rosario 173
chaos story 59, 61–62, 66, 73, 76
Charles, Marilyn 187
cognitive play 9–20, 27–38, 41–52, 64, 125, 133–143, 152–155, 170–175, 180–188, 192–194
Coleridge, Samuel 143
consciousness 19, 21, 25, 72–73, 81, 95, 98, 104, 112, 157, 166, 171, 173
The Contracts of Fiction 46
Cornwall 75
Cosmides, Leda 35–42
creation myth 20, 160
creativity 14, 17, 22, 30, 135, 144, 155, 162
Cunningham, Michael 191–194

216 INDEX

Dalloway, Clarissa 12, 16, 22, 26, 91–92, 95–112, 133, 139, 182–183
Dalloway, Elizabeth 102, 105–107
Dalloway, Richard 98, 104, 182
Darwin, Charles 3, 10–11, 28–29, 32, 36–38, 40, 42, 46, 50, 55, 60, 65, 90, 93–96, 102, 11, 114, 122, 152, 160–161, 175–176, 191
Darwinism 15, 27, 32, 36, 39–40, 46, 52, 98, 101, 114, 145, 148, 150, 152, 175, 178–179, 185
Darwin's Origin of Species 36
Darwin's Plots: Evolutionary Narrative in Darwin, George Eliot and Nineteenth-Century Fiction 39
deconstruction 46
de Gay, Jane 138
denouement 22, 26, 170, 186, 191
Derrida, Jacques 46, 50
The Descent of Man 3, 10, 36, 40, 93, 161
Diamond, Jared 42–43
The Diary of Virginia Woolf: Volume I 78, 153; Volume II 18, 60, 64, 99–100, 168; Volume III 18–19, 64, 77–79, 116, 136, 139, 154–155, 157, 159, 161, 168; Volume V 19, 113, 116–118
Dickens, Charles 16
Dissanyake, Ellen 134
Dodge, William 46, 126–128, 130, 181
Duckworth, Stella 63
Dunn, Jane 85
Durrant, Clara 68, 72
Durrant, Timmy 72
Dutton, Denis 41–42, 174

Eliot, George 40
Eliot, T.S. 60, 109
Elmer, Fanny 68
evolution 1, 4, 8, 10, 12, 15, 19, 26, 32–37, 39–44, 52–53, 55–57, 59, 71, 76, 82, 91–96, 108–109, 113–114, 119, 132, 134, 136–138, 141, 145, 151, 154, 173–177, 180–181, 188, 194
Evolution and Literary Theory 39, 47
The Expression of Emotion in Man and Animals 36

fairytales 4, 49, 92
Farwell, Marilyn 143
fiction 27, 31, 34, 36, 39–45, 49–52, 56–60, 64, 75, 78–80, 83, 85, 100, 102–103, 116–117, 122–125, 129–130, 132, 135–143, 145, 148, 151–158, 164, 173–175, 177–181, 184, 188–189, 191–193
Flanders, Jacob 72–73, 77, 133, 181–183
Flint, Kate 60
Florinda 68
Forster, E.M. 135
Frank, Arthur 14, 58–61, 74–76, 88, 178
Fromm, Harold 177
fugue 158–160

gender 23–24, 76, 96, 100, 119, 137, 139–144, 146–147, 150
genre 4, 11, 43, 47, 60, 139–140, 151, 175
Gilbert, Sandra 148
gods and goddesses 38, 69, 82–83, 109–110, 150
Gopnik, Alison 30, 134, 179
Gottschall, Jonathan 31, 38–39, 45, 49, 52, 129, 179
Gould, Stephen Jay 3
grand narrative 33, 41
Gubar, Susan 148

Haines, Rupert 126–128
Hamlet 28, 124
Hansel and Gretel 49
Hardy, Thomas 40
Harris, J.R. 31
The Heider–Simmel Illusion 50
Hera 24
hero/heroine 12, 23, 25, 27, 43, 45, 57, 62, 65–66, 68–70, 72–75, 81, 87, 108–110, 121, 126, 133, 137, 139, 150–151, 182, 184
hero quest 27, 67, 86, 110–115
The Hero with a Thousand Faces 91
Hickok, Greg 129
Hood, Randall 39
The Hours 191–194
Hulme, T.E. 161
human nature 4, 14, 17, 23, 27, 31–33, 36–37, 39, 44–45, 47–48, 52, 105, 132, 150, 156, 158, 161, 175, 177, 187
Hyde Park 5
Hyde Park Gate News 13

identity 45, 62, 69, 72, 81, 92, 101, 104, 113, 116, 118, 120, 127, 129, 137–141, 144–146, 150, 159, 185–186, 195

Index

Impressionist painting and writing 21, 87–88
indirect discourse 21, 80, 85, 180
It's Always Something 171–172

Jacob's Room 10–11, 16, 18–19, 20–23, 26, 55, 58–62, 64, 66–67, 69–71, 73, 76–77, 79, 81, 84, 88 90, 133, 178–179, 181–182, 186, 195
Jamison, K.R. 14, 58, 155
Jinny 151, 162, 164, 166–167, 170
journey motif 19, 21–22, 25, 27, 44, 57, 60, 67–68, 73–77, 81–82, 87–88, 91–97, 101–102, 105, 108–111, 120, 133, 156, 172, 181–185
Joyce, James 110, 174

Keats, John 53, 145
Kingsley, Charles 39–40
kinship 9, 21, 28, 52, 94, 96, 98, 103, 106, 119, 126, 128, 130, 148–149, 180, 185, 192, 194
Knole 5
Kristeva, Julia 148
Kübler-Ross, Elizabeth 58

LaCourarie, Chantal 84–85
LaTrobe, Miss 23, 117, 120, 122, 124–126, 128–129, 131–133, 186
Leaska, Mitchell 16
Lee, Hermione 7
Lehrer, Jonah 85, 112
Levine, George 40
Lilienfield, Jane 180
Literary Darwinism 4, 10–11, 32, 35, 38–39, 45–46, 48, 50, 176
The Literary Mind 46–48, 179
Little Red Riding Hood 49
London 5, 22, 69, 90, 96–98, 101, 105, 110–111, 140, 145, 182–183
Louis 151, 157, 159, 162, 164, 170, 193–194

manic-depression 155
Manresa, Mrs. 23, 117, 119, 123–124, 126–128, 131, 181
memoir 14, 20, 172
mental health 7, 10, 14, 16–18, 28, 56–57, 63, 95–97, 100, 118, 153, 175, 155–156
meta-story 12, 17, 26–27, 140, 181–183, 185–186, 191

Mirror 9, 15, 42, 52, 98, 113, 125, 127–131, 147–149, 181
"Modern Fiction" 18, 33, 161, 171
modernism 60, 105, 137
Moments of Being 29, 253, 155, 163, 166, 191
Mrs. Dalloway 5, 10, 11–12, 19–20, 22, 26, 41, 79, 89–90, 92–103, 108–110, 112, 140, 174, 178–180, 182, 186, 191–195
mutuality 9, 42, 52, 87, 98, 130, 148, 150, 180, 185–186, 192, 194
mystery 8, 121, 132, 169, 191
myth 20, 24, 38, 43, 91–92, 107–111, 121
myth-making 108, 121, 184

narrative 4, 9–10, 18–19, 21, 27, 30–31, 34, 40, 44, 46, 49, 51–52, 57, 59–60, 62, 64, 66, 69, 71–72, 74, 82–83, 85, 91–92, 98, 100–101, 106–108, 111, 114, 118, 121, 123, 130, 138, 140–141, 143, 154–158, 160–161, 163, 165, 168, 174–175, 178, 180–181, 194
"Narrow Bridge of Art" 155
nature/nurture 44
negative capability 145
Neville 151–162, 164–165, 168, 170
Nicolson, Nigel 5
Nietzsche, Friedrich 140
The Novel Cure: From Abandonment to Zestlessness 56

Odysseus 25, 110
Oliver, Bart 113, 119–120, 126, 128, 130
Oliver, Giles 23, 119, 121–124, 126–128, 186
Oliver, Isa 12, 23, 91, 113, 117, 119–128, 130, 132, 181, 186
On the Origin of Species 29, 36, 42, 90, 94
Orlando (novel and character) 10–12, 19–20, 23–27, 133–134, 136–152, 159, 175, 180, 184–185, 195
Out of Africa 184–185

Pater, Walter 140–167
Percival 26, 151, 167–168
Persephone 93, 108, 110–111
Phases of Fiction 17–18
Pinker, Steven 3, 42, 52, 187
plot 15, 21, 23, 26, 49, 56, 59, 61–63,

67, 70, 74, 96, 99–100, 111, 113, 115, 123–124, 126, 135, 137–138, 140–141, 152, 157–158, 163, 165, 174, 182–183, 193
poetry 43, 58, 116–117, 120, 123–125, 127, 142, 145, 149, 187, 193
Pointz Hall (title and name of house) 113, 118, 120, 124, 126
Pound, Ezra 60, 79, 109
prose 18, 20, 67, 75, 157, 165, 175, 187

quest (as in search) 15–18, 36, 74, 77, 80, 84–88, 149, 152, 174, 181, 186, 191
quest narrative 23, 59–60, 73–77, 81

Ramsey, Helen 16, 76, 80–81, 83, 87
reflection 20, 78, 85, 88, 112, 129, 130, 147, 149, 152, 166, 183
religion 36, 38, 183
The Renaissance: Studies in Art and Poetry 167
restitution narrative 59, 62, 74
Rhoda 151, 162, 164, 167–168, 170
rhythm 70, 82, 123, 153, 156, 158–166, 178, 180, 186, 188
Rising Strong 4
ritual 43, 58, 83, 92, 112
River Ouse 7
Rodmell 7, 116–117, 151, 170
A Room of One's Own 3, 5, 23–25, 95, 97, 141, 144, 175, 184

Sackville-West, Vita 5, 20, 23–24, 79, 142, 150
St. Ives 25, 75, 78
Sarraute, Natalie 173–174
Sasha 140, 145–146, 148, 185
Scherherezade 49
Schlain, Leonard 43, 128
Seton, Sally 22, 98–99, 103–104, 110, 183
Shakespeare, William 6, 24, 53, 106, 142, 188
Shel (Shelmerdine, Marmaduke Bonthrop) 143, 147–149, 185
Shelley, Percy 145
Sirens 110–111
"Sketch of the Past" 13–14
Smith, Rezia 22, 97, 102–103, 105, 108
Smith, Septimus 22, 26, 96–97, 99–103, 105–106, 108–112, 178
Smith, Timothy 159

Spengler, Oswald 161
Spolsky, Ellen 9, 11, 35, 38, 46, 50
Stephen family: Adrian 6; Julia 75, 80, 83, 180; Leslie 20, 63, 82, 180; Thoby 11, 13, 16, 20, 63–64, 71, 77, 178–179; Vanessa 13, 20, 60, 63, 71, 78, 85, 193
Storey, Robert 49
Story/story 1, 3–19, 21–23, 25–53, 55–58, 60–73, 77–78, 85–86
storyteller 10–16, 18, 27, 29–32, 34–38, 40–45, 52–53, 57, 60, 78, 84–86
The Storytelling Animal 39
stream of consciousness 25, 98, 180
survival of the fittest 9, 92, 180, 185
Susan 151, 162, 167, 170
Swithin, Lucy 113, 117, 119–123, 125–127, 130, 132, 181

testimony 59–60, 74, 76
Theory of Mind (ToM) 34, 41–42, 136, 141, 146, 179, 194
Thomas, Ben 129
Three Guineas 23
Tiresias 24
To the Lighthouse 5, 10–11, 16, 19–21, 25–27, 55, 58–60, 67, 73–82, 84–88, 90, 133, 139, 157, 178, 180, 183–184, 185–186, 195
Tooby, John 35, 38, 42
Touched with Fire: Manic-Depressive Illness and the Artistic Temperament 14, 155
Trollope, Anthony 40
Truth/truth 15, 31, 35, 46–47, 50, 87, 92, 95, 99, 107, 137–140, 156, 164, 167, 170, 181
Turner, Mark 46–48, 179

Ulysses 99, 110, 170
unconscious mind 161
An Unquiet Mind 58
Useful Fictions 41, 48

A Very Close Conspiracy 85
The Voyage Out 10, 21, 64, 131, 140, 153

Walsh, Peter 22, 90, 98, 102–105, 108, 110, 182–183, 193
The Waves 6, 10–11, 18–20, 24–26, 65, 133–134, 136–137, 150–160, 164, 166, 167, 170, 180, 185–186, 195
web of affinities 11, 40, 94–95, 101,

104–105, 11, 114–115, 124, 146, 149, 179, 185–186, 194
Who's Afraid of Virginia Woolf? 7
Williams, Sandra Wentworth 68–69
Woolf, Leonard 8, 25, 115–116
Wordsworth, William 53
World War I 21, 23, 60–61, 97, 182

World War II 6, 14, 23, 112, 115–116, 124, 192
Wyatt, Jean 92, 108

Zeus 24
Zunshine, Lisa 11, 34–35, 41, 136

www.ingramcontent.com/pod-product-compliance
Lightning Source LLC
Chambersburg PA
CBHW032054300426
44116CB00007B/729